Public Enterprise

First Published in 1937, *Public Enterprise* presents a broad overview of the numerous public boards and commissions established in Britain during early twentieth century. These bodies have been entrusted with the operation of vital public utilities and the regulation or organization of national industries. The book discusses leading examples such as the Port of London Authority; the British Broadcasting Corporation; the Central Electricity Board; the London Passenger Transport Board; the Coal Mines Reorganization Commission; and the Public Service Board, to showcase their importance in the economic and social life of the community. This book is a must read for scholars and researchers of business and economics, British politics, and political science.

T0371739

Public Enterprise

Developments in Social Ownership and Control in
Great Britain

Edited by William A. Robson

First published in 1937
by George Allen & Unwin Ltd.

This edition first published in 2022 by Routledge
2 Park Square, Milton Park, Abingdon, Oxon, OX14 4RN
and by Routledge
605 Third Avenue, New York, NY 10017

Routledge is an imprint of the Taylor & Francis Group, an informa business

© William A. Robson, 1937

Publisher's Note
The publisher has gone to great lengths to ensure the quality of this reprint but points
out that some imperfections in the original copies may be apparent.

Disclaimer
The publisher has made every effort to trace copyright holders and welcomes
correspondence from those they have been unable to contact.

A Library of Congress record exists under LCCN: 37020839

ISBN: 978-1-032-18467-8 (hbk)
ISBN: 978-1-003-25469-0 (ebk)
ISBN: 978-1-032-18468-5 (pbk)

Book DOI 10.4324/9781003254690

PUBLIC ENTERPRISE

DEVELOPMENTS IN SOCIAL OWNERSHIP
AND CONTROL IN GREAT BRITAIN

Edited for the New Fabian
Research Bureau by

WILLIAM A. ROBSON
B.Sc.(Econ.), LL.M., Ph.D.

LONDON
GEORGE ALLEN & UNWIN LTD
MUSEUM STREET

FIRST PUBLISHED IN 1937

CONTENTS

PREFACE

by

THE EDITOR

THIS book constitutes the first serious attempt which has been made to investigate the numerous public boards and commissions which have been set up in this country during the past thirty years, and especially in the last decade. These bodies have been entrusted with the operation of vital public utilities and the regulation or organization of great national industries, and it is impossible to over-estimate their importance in the economic and social life of the community. They form the most significant development in the field of political institutions which has taken place in Great Britain during the present century; yet, curiously enough, they have so far received hardly any systematic attention by social scientists or publicists.

It has not been possible, nor indeed would it have been desirable, to deal with every board or commission which exists. Only the leading examples have been considered; but it is believed that those selected are sufficiently typical to enable all the main aspects and problems of the subject to be explored and discussed. On the other hand, the net has been cast beyond the strict confines of the public board or commission so as to include for purposes of comparison two other types of collective organization which stand out in sharp contrast to the new type of board. In the first place, the Post Office, which represents the traditional method of organizing a socialized service; and in the second place, the Consumers' Co-operative Movement, which is the other great alternative method of producing and distributing goods and services without profit to the producers.

The work has been done by a group of contributors

*

belonging to, or associated with, the political section of the New Fabian Research Bureau, and the result reflects credit not only on those whom I was fortunate enough to enlist in the task, but also on the Bureau itself, which has acted as a focusing point and a stimulus for the effort.

The volume is, therefore, presented quite frankly as the work of a group of investigators holding certain basic ideas in common and sharing more or less the same assumptions of what is desirable. This common outlook makes the book not less but more useful than it would otherwise be. A collection of studies of this kind, if written from half a dozen different angles by students with as many different political philosophies, would confuse the issue rather than assist in its clarification. The result would form an incoherent *mélange* lacking any intelligible sign-posts by which to estimate the progress of the journey. The general level of the studies appears to me to reach a fair level of objectivity and accuracy in the presentation of facts, despite the unevenness inevitable in a book of this kind.

The common political philosophy of the contributors is offset by a wide variety of experience and occupation. One of our number is a distinguished engineer, one a financier; two of us are engaged in academic work in universities; we include a Member of Parliament and two or three candidates for election; two of us are engaged in the higher realms of journalism; one of our company is a member of the Bar; one occupies a leading position in the co-operative world; and, finally, we include a Rhodes scholar from a great centre of learning across the Atlantic.

There would, no doubt, be certain advantages if a book of this kind could be written by a single hand. But anyone who has attempted to master the vast mass of material necessary to study even one of the institutions here dealt with can have no illusions as to the magnitude of the task which would be involved. Even with several contributors the difficulty of keeping the essays up to date in a rapidly changing world has been formidable; and I doubt whether, with the present rate of change and flux, it would be practicable for a single author to deal with the various organs even in the relatively slight detail here attempted. However, if it can be done, so much the better; and I hope that success will attend the efforts of any bold and industrious spirit who makes the attempt.

In the meantime, the book is offered as a preliminary contribution to the solution of an interesting problem, to practical politicians of all parties; to teachers and students in the social sciences; to administrative officials in the civil service, the local government service, and on the boards themselves; and, last but not least, to the intelligent general reader.

I may add that each author is alone responsible for the views put forward in his particular contribution; and no one except myself is committed to the conclusions contained in the final chapter. Neither the Bureau nor its members are responsible for the opinions expressed in the book.

The offices of the New Fabian Research Bureau are at 37 Great James Street, London, W.C.1.

W. A. R.

LONDON

THE PORT OF LONDON AUTHORITY

by

LINCOLN GORDON

PUBLIC concerns as developed in Great Britain fall into two classes, broadly distinguished by the method of selection of their governing boards. The one, appointed from above, usually by a representative of the central Government, is wholly a creation of the post-war era; the other, more local in scope and for the greater part elected by its immediate consumers, was already a common feature in the Victorian economy. Nowhere is it more ubiquitous than in the field of port and harbour management. One third of Britain's 330 harbours are managed by such "public trusts,"[1] the form serving as the chief alternative to operation in conjunction with a railway system. Of the ten leading ports five are so managed, namely London, Liverpool, Glasgow, Newcastle-upon-Tyne, and Belfast; while railways manage three—Southampton, Hull, and Harwich. Manchester is administered by a mixed company, the Manchester Ship Canal Company, on which the municipality has a statutory majority of one director, and Bristol directly by the municipal corporation. The evolution of the Mersey Docks and Harbour Board and the Port of London Authority from opposite angles—municipal operation in the former case and private in the latter—is indicative of a guiding principle making the public concern a peculiarly suitable type of undertaking in this sphere.

The Liverpool docks[2] were from their inception in 1715

[1] *The Co-ordination and Development of Transport; Final Report of the Royal Commission on Transport;* Cmd. 3751 of 1931, par. 445.

[2] Cf. J. A. Picton: *Memorials of Liverpool, Historical and Topographical, Including a History of the Dock Estate;* 2nd ed., continued to the end of the Reign of Queen Victoria, by J. Allanson Picton (Liverpool, 1903), vol. i, pp. 551–607; vol. ii, pp. 539–50.

constructed by the municipal corporation, which had administered the port and provided facilities for shipping since the reign of King John. A rapidly growing trade led to continuous expansion in the number and size of dock units throughout the eighteenth century, and constituted a lucrative source of general revenue for the municipality. As the importance of the port increased, however, the mercantile community, both in Liverpool and elsewhere, became steadily less content with its management. A slight distinction between dock and other municipal affairs was introduced in 1811, when the administration of the former was delegated to a committee of twenty-one members of the common council, but the change in no way derogated from the complete authority of the unreformed, self-elected municipal governing body. Financial abuses were not infrequent, but more important, users of the port objected to the diversion of dock revenue to objects other than dock maintenance and improvement. The threat of a parliamentary contest in 1825 induced the corporation to concede eight places on the managing committee to dock ratepayers outside the council. In 1851 a further change in the same direction was effected at the instance of the American Chamber of Commerce, balancing the committee at twelve members each for the corporation and the port ratepayers, but leaving a veto in the hands of a two-thirds majority of the town council.

The dock facilities were meanwhile expanding beyond the limits of Liverpool. Supported by Cheshire landowners and railways, a rival enterprise sprang up across the Mersey in Birkenhead. Competition became keen, resulting not only in an outlay of capital not justified by the combined prospective revenues, but in frequent parliamentary contests wherein the promoters of each undertaking sought to limit the borrowing powers of the other. This unsatisfactory position was aggravated by the Liverpool "town dues," levied on the entire trade of the port, including Birkenhead and Runcorn, but not exclusively applied to harbour improvement. It was clear that only an administrative body covering the whole area, utilizing its revenue with the single purpose of maintaining and expanding port facilities, could render satisfactory service to the interested merchants and shipowners. Authority was given this viewpoint by a Royal Commission[1] in 1854 and a Select Committee of the House of Commons two years later. The outcome was the successful passage after a prolonged struggle in Parliament of a Bill promoted by Manchester traders and the Great Western Railway, establishing a new and independent board to manage the affairs of the entire port.

The Mersey Docks and Harbour Act, 1857,[2] slightly modified in the following year,[3] provides for the establishment of a Mersey Docks and Harbour Board, a non-profit-making public concern. Twenty-four of its twenty-eight members are elected for four-year terms by the payers of dock rates, who also select twelve audit commissioners to check in detail the financial administration. The elected members must themselves be ratepayers to a substantial sum. The remaining four were originally nominated by the Conservancy Commissioners of the River Mersey, namely, the First Lord of the Admiralty, the President of the Board of Trade, and the Chancellor of the Duchy of Lancaster acting *ex officio*; they have since been replaced by the Minister of Transport. In practice the entire complement of the Board has always been made up of Liverpool and Birkenhead shipowners and merchants. Control of the port is thus completely divorced from the corporation. The docks were consolidated under the Board's ownership, and it was in addition entrusted with the conservancy of the lower river, the control of pilotage, and the lighting and buoying of the

---

[1] *Royal Commission on Local Charges upon Shipping*, Parl. Papers, 1854, vol. xxxvii.

[2] 20 & 21 Vict., Ch. CLXII.

[3] The Mersey Dock Acts Consolidation Act, 1858, 21 & 22 Vict., Ch. XCII.

harbour. It took over from the municipality the capital debt on account of the docks, amounting to £6,100,000, and acquired the town dues for a further £1,500,000. Additional capital is borrowed by means of bonds, annuities, and debenture stock, all bearing a fixed return and carrying no proprietary interest in the management of the undertaking.

The members of the Board, serving without remuneration, have been drawn from the leaders of local enterprise. "The vigour, energy and prudence," writes the historian of the dock estate, "with which the vast and complicated affairs under their control are managed, place the Mersey Docks and Harbour Board in the first rank of administrators in the country."[1] Through its ten standing committees the Board proper exercises a steady guiding control over actual administration,[2] which is carried on by a permanent salaried general manager and a large executive staff. In contrast to the practice in London, almost all of the manual labour employed in the docks is engaged by private enterprise, and does not directly concern the Board.[3] Government supervision is limited to approval of new works through the machinery of private legislation, the setting of maximum charges, the appointment of a special auditor by the Minister of Transport, and the publication of annual accounts. On the whole, discretion in providing new facilities, as well as in day-to-day operation, has been left to the Board, guided by the direct interests of consumers of its services who choose its personnel.

The success in Liverpool of the representative public trust, which has accomplished a seven-fold increase in capital equipment, is undoubted. So impressed with it were the commercial leaders of London that when reconstitution

[1] Picton: *Memorials of Liverpool*, vol. i, p. 585.
[2] L. A. P. Warner (General Manager, Mersey Docks and Harbour Board): *The Mersey Dock Estate—Its Management and Principal Trades* (Pamphlet, Liverpool, 1932).
[3] F. G. Hanham: *Report of Enquiry into Casual Labour in the Merseyside Area* (Liverpool, 1930), p. 17.

of the administrative machinery for the metropolitan port was under discussion at the beginning of this century a similar body was advocated on behalf of all three of the most interested parties, local government, mercantile, and shipowning.[1] Its example was probably the most powerful single influence in determining the form finally adopted for the Port of London Authority.

In its early history[2] the development of Thames-side facilities presents a marked contrast to that on the Mersey. While here, too, the river conservancy was from time immemorial in the hands of the City Corporation, the limited number of "legal quays" and "sufferance wharves," with a monopoly on the landing of goods dating from the Tudor period, was owned by private entrepreneurs. When the need for enclosed docks became evident, private enterprise similarly undertook the new works. Under a series of local Acts beginning in 1799 Parliament granted twenty-one year monopolies over various sections of London trade to the West India, London, and East India Dock Companies, with statutory restrictions as to maximum charges and dividends. To secure the "benefits" of free competition upon the expiry of this period, however, the House of Commons refused renewal of the monopolies, and from 1825 onward a number of new companies entered the field. The remainder of the century witnessed successive periods of severe cut-throat competition as each dock was opened, followed by fusions into increasingly large corporate units. After 1864 the chief developments in the port were by-products of a struggle between the East and West India Dock Company on the one hand and the London and St. Katharine Company on the other, with the Millwall Dock affording a degree of annoyance to both. Only the Surrey Commercial Company, with its group of docks on the south

[1] *Royal Commission on the Port of London, Minutes of Evidence*, Cd. 1152 of 1902, Questions 1252, 2165, 2265, 2291–2, 7120–204, 7295, 7440, and pp. 590, 610.

[2] Sir Joseph G. Broodbank: *History of the Port of London*, 2 vols. (London, 1921).

shore, remained relatively aloof, concentrating on special facilities for the grain and timber trades. For two decades competition brought rapid expansion, in the construction of the South-West India, Royal Albert, and Tilbury Docks, but in its train came rate wars, general financial debility, and eventual bankruptcy for the India Company. A scheme for joint working was finally negotiated in 1888, consummated in 1901 by the formation of the London and India Docks Company. After 1885 capital development ceased entirely, although the amount of shipping entering the port continued to increase by 50 per cent every twenty years.

The weakness due to internecine strife among the companies was aggravated by the competition of public wharfingers and warehouse-keepers with tidal accommodation along the riverside. In compensation for the original dock monopolies, the early legislation always included a "free-water clause,"[1] exempting from dock charges on either vessel or goods lighters entering to load or discharge ships oversides. Repeal of these clauses failed to follow upon repeal of the monopolies; as a result there developed an immense trade utilizing the docks as shelter for large steamships but removing their cargoes in lighters to wharves and warehouses outside the jurisdiction of the dock companies. It is estimated[2] that in 1898 over 80 per cent of the goods entering the docks avoided the payment of dues in this manner.

These economic factors would themselves have been sufficient to impair the credit of the dock companies with the investing public; their effect was augmented by serious misgivings as to the administrative capacity and reliability of the directorates. "For many years," writes Sir Joseph Broodbank, the port's historian, "the directors were almost

---

[1] West India Dock Act, 1799, 39 Geo. III, Ch. LXIX, s. 138, and corresponding sections of other Dock Acts.

[2] Broodbank: *History of the Port of London*, vol. i, p. 268.

without exception chosen for the business which they could
influence to the company they were asked to serve; their
ability to manage a big undertaking was seldom considered."[1]
Falsification of accounts and swollen dividends paid from
capital consumption were discovered in the Millwall Company. The provision of new facilities by private enterprise
was impossible, but shipowners and merchants were universally dissatisfied with the existing state of affairs. In
1900 the Government was induced to institute a thorough
investigation into every aspect of the port's management
by a Royal Commission, under the chairmanship of Lord
Revelstoke.

The Commissioners found ample evidence to support
existing criticism. They summarized the position thus:

> The body of testimony as to the delays in the delivery of goods
> from the docks and the injury suffered in consequence by the
> trade of London is overwhelming. The conditions of modern
> trade and industry, and the increase of railway facilities in various
> parts of the world, have enabled enormous cargoes to be brought
> together and shipped for London. Mechanical invention and
> enterprise have provided ships equal to carrying these cargoes;
> and the immense growth in population and wealth of London
> and the country round it have afforded a market sufficient to
> attract and absorb them.
> The dock companies, however, for financial reasons which
> we have indicated, have not been able to adapt their receptive
> powers fully to the change of circumstances.[2]

Not only was dock accommodation inadequate, but dredging
and the general conservancy of the river had been neglected
as well. Since 1857, these latter functions had been assigned
to a body of "Conservators of the River Thames," nominated
by the City, Trinity House, the Admiralty, and the Board
of Trade. The lower channel and several of the dock
entrances were navigable for new ships of deep draught

---

[1] Broodbank: *History of the Port of London*, vol. i, pp. 198–9.
[2] *Report of the Royal Commission on the Port of London*, Cd. 1151 of 1902,
par. 209.

only at high tide, but the Conservators saw no reason to take action until the companies lowered the dock sills and the companies would not act until the channel was dredged. Under these conditions, London's trade, particularly in transhipments and goods deposited *en entrepôt*, was seriously threatened by the rising ports of the Continent, Antwerp, Bremen, Hamburg, and Rotterdam, which were financially aided by their municipalities or the State.

A twofold remedy was clearly indicated: consolidation of conservancy functions and dock administration under unified control, and the right to impose a tax on all goods entering the port. The Commission could not contemplate placing such powers in the hands either of the Thames Conservancy or of a private company. Here again, it was felt, only a body combining political independence with direct interest exclusively in the provision of adequate facilities could satisfy the requirements of the situation. With the example of Liverpool before them the Commissioners had no hesitation in recommending the establishment of a non-profit-making public trust. It was to be composed of forty members, twenty-six elected by merchants and shipowners paying dock and port dues, and the remainder appointed by Government departments and local authorities. Of the £7,000,000 capital expenditure considered immediately necessary for the complete rehabilitation of the port, it was expected that £2,500,000, allocated to river channel dredging, would be provided by the London County Council and the City Corporation; these bodies were, consequently, to appoint eight and two members respectively to the Board. The magnitude of private wharfinger and warehouse-keeper interests outside the dock system precluded their inclusion in the recommendations, but the new authority was to take over the entire dock estate, the conservancy of the tidal portion of the river, the licensing of watermen and lightermen, and the lighting of the harbour.

Several years elapsed before these proposals were implemented by statute. A Bill[1] introduced by the Government in 1903 followed the Revelstoke Report in all substantial points, including the municipal subsidy for river improvement and a municipal guarantee of port stock interest as well, but it was permitted to drop[2] when sentiment in the City crystallized against it on the ground that too close an association of the then Progressive County Council with the port might prove unduly favourable to labour. A Bill submitted by the L.C.C. in 1905 would have established a municipally appointed port authority, but was rejected by the Government on similar grounds.[3] When Mr. Lloyd George came to the Board of Trade in 1906, finally, he undertook negotiation with the dock companies for their purchase on agreed terms, and two years later introduced a Port of London Bill.[4] It included the cardinal recommendation of the Revelstoke Commission, namely, the establishment of a single authority predominantly representative of commercial interests to acquire the docks and powers of river conservancy. In its course through Parliament only details were substantially altered, by the competing claims of shareholders, shippers, traders, local authorities, and labour.[5] The Act of 1908,[6] modified from time to time and re-enacted in the Port of London (Consolidation) Act, 1920,[7] is the organic charter of the Port of London Authority.

[1] Port of London Bill, H.C. Bill 144 of 1903.
[2] *Official Report, Commons*, 4th series, vol. 137, cols. 1222–3 (July 11, 1904).
[3] The London Port and Docks Commission Bill, 1905. Rejected on second reading by 123 to 191. *Official Report, Commons*, 4th series, vol. 145, col. 188 (April 13, 1905).
[4] H.C. Bill 288 of 1908.
[5] *Joint Select Committee of the House of Lords and House of Commons on the Port of London Bill: Report, Minutes of Evidence, and Appendices*; H.C. No. 288 of 1908, *passim*.
[6] 8 Edw. VII, Ch. 68.
[7] 10 & 11 Geo. V, Ch. CLXXIII.

The P.L.A. is by statutory definition a body corporate, composed as follows:—[1]

ELECTED (18)

By payers of dues, wharfingers, and owners of river
craft   17
By wharfingers   1

APPOINTED (10)

By the Admiralty   1
By the Ministry of Transport (before 1920 the Board
of Trade)   2
By the L.C.C. (being members of the Council)   ..   2
By the L.C.C. (not being members of the Council) ..   2
By the City Corporation (being a member of the
Corporation)   1
By the City Corporation (not being a member of
the Corporation)   1
By the Trinity House   1
                                                           —
                  TOTAL   28

The Chairman and Vice-Chairman are elected by the Authority and may come from outside; hence the total membership varies from twenty-eight to thirty. Members' terms are for three years, the entire body going out of office together, but there is no restriction on reappointment or re-election. Non-British subjects and the Authority's own employees are ineligible, and members may not be concerned with or profit by any P.L.A. contract other than in the ordinary course of dock or warehousing business.[2] The Chairman, Vice-Chairman, and Chairmen of Committees may be remunerated at the Authority's discretion, but in practice only the Chairman is salaried, receiving £5,000 per annum. Lord Devonport received no salary as Chairman, but during his régime the Dock and Warehouse Committee Chairman was paid a stipend.

It will be seen that payers of port and dock charges elect well over half the entire Board. Under statutory regulations

[1] 1920 Act, s. 6; 1908 Act, s. 1.   [2] 1920 Act, 2nd Schedule.

governing elections to the P.L.A.,[1] eight of the seventeen places in this category go to shipowners, eight to merchants, and one to river craft owners. The advantages in principle of such a composition are clear. To regulate the policy and control the administration of a semi-technical enterprise of localized scope there is required an intimate acquaintance with the work of the undertaking and continuous criticism by interests immediately affected. A port is in essence a transport link between shippers carrying goods to and from the rest of the world, and merchants and manufacturers disposing of imports and supplying exports. Their concern as users of the port is to ensure adequate development of facilities, while as payers of dues they benefit by efficient management and avoidance of uneconomic capital outlay. Nevertheless, specific commercial interests may often conflict with the best advantage of the port as a whole. Fear of such sectionalism led the Revelstoke Commission to recommend nomination of a number of members by the Bank of England and the Chamber of Commerce,[2] but the Liverpool example favoured direct election. The Government hoped that the device of a general register of electors, containing everyone with a substantial pecuniary interest and voting *en bloc*, would secure representatives more likely to act for the general welfare than men chosen to represent particular trades. Voting power varies, although not in direct proportion, with the amount of dues paid to the Authority.

In practice, while sectional advocacy of the brand encouraged by direct representation of particular interests has been avoided, no substantial group of merchants or shippers can afford the possibility of complete exclusion from P.L.A. meetings. Not only are the shipowning and mercantile sections equally balanced as against one another,

[1] "Method of Election of Elected Members of the P.L.A. Regulations of the Minister of Transport," *Statutory Rules and Orders*, 1930, No. 332.
[2] *Report*, 1902, par. 313.

but adjustments are made through unofficial machinery to allocate places to the most important sections within these categories. The merchants' nominees are selected in advance through the London Chamber of Commerce, and the shipowners' through the London General Shipowners' Society. In most cases, as a result, the triennial election is a mere formality. Only four have been contested at all, and not since 1913 have there been more than twenty-one nominees for the seventeen places. On the merchants' side, members have for several years discussed P.L.A. policy with Chamber of Commerce officials at regular intervals.[1] On the whole, conflicts are better informally resolved within the trade organizations before nomination than left to find expression after the election, among members chosen each by his own trade.

Special representation for the wharfingers is a by-product of the most difficult single problem encountered by the Liberal Government in its negotiations leading to the Act of 1908. Private riverside interests are far more substantial in London than at other British ports, for the rise and fall of the tide and the nature of the estuary are just at that margin where expensive locked docks are essential for handling large liners but small vessels and lighters can be adequately cared for at tidal wharves. The Government would not purchase the latter, but it was loath to leave them to compete with a public authority empowered to collect rates on all goods entering the port, whether destined for docks or wharves. This anomalous remedy was therefore applied to an anomalous situation, a member on the governing body being granted the wharfingers to protect their trade from unfair competition.[2]

The appointed minority falls into two groups, one to supplement the trading representation and the other to

[1] *London Chamber of Commerce, 49th Annual Report of the Council* (London, 1930), pp. 21–2.
[2] *Joint Select Committee*, 1908, p. 18.

represent special interests of a semi-public nature. Lest the size of the London mercantile community cause electing interests to overlook distinguished outside experts in finance, engineering, or administration who might prove of value to the Authority, the City and the L.C.C. each appoint a non-member of their bodies to the Board and the Minister of Transport has a single nominee without special statutory qualification. This group has in fact comprised some of the most prominent members of the P.L.A., including from 1909 to 1925 Lord Ritchie of Dundee, the present Chairman, and from 1909 to 1920 Sir Joseph Broodbank, Chairman of the influential Dock and Warehouse Committee.

In the other class of appointed members the Admiralty and Trinity House are represented as a matter of course. Local geographical representation was resisted on principle in 1908, but a member of the City Corporation was held to stand for the financial interest and to represent the City in its character of Port Sanitary Authority, while the L.C.C. member stood for the body of consumers served by the port, a supra-sectional interest. These latter appointees have tended to be more or less real delegates, reporting to their constituent authorities on the work of the P.L.A., but not receiving instructions as to their own action.

The two remaining members are chosen respectively by the Minister of Transport and the L.C.C. "after consultation with such organizations representative of labour as [they] think best qualified to advise them on the matter."[1] Labour representation was a novel conception when the P.L.A. was formed, but it was justified in these terms by Mr. Winston Churchill, then Liberal President of the Board of Trade:

Although I am quite ready to admit that the representation of Labour on a port authority is introduced in this Bill for the first time, I am perfectly certain it is defensible, because, although it is an interest of a particular class, that class is so

[1] 1920 Act, s. 6 (6).

large, and its interests are so interwoven that it cannot be dismissed as wholly sectional; it is a human, moral, and national interest of a large and responsible character.[1]

Added justification was found in the special statutory requirement that the P.L.A. take steps to reduce the evils of casual employment. The L.C.C. appointee has always been chosen from dockers' organizations and the Minister's from the watermen, after recommendations from the trade unions concerned. This indirect representation of labour, contrasted with the direct election of trading members, has at times been considered invidious by labour spokesmen,[2] but a change would probably not affect the personnel and might raise administrative difficulties offsetting any increment in goodwill.

More controversial is the basic principle of labour representation and its proper weight on the managing board. Lord Devonport, when Chairman of the P.L.A., was more or less indifferent, considering the experiment "not detrimental,"[3] but Sir Joseph Broodbank has described it as an utter failure, on the ground that labour members devote their energies solely to improving the lot of the workpeople, with no concern for the larger issues of port administration.[4] This judgment is the product of experience on the Authority in its first decade, when disputes were common and the labour members were ranged as strike leaders against the P.L.A. Chairman at the head of the port employers. Lord Devonport's known hostility also made collaboration on wider topics difficult. In the happier phase of labour relations which followed the war, the men's representatives have played a fuller part in P.L.A. administration, culminating with an appointment in 1930 to the Chairmanship of the

---

[1] *Official Report, Commons*, 4th series, vol. 196, col. 395 (November 11, 1908).

[2] *Transport Workers—Court of Inquiry (Shaw Court): Report and Minutes of Evidence*, Cmd. 936 of 1920, p. 30.

[3] *Coal Industry Commission—Reports and Minutes of Evidence on Second Stage*, Cmd. 360 of 1919, Question 26108.

[4] Sir Joseph G. Broodbank: "The Appropriate Type of Authority," 4 *Public Administration*, 309, 313 (October 1926).

Authority's Maintenance Committee, which carries with it a place on the guiding General Purposes Committee. It is now widely recognized[1] that the intimate acquaintance of the labourer with the physical working of a port enables him to make a substantial contribution to efficient administration, while direct representation on the governing body has a tonic effect upon his co-operative spirit and willingness to exploit such knowledge. From such considerations a moderate increase in labour representation would be a valuable modification of the P.L.A. constitution.

An entirely distinct question of principle is raised by the single legislative attempt in the Authority's history to alter the composition of the Board. On behalf of the Transport and General Workers' Union a Private Member's Bill was submitted in 1924 and 1925[2] to increase the membership to thirty-one, nine representing labour, nine elected by trading interests, nine appointed by various local authorities, and four by Government departments and Trinity House. The general question of workers' control is not within the bounds of this study, but given the present economic contexture it is clear that the interest of labour taken as a whole is sectional in a deeper sense than that of the shippers and merchants as a whole. It is rather comparable to the interest of the Authority's creditors, and it must be remembered that holders of port stock have no voice in the port's control. In theory, at least, while it is admitted that each group of traders has sectional interests against the others, they share in common a prime and direct concern for the optimum use and development of port facilities as an efficient link in the general transport system, as contrasted with the anti-social interest of a producers' monopoly. Of the proposal for local authority representation

[1] Cf. *Transport Workers—Court of Inquiry*, 1920, *Report*, par. 27. Also F. M. Du-Plat-Taylor: *The Design, Construction and Maintenance of Docks, Wharves, and Piers*, 2nd ed. (London, 1934), p. 30.

[2] Port of London Authority (Constitution) Bill, H.C. Bill 231 of 1924, H.C. Bill 150 of 1924-5.

it need only be said that although P.L.A. policy undoubtedly reacts upon housing, poor law, and other local government functions, at a time when it is seriously being considered how far localism in one great port as against another is detrimental to national transport as a whole, there is a case *a fortiori* against representation of geographical interests within a single port.

It is the broad task of the appointed membership of a port trust to exercise a leavening effect upon the whole body, displacing the equilibrium between particular and general interests of the elected members in the latter direction. On the whole it has succeeded in this object with the P.L.A. While action specifically affecting a given trade or shipping line is always closely scrutinized by its representative on the Authority, minor differences are generally sunk in the wider effort, particularly when guided by Chairmen both of whom have been appointed members.

Thus constituted, the P.L.A. exercises a broad statutory jurisdiction over the entire tidal portion of the Thames estuary, a river distance of sixty-nine miles, excluding only the rivers Medway, Swale, and Lee, and the Grand Junction Canal.[1] Its powers may be roughly classified into three divisions. As a quasi-governmental authority it registers and licenses river craft, houseboats, and lightermen and watermen.[2] As a river conservancy it maintains and improves the channel, removes wrecks, formulates by-laws for navigation, licenses the construction of works by other entrepreneurs, ensures the river's flow and purity, and undertakes surveys.[3] As a commercial enterprise, finally, it administers and improves the dock and warehousing system of the former companies, constructs new facilities, and may acquire existing facilities not already within its control.[4]

---

[1] 1920 Act, 1st Schedule, as amended by Port of London (Various Powers) Act, 1932, 22 & 23 Geo. V, Ch. XXXVIII, s. 22.

[2] 1920 Act, ss. 318–31, 348–55; Port of London Act, 1935, 25 & 26 Geo. V, Ch. CXVI, s. 38.

[3] 1920 Act, ss. 197–314.   [4] Ibid., ss. 9–12, 112–96.

To implement these grants of authority is a host of financial powers, governing the Authority's revenue, expenditure, and borrowing.

Autonomy is the keynote of the financial structure. P.L.A. capital is obtained in the open market; its revenue from charges on goods and vessels entering the port and docks; it is reasonably free in the allocation of expenditure. In each of these related activities, however, there is a degree of control by the Ministry of Transport, and in each only a limited grant of statutory powers.

The Authority may borrow money on short term by means of overdrafts and bonds, and on long term through the creation of port stock, for the following purposes: (a) purchase of other undertakings; (b) dredging and improving the river; (c) acquisition of land and construction of new works, including interest charges during the period of construction; (d) land and buildings; and (e) any other payment which in the opinion of the Ministry of Transport ought to be spread over a term of years.[1] Stock must all bear fixed interest and be redeemed through sinking funds within a period approved by the Ministry, but ninety years at the latest (sixty years for river works).[2] When the redemption period is ninety years, sinking fund payments may be suspended during the first decade. There are of course no voting rights. For the protection of stockholders, after three months' default owners of not less than £500,000 nominal value may apply for the appointment of a receiver and manager,[3] but the latter can administer the port only in accordance with the Port of London Acts and not specifically in the interest of holders.[4] In contrast to the senior issues of the London Transport Board, port stocks are not trustee securities. Total borrowing is quantitatively limited by statute, the amount being raised from time to time as new

[1] 1920 Act, s. 95.　　[2] Ibid., ss. 96, 104.　　[3] Ibid., s. 96 (4) (A).
[4] Port of London Authority v. Commissioners of Inland Revenue, [1922] 2 K.B. 599, 618 (Younger, L.J.).

works are authorized. At present it stands at £45,000,000,[1] leaving a margin of £3,000,000 over existing needs and immediate commitments.

The chief sources of working revenue are port rates on all goods, dock and warehousing charges on goods handled in the docks, river tonnage dues on all vessels, discharging charges and tonnage dues on vessels entering the docks, and rents for the hire of land, fixed berths, plant, and supplies. The port rate on goods was a novelty in London in 1908, introduced to enable the new Authority to establish its credit on a sound basis and obtain money from the public for much-needed development. Unlimited discretion in fixing the amount of the charge on various commodities would have given the P.L.A. tremendous power to injure specific trades, a danger by no means outbalanced in merchants' minds by the representative composition of the governing board. At their insistence, a schedule of maxima was established by Provisional Order and confirmed by Parliament,[2] while in addition the total sum collected was not to exceed one-thousandth the value of London's aggregate foreign trade.[3] The latter limitation proved too narrow during the severe trade contraction of the last few years and was repealed in 1932.[4] In exchange, a "revision clause"[5] was enacted, giving the Minister power on application from a trade association or from the Authority itself, and after inquiry and report by a rates advisory committee, to alter the maxima downward or upward but not above those scheduled to the Act, which comprised the rates then in force. In effect, the Authority's discretion was limited to making voluntary reductions.

Statutory maxima also limit the other major charging powers of the P.L.A., except for warehousing and special services like sampling, examining, appraising, and repacking,

---

[1] 1932 Act, s. 14.
[2] Port of London (Port Rates on Goods) Provisional Order Act, 1910, 10 Edw. VII & 1 Geo. V, Ch. C.   [3] 1920 Act, s. 14 (2).
[4] 1932 Act, s. 16 (1).   [5] Ibid., s. 16 (3–9).

where the Authority is in direct competition with private wharfingers and warehouse-keepers. Dock charges on goods, the most lucrative item, were revised steadily upwards during the war-time inflation, and finally settled on a new statutory basis in 1922,[1] with a "revision clause" identical with that later adopted for port rates. On most commodities there is sufficient margin between actual and maximum charges to leave the Authority a modicum of discretion in the allocation of burden, but it is relatively slight.

The order of application of revenue is also fixed by statute in the usual manner, i.e. to: (a) working expenditure; (b) interest on "A" Stock, the Authority's senior security; (c) interest on other stock; (d) interest on loans raised otherwise than by stock; (e) sinking funds; and (f) a general reserve fund.[2] This latter fund is limited to £2,000,000,[3] and without special authorization from the Minister may be applied only toward deficiencies on revenue account.[4] Any remaining surplus after the reserve is established may be devoted "to such purposes and in such manner for the benefit of the Port of London as the Port Authority may determine." Since no element of profit enters into P.L.A. finance, this can include only capital development, wage increases, or reduced charges.

In its general operations, likewise, the P.L.A. is as a public concern a fundamentally independent body. Like other public concerns it is subject to ultimate potential control by Parliament, its begetter, while in a number of matters the Ministry of Transport exercises special controlling supervision.

Every enterprise, public or private, is within the shadow of possible statutory regulation, but in the case of the P.L.A. grants of power are ordinarily in limited terms, inherited from the private legislation of the old companies. The 480 sections and fourteen schedules of the Act of

---

[1] Port of London (Dock Charges) Act, 1923, 13 & 14 Geo. V, Ch. XXXIV.
[2] 1920 Act, s. 106.   [3] 1932 Act, s. 15.   [4] 1920 Act, s. 107.

1920 are sprinkled with specific provisions governing such
particulars as the placing of lights and buoys, the duties
and jurisdiction of dock and harbour masters, obligations
to merchants and shipowners in handling their goods and
vessels, and savings for the rights of sewage commissioners,
water boards, railways, fisheries, local authorities, and other
bodies with which the P.L.A. may come in contact. In the
ordinary course of events, however, the most important
statutory restrictions concern compulsory acquisition of
land and other undertakings in the port, construction of
new works, and the matters of finance above described.
The Minister alone may by order authorize new works or
compulsory acquisition of land, but only after public
inquiry by an impartial deputy;[1] in cases where he considers parliamentary sanction desirable the order must be
confirmed by both Houses. It has in practice been found
more convenient to apply directly to Parliament by way of
Private Bills. Such sanction is also necessary for purchasing
other undertakings, except by agreement.[2] Since the organic
Act was passed in 1908, the Authority has brought fifteen
Bills before Parliament, all of which have been passed
substantially as deposited and frequently unopposed. Ten
contained financial provisions; three related to the compulsory acquisition of land; and clauses for new works were
in six. Two were to rectify minor ambiguities or anomalies
in the law. Only once has there been submitted a proposal
to acquire another undertaking, namely, Hay's Wharf and
its subsidiary properties in 1932, but the matter was re-
considered by the P.L.A. in view of the expense involved
and objections by certain traders, and the clause voluntarily
withdrawn.[3]

Opportunity for debate on the Authority in the House
of Commons is very limited. The Minister of Transport is
its spokesman, but financial autonomy precludes its dis-

[1] 1920 Act, s. 11.   [2] Ibid., s. 10.
[3] P.L.A.—23rd Annual Report, 1931–2, p. 7.

cussion on his vote. The constitutional position was clearly enunciated by the Speaker in 1912, when the Board of Trade occupied the position *vis-à-vis* the P.L.A. now held by the Ministry, in refusing a motion to adjourn to consider the alleged failure of the Authority to relieve traffic congestion and decasualize labour:

I regret that I am not able to accept the motion of the honourable Member. The Port of London is an Authority set up by Parliament, and quite independent of the Board of Trade. . . . That being so, it is clear that the Board of Trade have no such control as the honourable Gentleman would wish to imply in his motion. . . . It is true that the Board of Trade have certain representatives on the Port Authority, but they have no controlling power through those representatives. . . . I do not know whether they have given instructions or not, but it seems to me that even if they have given instructions they have no control, and they cannot compel the independent Authority to take a particular line.[1]

At question time the Minister gives full replies where his own duties in relation to the Authority are concerned, or on simple matters of fact already open to the public, as he does when the Government takes positive action in regard to a labour dispute or in aiding the finance of capital construction. The day-to-day conduct of the Authority's business, however, is left to its own discretion, and if any reply whatever is given it follows the formula, "I am informed by the P.L.A. that . . ."[2] Complaints are referred back to the Authority, even when alleging non-feasance of statutory obligations,[3] for the Minister has no general authority to require compliance with the law comparable with that of the Postmaster General under the Charter of the British Broadcasting Corporation. As a result, five or six years have passed without the slightest mention of the P.L.A. on the floor of the House.

[1] *Official Report, Commons*, 5th series, vol. 41, col. 816 (July 22, 1912).
[2] Ibid., vol. 44, cols. 1097–8 (December 16, 1912).
[3] Ibid., vol. 60, col. 548 (March 26, 1914).

Legal limitations and Parliamentary discussion offer no machinery for continuing control, which, so far as it is provided, rests with the Minister of Transport or, in a few cases, with the Board of Trade. One of these departments has revisory jurisdiction over almost all the P.L.A.'s administrative functions, hearing appeals on river craft licences and licences to construct works in the port, and, after a full hearing, confirming all bye-laws.[1] The Authority is also limited by Ministerial powers in a number of its operations as a commercial enterprise. New works not requiring parliamentary sanction and the acquisition of other undertakings even by agreement require authorization by the Minister.[2] In regard to P.L.A. finance he serves as a watchdog on behalf of the stockholders, framing regulations[3] for the due payment of interest and management of sinking funds and enforcing the Authority's compliance. Moreover, lest the need to maintain credit for future borrowings be insufficient inducement to the Board to achieve financial equilibrium and to prevent a sacrifice of stockholders to the transitory advantage of uneconomically low charges, the Authority must at the beginning of each year submit to the Minister an estimate of receipts and expenditure for the coming period; if he considers a satisfactory balance unlikely he may require an increase in any or all rates, within the maxima set by law.[4] Needless to say this power has never been exercised, but its implications are significant. It appears that in the eyes of the legislators of 1908 the representative constitution without voting rights for stockholders did not alone afford sufficient protection to these lenders of capital. In practical terms the clause was directed toward improving P.L.A. credit in the money market.

The Minister is also endowed with special authority in the interest of users of the port. The "revision clause" for

---

[1] 1920 Act, ss. 359, 248, 449.   [2] Ibid., ss. 10 (1), 11.
[3] "Port of London Stock Regulations, 1921," *Statutory Rules and Orders*, 1921, No. 1700.   [4] 1920 Act, s. 108.

port rates and dock charges has already been described; in addition he may act on complaints of "unfairly oppressive" action by the P.L.A. in any aspect, including charges, of its dock or warehousing business. If satisfied that the complaint is reasonable, he

shall call upon the Port Authority for an explanation and shall endeavour to settle amicably the differences between the complainant and the Port Authority and shall from time to time submit to Parliament such reports with regard thereto as [he] thinks fit.[1]

If no settlement is reached and the complaint emanates from a Government department, the London Chamber of Commerce, or any representative trade association, and refers to the warehousing business of the Authority, the Minister may after a hearing "make such order as in his opinion the circumstances require."

In the early years a few complaints of discrimination were submitted under this right of appeal, but no formal action was taken and no compulsion exercised on the P.L.A. An ex-member of the Authority says of the provision that it "has worked admirably in that it has scarcely been worked at all."[2] Nevertheless, its potential use is probably of considerable influence in preventing discrimination or other arbitrary action; indeed, when a rate advance was under consideration in 1924 the Authority, under the London Chamber of Commerce's threat to institute a Ministerial inquiry, went so far as to permit an accountant appointed by the Chamber to examine its books.[3] In general, sufficient protection is afforded by the constitution of the P.L.A. and the close and continuous watchfulness of merchants' and shippers' trade organizations, which are never reluctant to make direct representations[4] and are on excellent terms with the Authority.

[1] 1920 Act, s. 195.   [2] Broodbank, in 4 *Public Administration*, 314.
[3] *London Chamber of Commerce, 43rd Annual Report of the Council*, 1924, p. 46.
[4] Cf. *Annual Reports* of the London Chamber of Commerce and the London General Shipowners' Society.

Audit and published accounts provide a retrospective
check over the Authority's operations and a degree of public
insight into its working. The Minister appoints an auditor
each year and prescribes the form and detail of the accounts.[1]
In addition, the Authority submits an annual report sur-
veying the work and results of the previous year.[2] In their
degree of detail, particularly in regard to capital expenditure
and revenue account, these documents are in happy contrast
with the corresponding reports of the B.B.C.; the P.L.A.
has not feared to reveal to the public its financial structure.
Within the published classifications, however, P.L.A. expenditure and salaries are private, and cannot be obtained even
by question in Parliament.[3]

In form the P.L.A. is probably surrounded with more
restrictions than any other public concern, but they are
rarely called into operation. Initiative almost always rests
with the Authority, and where the Minister's approval is
required it is never extended beyond the safeguarding of
other interests. Direct political influence is negligible; the
Authority has, on the contrary, at times shown itself distinctly antagonistic to Governments of the day. Lord
Devonport stated its attitude to political interference in
labour disputes:

We tell the Government to leave us to settle our disputes,
and if we fail then bring whatever machinery they like into
play. We are not going to have the Government running our
labour affairs; we are going to resist it vehemently at all times.[4]

A similar hostility was expressed toward regulation from
Whitehall of trade routes in certain commodities immediately after the war.[5] Again, when Sir Eric Geddes proposed
to invest the Minister of Transport with general regulatory

----

[1] 1920 Act, s. 109, and *Statutory Rules and Orders*, 1929, No. 212; 1933,
No. 329.   [2] 1920 Act, s. 441.
[3] *Official Report, Commons*, 5th series, vol. 44, cols. 1097–8 (December 16,
1912).
[4] *Transport Workers—Court of Inquiry*, 1920, *Minutes of Evidence*, p. 341.
[5] Ibid., p. 338.

power over port trusts in the interest of general transport co-ordination he was vigorously resisted by the P.L.A.[1] Such outside control as exists is devised merely to offset the character of the Authority as a miscellany of interests. Since it is impossible so to balance a governing board that everyone concerned is assured just treatment, appeal must lie to some impartial organ. A small, independently appointed board might well be trusted with more discretion, but its advantages have been judged inferior to those of experience and of satisfaction and confidence among the trading community, derived from the existing constitution.

The day-to-day operations of the P.L.A. are performed by its administrative staff of over four thousand and a force of skilled and unskilled labour numbering some seven thousand, partially employed direct and partially through contractors. Unlike many other public concerns, however, the P.L.A. Board follows the common practice among port trusts of exercising very close supervision over all matters of administration other than routine, and concentrating in its own hands the determination even of minor questions of policy. Meeting as a full body only fortnightly, its active work is devolved upon eight committees, namely, General Purposes, Dock and Warehouse, River, Finance, Staff, Stores, Law and Parliamentary, and Maintenance. The ordinary member sits on at least two committees and hence appears at the head office some three or four times each week, while the Chairman and Vice-Chairman devote considerably more time to the work of the Authority. Before 1920 the committees supervised many details of routine administration, but in that year executive reorganization under a new general manager removed much of the burden from the directing members. Even to-day any operation involving a departure from regular working under agreed principles must be referred to the appropriate committee

[1] *Port of London Authority—Ways and Communications Bill—Observations on the Proposals—March* 1919 (Pamphlet).

for approval. Ultimate decisions of the P.L.A. are made not only *de jure* but *de facto* by the Board.

In the earlier period administrative responsibility bifurcated at the head into engineering functions, including new construction, maintenance, and river improvement, under a Chief Engineer, and commercial and administrative functions under a General Manager and Secretary. After the war, however, a new policy was introduced of sub-contracting dredging and maintenance work and carrying on new developments under the supervision of outside consultants with their own technical and labour force, thus greatly reducing the importance of the Authority's own engineers. A complete reorganization followed, consolidating the entire administration under the newly appointed General Manager, Mr. D. J. (now Sir David) Owen, upon whom all formal responsibility and most of the work of co-ordination is concentrated. Every matter going before a committee receives at least his nominal consideration. Below him are a number of chief officers, including the Secretary and Solicitor, Dock and Traffic Manager, River Superintendent and Chief Harbour Master, Chief Engineer, Chief Draughtsman, Treasurer, Chief Accountant, Land and Estates Manager, Establishment Officer, Stores Officer, Chief Police Officer, Medical Officer, and Publicity Officer.[1]

The supervisory and administrative staff of 4,500 is divided into Upper and Lower Divisions, with some 1,400 in the former. It is recruited from the secondary schools by examination and paid monthly. Its members fill indoor administrative posts. The Lower Division comes from the elementary schools, being largely recruited from P.L.A. messengers and the sons of the permanent labour force by examination, failing which they may enter the labour ranks. It is paid weekly and concerned for the most part with outdoor supervision and a modicum of routine clerical work. Promotion to the Upper Division is not barred but is

---

[1] A. Bell: *The Port of London, 1909-34*, p. 74.

extremely rare, since the Authority has made no provision for regular advancement. The preservation of this sharp distinction is ground for justifiable minor criticism. Before 1926 both Divisions were organized in the non-manual section of the Transport and General Workers' Union. In the General Strike of that year, however, almost half of the Lower Division followed the manual forces in the stoppage of work, while 95 per cent of the Upper Division stayed in; the consequent complications led to the almost complete withdrawal from the Union of the latter body, which later joined the National Association of Local Government Officers.

Some 4,000 of the 34,000 registered port transport workers in London find their employment regularly with the P.L.A., along with several thousand in allied fields. In this respect the port stands midway in British practice, contrasting both with Liverpool, where the Mersey Board employs no labour directly, and with Manchester, where the Ship Canal Company enjoys a legal monopoly over employment. Almost all the dock warehousing operations are performed by the Authority's employees, together with the discharge of vessels and quay handling of goods in the upper docks. Men under contract with the shippers themselves load vessels throughout the system and perform most other operations in the lower docks, although the P.L.A. is always ready to supply labour anywhere on its estate.[1]

Under the Act of 1908 special obligations were imposed upon the P.L.A. in regard to casual labour, the notorious sociological feature of the dock industry:

The Port Authority shall take into consideration the existing methods and conditions of engagement of workmen employed in dock, riverside, and warehouse labour in connection with the Port of London, and shall, either by themselves or in co-operation with other bodies or persons, by establishing or maintaining or

[1] E. C. P. Lascelles and S. S. Bullock: *Dock Labour and Decasualization* (London, 1924), p. 10.

assisting in the establishment or maintenance of offices, waiting-rooms, and employment registers, and by the collection and communication of information and otherwise, take such steps as they think best calculated to diminish the evils of casual employment, and to promote the more convenient and regular engagement of such workmen or any class thereof.[1]

An emasculating proviso, however, made impossible any thorough-going reform over the whole port, for "nothing in this section shall deprive any person of any legal right which he would otherwise possess with regard to the engagement of labour." Within the limits of its own staff the Authority has extended and improved the regularization of employment along the lines set out by its chief predecessor, the London and India Docks Company. About 2,800 men form a permanent force, paid weekly and under direct contract with the General Manager, a number roughly equivalent to the Authority's minimum needs on any day. As determined by the daily fluctuations of shipping, casual labourers are taken on in addition, averaging 800 to 1,000 in number. They are divided into "B" or preference men, with numbered tickets, always looking to the Authority for employment in the first instance, and "C" men or ordinary casuals. Handbills are posted each evening detailing the expected places and ticket numbers of men wanted for the following day. Only by thus maximizing mobility within each group of docks has the P.L.A. been able to employ permanently as many as 80 per cent of its staff. It is true that the position of "B" men is made correspondingly more uncertain and their opportunities for regular work diminished, while "C" men are hardly ever employed by the Authority, but the scheme has proved the feasibility of mobilizing labour over a large and geographically unfavourable area, capable of extension, were there but a single employer in the port, to the whole of London.

In fact, however, there are 300 employers, each with

---

[1] 1908 Act, s. 28 (1); 1920 Act, s. 440 (1).

his own pool of labour, and the proviso to the decasualization provision of the Act of 1908 has effectually prevented any action by the P.L.A. to regularize work for the remaining 30,000 men. Since the war important steps have been taken in this direction through port worker registration and the exclusion of unemployed from other industries,[1] but not on the initiative of the P.L.A. The radical solution, a labour monopoly for the Authority, does not commend itself either to shipowners, who fear a strengthening of labour's bargaining position, or to the workers themselves, who remember the P.L.A. as a difficult opponent in past disputes. The problem remains serious.

Both wages and hours of work have undergone substantial improvement during the Authority's régime, largely as a consequence of the formation of a powerful trade union organization, the Transport and General Workers' Union, which includes over 90 per cent of the workers in the port. Ordinary time wage rates, now determined by agreements on a nation-wide scale, are at a minimum of £3 6s. for a forty-four hour week, but 85 per cent of P.L.A. employment is at piece rates, often yielding more than £5 for a full working week. The minimum rate represents an increase of 157 per cent over pre-war standards, compared with a rise in the cost of living of only 45 per cent. The regularly employed docker is thus somewhat favoured by comparison with other industrial workers, even taking into account the danger element, which is greater only in mining.[2] The ground for these high rates is the prevalence of casual employment, necessitating a wage to permit adequate subsistence upon an average of only four days' work out of a possible five and one-half.[3] Thus casual labour, in addition to its social evils, is indirectly responsible for an unneces-

[1] Lascelles and Bullock: *Dock Labour and Decasualization* (London, 1924), Ch. XII; *New Survey of London Life and Labour* (London, 1931), vol. ii, pp. 394–9; *Report of the Committee of Inquiry on Port Labour*, 1931, pars. 21–54.
[2] *New Survey of London Life and Labour*, vol. ii, p. 418.
[3] *Transport Workers—Court of Inquiry, Report*, p. 12.

*

sarily high burden of labour costs upon this port, as upon all the ports of Great Britain.

In the general character of its labour relations the P.L.A. has had a very chequered career. Its infancy was marred by the severe strikes of 1911 and 1912, of which the latter was prolonged for almost ten weeks by the employers' refusal to undertake any negotiations prior to resumption of work, despite a number of governmental efforts to find a settlement.[1] P.L.A. conditions and wage rates had no share in its origin, but the activities of Lord Devonport as leader of the employers and the reduction of former permanent men to casual status upon termination of the strike so embittered the workpeople that resulting animosities were not healed for a decade.[2] Since the war, however, there have developed evidences of a happier relationship. An unofficial strike in 1923 was brought to an end at the instance of the union officials themselves,[3] while the official and successful stoppage of the following year[4] involved no breach of agreement and lasted only a week. Since then the whole body of port workers has been called out only in the general strike of 1926,[5] for which this industry had no direct responsibility. Meanwhile a port employers' association has brought security for the observance of agreements by other employers in conjunction with the P.L.A., while a full-blown system of Whitley Councils,

[1] *Report upon the Present Disputes affecting Transport Workers in the Port of London and on the Medway, with Minutes of Evidence (Clarke Report)*, Cd. 6229 of 1912; Board of Trade: *Report on Strikes and Lock-outs and on Conciliation and Arbitration Boards in the United Kingdom in 1912*, Cd. 7089 of 1913, pp. xxxiv–xxxix; Lord Askwith: *Industrial Problems and Disputes* (London, 1920), Ch. xxii; C. Watney and J. A. Little: *Industrial Warfare—The Aims and Claims of Capital and Labour* (London, 1912), Ch. vii.

[2] H. Gosling: *Up and Down Stream* (London, 1927), pp. 157–72; *Transport Workers—Court of Inquiry, 1920, Minutes of Evidence*, p. 342.

[3] 31 *Ministry of Labour Gazette*, 239, 280 (July and August 1923).

[4] *Report of the Ministry of Labour for the Years 1923 and 1924*, Cmd. 2481 of 1925, pp. 54–8.

[5] *P.L.A. Monthly*, No. 8, pp. 271, 275 (June 1926), and No. 10, pp. 357–60 (August 1926); *P.L.A.—18th Annual Report, 1926–7*, pp. 9–15.

including a Port of London Local Joint Committee and five Group Joint Committees within the port, one of which is devoted exclusively to the P.L.A. and its employees, provides machinery for continuous and effective co-operation.[1] Joint action has been taken in reducing accidents, improving conditions in specific types of work, and above all in steps toward the decasualization of employment. In these conciliatory developments the Authority has played its full part, and sympathy between employer and employee is now evident on both sides.

The Authority began its career on March 31, 1909, with capital valued at about £23,000,000, the sum paid the London and India, Surrey Commercial, and Millwall Dock Companies for their undertakings. Under the terms of their agreements with the Government, the shareholders were given Port of London "A" and "B" Stock, bearing interest at 3 and 4 per cent respectively, in amounts sufficient to yield an income equal to that received on the average from 1901 to 1907.[2] Some consideration was also given for the most junior securities, which had paid no interest or dividends for years. As in the case of London Transport a quarter-century later, no allowance was made for increased security and none for the improbability of maintenance of existing profits without consolidation of ownership, so that a degree of unnecessary and unjustified burden was placed on the P.L.A. for ninety years. The dock companies were given the extraordinarily generous treatment of twenty-six years' purchase of existing revenue,[3] although its maintainability was particularly doubtful, for a thorough examination of the estate by the new Authority's Chief Engineer shortly after the transfer revealed that the properties "had not been maintained in a proper state of repair, and to ensure the efficient and safe working of the undertakings a

---

[1] *New Survey of London Life and Labour*, vol. ii, pp. 413–16.

[2] *Joint Select Committee*, 1908, pp. 153–85; *Memorandum in Reference to the Port of London Bill*, H.C. No. 109 of 1908, p. 7.

[3] *Coal Industry Commission*, 1919, vol. ii, p. 1112.

large and immediate expenditure was absolutely necessary," estimated at £736,000.[1]

Faced at the outset with the necessity for redeeming the companies' delinquencies, the P.L.A. had also to plan immediate large-scale expansion of the port's accommodation. Its very *raison d'être* was London's relative decline in comparison with the ports of the Continent and the universal dissatisfaction of shippers and merchants with both the river channel and the equipment for handling goods and vessels. The Act of 1908, therefore, laid upon the Authority an injunction

to take into consideration the state of the river and the accommodation and facilities afforded in the Port of London, and, subject to the provisions of this Act, to take such steps as they may consider necessary for the improvement thereof.[2]

The new body set about its task with vigour. The rate of dredging in the river channel set by the Thames Conservancy from 1907 to 1909 was immediately doubled, and rapid improvement followed until the war, when all new works were necessarily curtailed. In 1928 the programme was completed, except for dredging to maintain a constant depth, after the removal of 47,000,000 tons of material at a cost of over £2,000,000.[3] While in 1909 the ruling depth of the channel at low water ordinary spring tides was only 25 feet from the Nore to Tilbury, 18 feet from Tilbury to Coldharbour Point, 15 feet to the Royal Albert Dock, and 13 feet beyond, the present depths for the corresponding segments of the Thames are 30, 30, 27, and 20 feet, as far as the Surrey Commercial Docks, and from 14 to 16 feet beyond. The channel will admit to Tilbury any ship afloat within the dimensions of the new entrance lock, which is

[1] *P.L.A.—1st Annual Report*, 1909–10, p. 13.
[2] 1908 Act, s. 2 (1).
[3] D. J. Owen: "The Port of London Authority—A Survey of Twenty Years' Work and Trade," *P.L.A. Monthly*, No. 42, p. 191 (April 1929).

to except only the liners *Normandie* and *Queen Mary*, save for a brief period before and after low tide.

The Authority's chief concern, however, was naturally its dock and warehouse system. Restoration of the earning power and physical condition of existing plant was first undertaken, financed out of revenue and absorbing up to the outbreak of the war £437,000. During the period of hostilities this programme of special repairs was suspended, along with much of the ordinary annual maintenance work. Funds to cover both these objects were consolidated in 1924,[1] totalling £3,000,000, and rapid progress ensued. By 1931 both the laxness of the old companies and the delays caused by the war had been wholly made good.

As a basis for large-scale capital development the Chief Engineer submitted in 1910 a comprehensive report covering "all possible improvements," classified into an urgent programme, a prospective programme, and a contingent programme, and estimated to cost in all about £14,500,000.[2] The general scheme was accepted by the Authority, and the first great phase of expansion carried through from 1911 to 1922, delayed by the war for an average of three to four years. About £8,000,000 was expended during this period, an amount heavily swollen by the additional post-war costs of construction. Taking pride of place among the new works was the King George V Dock, sixty-four acres in extent, with an entrance lock 100 by 800 feet, described by an independent committee of shippers as "particularly well designed and excellently equipped."[3] Improvements were also undertaken at the London, East and West India, Royal Albert, and Tilbury Docks, including a very large addition to cold-storage facilities to accommodate the growing trade in frozen meat.

[1] *P.L.A.—16th Annual Report*, 1924–5, p. 4.

[2] *P.L.A.—2nd Annual Report*, 1910–11, pp. 7–8.

[3] *Report of the Port Facilities Committee appointed by the Chamber of Shipping of the United Kingdom, with Representatives of the Association of British Chambers of Commerce and of the Federation of British Industries*, 2nd ed. (London, 1924), p. 253.

War-time conditions dislocated the whole of the normal trade, the Authority placing itself at the Government's disposal. The gradual restoration of equilibrium from 1919 to 1922 found persistent congestion in the Surrey Docks, not attributable solely to war circumstances, while rapid growth in the size and draught of ships continued to encroach upon facilities further down the river. Well before the completion of the first improvement scheme, plans were under consideration for a second phase of development, at a cost of £5,000,000.[1] Completed in 1931, it involved the extension of Tilbury Dock by fifteen acres, with a new entrance lock 110 by 1,000 feet and a new dry dock, the Tilbury passenger landing stage, a new entrance lock for the West India Dock system, and thorough modernization of the India and Millwall group. On the Surrey side two new docks were constructed for the timber trade and congestion was eliminated by 1926.

These improvements constituted a major revolution in London's physical equipment. In contrast with the "universal dissatisfaction" found by the Revelstoke Commission in 1902, a shipowners' representative testified in 1929 that the P.L.A. had "got all the schemes in hand that one can see," and that "the equipment is as fine as at any port in the world."[2] Nevertheless, after a few years' lull, continued increase in trade was felt to justify a further extensive scheme of modernization at the Royal Albert and Victoria Docks, authorized in 1935 at an estimated cost of £1,750,000.[3] On the side of physical development, therefore, the Authority has shown a forward-looking attitude in marked contrast to that of the old companies. Despite the need of anticipating expansion by at least five years,

[1] A. Binns: "Twenty-five Years' Engineering Developments of the Port of London Authority," *P.L.A. Monthly*, No. 102, pp. 163–70 (April 1934).

[2] *Royal Commission on Transport*, 1929–31, *Minutes of Evidence*, vol. iii, Questions 12359, 12617.

[3] *P.L.A.—26th Annual Report*, 1934–5, p. 5; Port of London Act, 1935, ss. 6–30.

the average period between the evolution of plans for major works and their completion, it has with the sole exception of the irregular war period successfully responded to calls upon its facilities.

Money for capital development was obtained through the creation of £14,000,000[1] of port stock, bearing interest at from 3½ to 6 per cent. Issues floated during the unfavourable post-war market conditions, when high rates were inevitable, carried provisions for early optional redemption, fully exploited by the Authority in the subsequent era of cheap money. Three conversion operations since 1924 have reduced annual interest charges by £95,000, or 7½ per cent. In general port stock has been very well received by the public, being ranked for security among the lowest yielding non-trustee investments.[2] With all the disturbances of war, post-war inflation, and more recent general depression, there has never been the slightest possibility of default on interest. The general reserve fund has stood untouched at £1,000,000 since 1921, and steady progress has been maintained with the ultimate redemption of stock through sinking funds, which will leave the port in 1999 with much of its relatively imperishable capital free of charge. The financial management of the undertaking has been of the highest calibre.

Despite the quality of its credit, the P.L.A. felt unable in 1922 to finance unaided the second phase of its programme of expansion.[3] A new dock must be built with an eye to the needs of a quarter-century, and may not become fully remunerative for a decade or two. The right to charge interest to capital and postpone sinking fund payments for ten years were insufficient safeguards to allow the P.L.A. to commit itself to the payment of heavy charges in the abnormally stimulated money market, even when it expected the works to be economic in the long run. Eager to grasp

---

[1] Excluding issues to redeem stock previously issued.
[2] Cf. 109 *Economist*, 582 (September 28, 1929); 115 Ibid., 365 (August 20, 1932).   [3] *P.L.A.*—14th *Annual Report*, 1922–3, p. 9.

any opportunity for constructive employment, the Government arranged through its Unemployment Grants Committee to provide half interest on the necessary borrowings for fifteen years,[1] amounting at present to £120,000 annually. In accepting this assistance the Authority in no way compromised its independence, for similar grants were given a large number of privately owned companies as well as other public authorities. In effect it merely accelerated works which would otherwise have been postponed pending more favourable borrowing conditions, and it is worthy of note that with the restoration of such conditions the Authority is undertaking its contemporary development programme without outside support.

In its normal operations, outside of development work, the P.L.A. has in principle simply carried on the work of the dock companies, extending it from time to time to cater for new trades. No fundamental matters of policy arise in this field. The Authority was at its inception, and remains, the greatest warehouse-keeper in the world, providing services of a variety and quality unique among harbour authorities.[2] It is not open to question that it has administered this undertaking with efficiency, unceasingly exploring new possibilities, whether in mechanization of clerical and operative work or in administrative reorganization, of reducing its operating charges. Over the last six years it has effected a reduction of £600,000, or 13 per cent of the annual working costs. After allowing for £150,000 saved on rates under the general de-rating of transport undertakings in 1929,[3] almost 10 per cent remains, attributable to a general tightening of expenditure on maintenance and in organization.

Operating efficiency is reflected in the general level of

[1] *P.L.A.—15th Annual Report*, 1923-4, p. 8; *Official Report, Commons*, 5th series, vol. 169, col. 2012 (February 21, 1924).
[2] D. J. Owen: *The Port of London—Yesterday and To-day* (London, 1927), pp. 30-72.
[3] Local Government Act, 1929, 19 Geo. V, Ch. 17, ss. 68, 136.

port rates and other charges on vessels and goods. The disparities in wage levels and other costs forbid comparison with the dock companies or the pre-war years of the P.L.A. itself, but comparison with other British ports shows London in a favourable light. Thus in a study made in 1926 for the London General Shipowners' Society, comparing charges on nine representative commodities at London, Liverpool, Glasgow, Avonmouth, and Hull, it was found that the weighted average aggregate dues for London were the lowest, at 8s. 9d. per ton, compared with an average of 10s. 9d. for the other four ports.[1] An unusually heavy proportion of the total falls on the shipowner instead of the merchant, leading the former frequently to describe London as "the most expensive port in the world," but by the general British standard London is comparatively inexpensive with regard to the whole sum of costs added at this stage of transport to the final price to the consumer. It is true that London shares with other British ports a general level of charges far exceeding those in force on the Continent.[2] Much of this differential is due to necessary differences in physical structure, for small tidal ranges abroad obviate the necessity for enclosed docks. A portion of the capital cost in Hamburg, Rotterdam, and Antwerp is borne by the State or municipality, and the equipment is generally more modern. A larger proportion of bulk as against mixed cargoes reduces operating costs. Wages are noticeably higher in Britain by virtue of the shorter regular working week and higher increments for overtime. Most important, however, is the industry's general over-equipment with capital when viewed from a national standpoint. Fresh port capital

[1] The data on which these figures are based were kindly supplied by the Secretary to the Society, but for the calculation of the averages and method of weighting I am alone responsible.

[2] Sir David J. Owen: "The Problem of Port Costs," 13 *Dock and Harbour Authority*, 49–52 (December 1932); A. H. Roberts: "Modern Dock Facilities—Some Comparisons of British and Continental Facilities," ibid., pp. 365–8 (October 1933); *Royal Commission on Transport*, 1929–31, *Minutes of Evidence*, vol. iii, Questions 11933–5.

since the war has been estimated at about £40,000,000, despite a 4½ per cent decrease in shipping from 1913 to 1933.[1] With the steady growth in the size of ships a measure of new construction would have been necessary in any case, but a considerable portion seems imputable to competition among British ports for a contracting trade.

Such a hindrance to national transport efficiency raises problems outside the sphere of any single local authority like the P.L.A. Within the present framework its success must be measured by the criterion of London trade during its régime. The following table summarizes the development:[2]

	1909–10 Tons	1923–24 Tons	1934–35 Tons
Vessels entering and clearing the port	38,510,989	41,214,928	58,947,642
Vessels paying river tonnage dues	28,579,648	30,748,768	42,322,588
Vessels using wet docks	17,436,097	19,195,799	24,764,600
Import goods handled by the P.L.A.	2,050,795	2,293,180	2,215,868
Export goods handled by the P.L.A.	640,769	615,349	615,501
Stocks warehoused by the P.L.A.	440,531	514,000	578,695

As guardian of the river channel and recipient of port rates and river tonnage dues the Authority is interested in the trade of the port as a whole, which has shown continuous expansion counterbalancing even the severe depression following 1931. As dock and warehouse-keeper, however, its chief interest is in that proportion of shipping which enters the docks, which has remained throughout at about 45 per cent of the total, although falling off slightly in recent years. The P.L.A. has thus received the lion's share of the general increase.

More enlightening is a comparison of London trends with those of other leading ports. The following table indicates

---

[1] D. Ross-Johnson: "English Port Ownership and Control," 13 *Journal of the Institute of Transport*, 107, 109 (January 1932).

[2] Statistics from the Annual Reports of the P.L.A.

the respective percentages of United Kingdom shipping and
value of trade at the six leading ports, with the Kingdom figures for scale:[1]

	1909	1923	1934
UNITED KINGDOM			
Shipping tonnage ..	253,894,704	274,893,997	289,494,073
Value of goods (£) ..	1,094,230,123	1,982,027,790	1,178,642,651
	Percentage of U.K.	*Percentage of U.K.*	*Percentage of U.K.*
LONDON			
Shipping	15·2	15·0	20·4
Goods	29·5	29·1	37·8
LIVERPOOL			
Shipping	11·0	11·1	11·6
Goods	27·3	26·7	21·9
HULL			
Shipping	4·1	4·8	3·8
Goods	6·1	5·1	5·6
MANCHESTER			
Shipping	2·1	2·3	2·5
Goods	4·0	4·7	4·2
SOUTHAMPTON			
Shipping	5·0	7·2	8·3
Goods	3·9	3·6	4·6
GLASGOW			
Shipping	4·4	4·4	3·8
Goods	3·8	4·0	3·9

It will be seen that despite a considerable initial supe-
riority in size, London's rate of development is beyond
comparison with any other port except Southampton.
London has, of course, enjoyed certain advantages for
which the port proper is not primarily responsible. The
basis of its import trade is the supply of food and raw
materials to a centre of population of 10,000,000, which
has expanded steadily during the present century. The
international wholesale markets for important commodities
like wool and tea, with exchanges and financial services
accompanying them, have been concentrated in the metropolis for decades, and could be removed only with the

[1] Calculated from statistics in the Board of Trade's *Statistical Abstracts for
the United Kingdom.*

greatest difficulty. Nevertheless, many other trade items which have also notably increased, such as tobacco, paper and paper-making material, wheat before milling, and un-refined sugar, are in no way London monopolies, and port efficiency must be held to have played a part in their attraction. Much of the increase in raw materials and in exports is related to the general southward movement of industry. Here again the primary causal factors are not relative adequacy of port services, but the Chief Inspector of Factories has considered as worthy of mention "the facilities for export furnished by the Port of London, and excellent transport facilities for raw materials and for finished products."[1] Taken in their *ensemble* the trade statistics present practical proof that the port has been equal to calls upon it and evidence of positive stimulation of the capital's commerce and industry. Viewed in this light it is clear that the satisfactory financial position of the P.L.A. contains no element of restrictive exploitation of such monopoly powers as it enjoys.

Its general success does not imply complete freedom from criticism, either in policy or in the form of its constitution. Specific complaints on matters of detail, continuously raised by the port's users and considered by the Authority, need not concern us here, but three more basic criticisms affect the administrative and constitutional structure of the P.L.A. The practice of contracting out dredging, repair, and maintenance work instituted in 1921, replacing direct execution by P.L.A. staff,[2] is found objectionable by certain engineering experts as incompatible with the most prompt and effective attention to emergency repairs and unlikely to result in economies.[3] Since any addition to the number

---

[1] *Annual Report of the Chief Inspector of Factories and Workshops for the Year* 1928, Cmd. 3360 of 1929, p. 6.

[2] *P.L.A.—12th Annual Report*, 1920-1, p. 9.

[3] Du-Plat-Taylor: *The Design, Construction and Maintenance of Docks, Wharves and Piers*, 2nd. Ed. (London, 1934), pp. 456-7; B. Cunningham: *Port Administration and Operation* (London, 1925), p. 80.

of separate employers in a port reduces labour mobility and militates against decasualization,[1] the change in policy must be judged unfortunate.

On the constitutional side there are possibilities of conflict between the P.L.A.'s administrative and commercial functions.[2] In particular, in hearing applications from other undertakers, possibly its competitors, for licences to construct works in the port, the Authority appears to be judge in its own case, raising objections not wholly removed by the right of appeal to the Minister of Transport. Towards the end of the war both municipalities and private companies were refused licences for deep-water wharves, and a Parliamentary Bill for the same purpose was opposed by the Authority. It was charged at the time that the P.L.A. was hindering the proper development of the port by vetoing such schemes for tidal facilities, and aggravating the congestion of the post-war years.[3] In retrospect its judgment was vindicated, for congestion proved temporary and abnormal, while its own experiment in a deep-water jetty, opened at Tilbury in 1920, required many years to attain full utilization.[4] As a matter of policy, moreover, the P.L.A. was established to eliminate pre-existing competition, owing to its demonstrated wastefulness, and it was hardly the Authority's duty to reverse this decision. The Board of Trade put this viewpoint in a statement that

by the Port of London Act, 1908, a single authority was established to administer, preserve, and improve the Port, and the scheme does not present any engineering or commercial advantages which would outweigh the desirability of maintaining the principle of a single representative authority for the whole Port.[5]

Indeed, the major defect in Port of London administration

---

[1] *Royal Commission on Transport*, 1929–31, *Minutes of Evidence*, vol. iii, pp. 933–48, "Memorandum of the Transport and General Workers' Union," par. 14.   [2] Broodbank, in 4 *Public Administration*, 309, 314.

[3] *Official Report, Commons*, 5th series, vol. 133, cols. 2064–6, 2099 (October 28, 1920).   [4] *Port Facilities Committee Report*, 1924, p. 265.

[5] *P.L.A.—10th Annual Report*, 1918–19, p. 20.

as it exists to-day is rather that the P.L.A. still lacks control over many of the facilities of the port. Over half the shipping tonnage is either received directly at the wharves of manufacturers or handled by the large number of private concerns managing "public" wharves. For several years the Association of Public Wharfingers has agreed to follow the P.L.A. in its rate making, but competition in facilities for the same trade remains. It is impossible to achieve maximum efficiency unless rationalization is extended to include river facilities as well as the dock system. Purchase of the wharves by the P.L.A., as strongly advocated by Sir Joseph Broodbank,[1] would remove several anomalies: the presence of a competitor on the governing board, the dredging by the Authority of a river channel above the docks to the direct benefit of its competitors, administrative decisions involving judgment over competitors, and the uneconomic "freewater" clause. The beneficial effects of reducing the number of port employers upon the problem of labour decasualization would be incalculable. Elimination of redundant capital would be of advantage to merchants and the ultimate consuming public alike. The present influence of competition upon rates is too slight to warrant traders' objection in 1932 to the P.L.A.'s proposal to acquire Hay's Wharf, an objection apparently based on a dogmatic "broad principle involved in a public authority compulsorily acquiring a private undertaking."[2] If at some future date the growth in London trade is decelerated and the wharves lose some of their present prosperity, acquisition may again be feasible.

Even greater potentialities for improved transport efficiency inhere in the possibility of port co-ordination over the nation as a whole. Sir Eric Geddes' scheme for general control by the Ministry of Transport was hotly and successfully resisted by the port trusts themselves in 1919.[3] Since

[1] In the *History of the Port of London*, vol. ii, pp. 509–10.
[2] *London Chamber of Commerce, 51st Annual Report of the Council*, 1932, p. 194.
[3] Cf. s. 4 of the Ministry of Transport Act, 1919, 9 & 10 Geo. V, Ch. 50, inserted at the instance of the dock and harbour authorities.

their financial responsibilities would have been left un-affected, the resistance was probably justified. The Royal Commission on Transport of 1931 was very inconclusive in regard to dock and harbour reform, making only a bare reference to regional consolidation and none to national co-ordination.[1] Nevertheless, opinion among both adminis-trators and users of the ports is rapidly coming to favour a move in this direction.[2] If associated with unification and nationalization of the railways, as in South Africa, the reform would involve administration by a central agency, either a Government department or a public concern on the model of the Electricity Board. A more feasible scheme would co-ordinate extensions, abandonments, and rate-making through a body similar to the Electricity Commis-sioners, leaving administration proper in the hands of existing and newly created regional port trusts. Under this plan the P.L.A. would constitute a single such regional authority. In any case, the time is ripe for an inquiry into this problem, which, if British trade is to be spared an unnecessary impediment, demands solution in the near future.

As far as London alone is concerned, the representative public concern has proved its value. Doubtless much of the P.L.A.'s success is due simply to its monopoly over the docks, which under any form of administration would have permitted rationalization of trade and freedom in rate-making not open to the former competitors, perhaps sufficient to restore the financial credit of the port. Never-

[1] *The Co-ordination and Development of Transport—Final Report of the Royal Commission on Transport*, Cmd. 3751 of 1931, pars. 479–80.

[2] Cf. Sir David J. Owen: "Great Britain and South Africa—The Questions of Trade and Transport," 26 *United Empire*, 104, 106 (February 1935); 92 *Shipping World*, 147 (January 30, 1935); A. A. Logan: "Port Ownership and Control," 15 *Journal of the Institute of Transport*, 33 (November 1933); F. W. P. Hampton: "The Probable Effects on Ports if included in a Scheme of Trans-port Rationalization," ibid., 386 (June 1934); F. Brown: "Port Reorganization —A National Problem," ibid., 132 (January 1934); *Royal Commission on Transport*, 1929–31, *Minutes of Evidence*, vol. iii, pp. 933-5, "Memorandum of the Transport and General Workers' Union," par. 16.

theless Parliament was justified in refusing to grant monopoly powers to any but a publicly constituted authority. For the essence of the representative public concern, responsible not to shareholders but to direct consumers of its services, and through its appointed members to local and national governmental authorities, is elimination of a choice among increased facilities, reduced charges, and increased dividends, by beneficiaries of the last alternative with no interest in the other two. This consideration vitiates Sir Joseph Brood-bank's proposal to restore the port to a private, monopolistic, statutory company, with limited dividends and appeals to an independent tribunal on rates and operations.[1] If maximum dividends were easily earned the incentive to efficient management would be destroyed; if earned with difficulty the port's users would have no security against restriction of services and sacrifice of necessary development, or even, as pre-1909 experience indicates, of maintenance. Expansion in the dock industry, moreover, requires anticipation of demands by many years, a factor not likely to receive full weight from importunate holders of equity shares. A public concern was introduced into the Port of London largely because profit-making was an unsatisfactory criterion of administration for the enterprise.

In its place was substituted a direct interest of shippers and merchants in optimum facilities at minimum cost, an incentive which has secured the services of competent business men and produced a highly successful régime. Only an unusual concomitance of circumstances makes such a constitution possible. It is dependent upon a clear, direct, common interest among P.L.A. electors and upon their organization into powerful trade associations coinciding with the area of the port and affording general acquaintanceship with leading personalities in the community. Without such associations, particularism would have a free hand, and might easily lead to complete dead-

[1] At 4 *Public Administration*, 315–17.

lock or the resignation of all power to a strong chairman or general manager. The filtering of more individual ends within the Chamber of Commerce and Shipowners' Society, aided by the leavening of appointed members, has permitted the broadest general interest of the port to be made paramount, while keeping the administrative machine under constant supervision by members of the Authority concerned to safeguard their constituents' rights and privileges.

Only because the port transport industry caters to the general public indirectly, by way of a limited number of merchants and shipowners, can the public interest find such complete expression through the medium of organized private interests. The representative public concern can be applied only to a narrow field of enterprise, restricted to industries fulfilling this peculiar condition and limited in geographical area. Where utilities of national scope are involved, or where the service is utilized by unorganized bodies of consumers, the public concern must take a different form, more closely related to the national legislature and dependent upon other motives for its effectiveness.

3

THE FORESTRY COMMISSION

by

JOHN PARKER, M.P.

THE German submarine campaign against British merchant-men in 1917 compelled the Government drastically to ration the tonnage allotted to each essential import. It was found then that timber needed more tonnage than any other single commodity, for it was quite impossible to curtail timber supplies which were required for vital military and civil purposes.

At the same time foreign timber merchants emptied the British exchequer and prices soared. If the price index figure for wood pulp for 1909–12 is taken as 100, the similar figure for 1916 was 228. In the critical war years it was difficult to utilize British-grown timber. There were no foresters or sawing machinery, and lumbermen had to be brought over from Canada. Nor were the consumers ready to absorb timber from new sources of supply, and serious dislocation was caused when the railways were unable to get "Baltic blocks" for sleepers.

The difficulties of this period led the Reconstruction Committee to appoint a Forestry Sub-Committee, the Acland Committee, which reported in May 1917. The Forestry Act of 1919, which created the Commission, was based largely upon its recommendations.

It had required the crisis of 1917 to drive home the danger of timber shortage and the necessity of action to remedy it. The matter had, however, been discussed at considerable length by a Royal Commission[1] which reported in 1909. It had then been suggested that a million acres of waste and infertile land in Great Britain and Ireland might

---

[1] Royal Commission on Coast Erosion and Afforestation.

be profitably afforested as a first step and, if that were a successful experiment, a much larger area could be put under trees at a later date. The Acland Committee drew up a more specific eighty-year programme of planting which the Forestry Commission has since used as a yardstick in carrying out its work.

In justifying the proposed creation of the Forestry Commission, the Acland Committee showed that, apart from articles of which wood was the main constituent, during 1909–13 this country had imported yearly 10,204,000 loads of wood and 859,000 tons of wood pulp. The latest figures, for 1934, show an even greater dependence on imported supplies, being 11,096,000 loads of wood and 2,244,000 tons of wood pulp. Not only is the total consumption of wood rising, but there is considerable evidence of a growing world shortage of softwood, which forms over 90 per cent of British timber imports. Only in Finland and Sweden of the European countries is planting equal to the cut. In Canada equilibrium may just be attained, but Canadian supplies are being steadily diverted to the United States, where the cut is 8·6 times greater than planting or natural regeneration. Many of the Russian, and all the Siberian, forests are at present too inaccessible to be useful. The case for setting up some body in this country to increase home timber supplies, which came to the fore in wartime, has since been strengthened by the growing world shortage of easily obtainable softwoods.

The Forestry Commission was created by the Forestry Act of 1919[1] following the recommendation of the Acland Committee, which had insisted on the necessity of some kind of central forestry organization in this country to make good the national timber deficiency. Parliament thus recognized that private landlords had neither the capital nor the desire to invest in afforestation for which returns were so far distant. It was thus compelled to establish machinery to

[1] 9 & 10 Geo. V, Ch. 58.

do the essential work of planting new forests, but it still hoped that private landlords would be able to maintain the existing woodlands.

The Ecclesiastical and Charity Commissions were chosen as models for the new Forestry Commission. This body originally consisted of eight commissioners and two assistant commissioners. The number of commissioners has now been increased to ten,[1] although the two new posts need not necessarily be filled. To enable it to carry out its multifarious duties the position and attainments of some of its members were defined in the Act of 1919.

One commissioner must be a Member of Parliament to answer questions put to him in the House about the work of the Commission. One must be "a person having scientific attainments and a technical knowledge of forestry." Two commissioners must possess knowledge and experience of forestry in Scotland. Although the commissioner who answers questions in the House cannot receive a salary, three of the other commissioners may be paid in the aggregate as much as £4,500 annually.

More than the statutory one are Members of Parliament. At present there are three Members of Parliament belonging to the three largest parties, and a fourth is a former Member. One has had experience of forestry in India. Landowners who have practised silviculture on their own estates or have had experience in agriculture form a large proportion of the Commission.

The commissioners hold office for five years, but are usually reappointed. Some who have been unable to do the work have resigned before the end of their term of office; others who have proved unsuitable have not been reappointed when they completed their term. Membership is part-time, but those who are paid now devote full time to the Commission's work; part-time paid work has been found unsatisfactory. The chairman is appointed by the

[1] Forestry Act, 1927, Ch. 6.

Government. It is of interest that whereas the earlier chairmen were appointed from among the ordinary non-specialist members of the Commission, the present chairman, a member of the Commission from the beginning, is a former civil servant who has specialized in forestry. Despite its heterogeneous personnel of amateurs and specialists, of scientists and politicians, the Commission has worked very smoothly for the furtherance of British forestry policy. Difficulties which have arisen in the Commission's work have not been due to the mixed character of its personnel.

Of necessity the Forestry Commission delegates much of its work. There are two statutory assistant commissioners, one for England and Wales and one for Scotland, who attend and take part in the meetings of the Commission but do not record votes in its decisions. They usually exercise all its powers of purchasing and planting land, but have no control over the educational and research activities of the Commission.

The primary function of the Commission, as laid down by the Forestry Act of 1919, is to create and maintain State forests in order to supply part of the country's timber requirements. In carrying out its work the Commission has obtained possession of nearly 1,000,000 acres of land;[1] 809,163 acres were acquired up to September 1935, and 120,000 acres of Crown woodlands were transferred to the Commission by the Forestry Act of 1923. Only 498,146 acres of those acquired in this period and 60,000 acres of those transferred were plantable. The programme of the Acland Committee, which was accepted by the Commission, envisaged the planting of 1,770,000 acres of new forest within eighty years, of which the bulk was to be done in the first forty years. This would have required acquisition of 607,800 acres for new planting up to September 1935. A comparison of this figure with that given above for the total plantable acreage acquired in the same period does

[1] *Sixteenth Report of the Forestry Commission.*

not reveal the programme's full deficit, as much of the plantable land acquired was derelict woodland,[1] which the Acland Committee had intended to be replanted by private enterprise. The total acreage planted or replanted up to September 1935 amounted to 275,876 acres. This is only a small part of what should have been accomplished, if the original planting programme had been implemented.

Successful afforestation can only be carried out under a series of long-term programmes. The number of young trees required in any year have to be planted in seedbeds some years before the trees are required; staffs have to be trained to be ready when necessary. The failure of the Forestry Commission to carry out the full programme originally laid down has been primarily due to short-sighted outside inter-ference with its work twice within the past sixteen years. In 1922 the Geddes Committee reported unfavourably on the Commission's expenditure, and their income and pro-gramme were curtailed by the Government. The result was considerable administrative confusion; ten forest officers had to be dismissed. This confusion was only increased in 1924 when the Labour Government returned to the original programme, as there were not enough seedlings or land ready.

It was decided in June 1928 to draw up a new working programme for the Commission's second decade. This was expanded in 1929 to include a scheme for dealing with the unemployed. Fortunately the expansion was to be concen-trated largely at the end of the decade, so that the drastic scaling down of the Commission's financial resources in 1931 did not cause such complete confusion as in 1922. Pressure was brought to bear on the Treasury, and the cuts were not so large as proposed by the May Committee. On both occasions, however, many millions[2] of young trees

[1] 74,190 acres of derelict woodland were replanted by the Commission during its first fifteen years (*Fifteenth Report*).

[2] In 1931–32 50,000,000 seedlings and transplants had to be destroyed.

which had been got ready for the planting programme drawn up by the Commission had to be destroyed. Now, in the boom year 1936, expansion of the ordinary programme has been undertaken at the Government's instigation, and the Commission promised an extra £200,000 yearly to carry through a separate afforestation scheme within fifteen miles of the special areas for the relief of unemployment. Past experience suggests that this scheme will probably be withdrawn in the early days of the next slump and further dislocation of the Commission's work caused just when its operation would be beginning to benefit the special areas.

The Forestry Commission has thus suffered from direct control and interference by Parliament and the Treasury. No planned forestry programme, such as was envisaged by the Acland Committee, can possibly be carried out successfully without a continuity of financial policy. The failure of Parliament to preserve such a continuity has been due to a variety of reasons. Few members, apart from those who are commissioners, have been interested in forestry; there is no vested interest to stiffen the Commission's resistance to outside interference. Afforestation has been looked upon more as an immediate remedy for unemployment than as a form of national development. However, the amount of employment provided is small in the early days of a new forest, and the great majority of members in times of difficulty have preferred to sacrifice long-term benefits to what they thought were the necessities of the moment. As a form of national planning in one industry alone afforestation is unlikely to secure continuity; it must be part of a national plan covering a large range of industries.

The Forestry Commission has attempted to distribute their activities over all parts of the country where the land is suitable. Of the plantable land they have bought 60 per cent is in England and Wales, and 40 per cent in Scotland. In 1935 the Commission possessed 105 forest units in England and Wales, and 86 in Scotland. Their largest units in

England were the new forests of Thetford Chase (37,000 acres) and Kielder (28,000 acres). In Scotland their largest forest was Loch Ard (11,000 acres).

The original planting programme had dealt only with softwoods, although it had been intended that there should be a supplementary hardwood programme. Of the 275,876 acres planted only 18,324 acres are under hardwoods. This is due to the more rapid maturity of softwoods and the fact that the Commission's resources have not enabled them to purchase the more fertile land suitable for hardwoods.

The Acland Committee recommended that the Forestry .Commission should also be responsible for encouraging the maintenance of existing private woodlands and the replanting of those felled during the war. Considerable grants have therefore been given to private owners and local authorities, to encourage replanting. The total area so replanted is 106,115 acres. When the fellings since the war are taken into account little leeway appears to have been made up on the 400,000 odd acres of felled or devastated private woodland left derelict after the war. Despite all the activities of the Commission, including its own planting programme, much still remains to be done to make good losses during the war before anything is done to create new timber resources. Report after report of the commissioners has drawn attention to the fact that the State alone can afford to finance afforestation.

At an early date the promotion of schemes of land settlement in connection with forestry was considered by the Commission. In 1925 it began to create smallholdings of about 10 acres in its forests. To the lessors it guaranteed 150 days' labour. Since this labour occurs mainly in the winter, it cannot interfere with agriculture. In 1935 there were 1,253 of these forest workers' holdings and the tenants owned stock worth £44,000. In 1931 the Government restricted the creation of further holdings. A considerable increase in their number is now to take place, and 70 per cent are to be allotted to families from the special areas. It is claimed that the Commission's experiment in land settlement[1] has been the most successful of the many attempts to stop rural depopulation. The guaranteed period of work in the forests provides the smallholders with a welcome sense of security. One or two attempts to foster marketing schemes for the Commission's smallholders have not been a success. In few areas are there a large number in close proximity and marketing problems in any locality cover other producers besides the tenants of the Commission.

A number of camps for the unemployed have been formed in or near some of the forests. These are run by the Ministry of Labour to enable men long unemployed to become fit. They carry out work for the Commission such as clearing and draining land and road building, much of which may not be needed immediately.

Other functions of the Commission have been the encouragement of forestry education, the building up of a British forestry service and the promotion of research. Schools for apprentices are run by the Commission at Parkend and Benmore, and grants are made to various universities and colleges, including the Imperial Forestry Institute. The Commission has also investigated problems associated with timber utilization, issued useful and important bulletins on this subject, and established an advisory committee to help market British-grown timber. Such subjects will become of increasing importance to the Commission as its forests begin to mature.

The 1919 Act, as strengthened by subsequent Acts, gives the Forestry Commission powers to buy, sell, lease, and manage land to enable it to carry out its primary duties of planting. It was also given power to inaugurate and manage woodland industries, to carry out research and educational work, and to enter property to inspect the land or to destroy

[1] *Fifteenth Report.*

rabbits endangering its forests. It was originally empowered to advance money to individuals or local authorities on strict conditions. These powers were subsequently modified. Under the Act of 1923 the Commission took over most of the woodland properties of the Commissioners of Crown Lands, and it may take over similar properties of other Government departments. It has power to make by-laws for the regulation of its forests.

The 1919 Act gave the Commission the power to purchase land compulsorily. Despite continual threats in its annual reports the Commission has not yet used this right. Fear of having to pay very high compensation has so far prevented such action; the difficulty of obtaining plantable land within fifteen miles of the special areas, however, will probably make it necessary to use these powers in the near future. Had they been exercised in the past it would probably have enabled the Commission to buy less unplantable land and to acquire more suitable units for afforestation than it has been able to do when under the frequent necessity of buying whole existing estates.

The Forestry Commission works through a variety of committees. Those concerned with personnel, technical questions, and forest holdings are sub-committees of the Commission itself. Other committees, which deal with sales, amenities, and housing, consist of five members of the Commission on each, together with a number of co-opted specialists. Consultative committees were set up for England, Scotland, and Wales as a result of the Act of 1919. They must include representatives of the county councils, of labour, of societies interested in forestry and of woodland owners. They have considered particularly subjects which interest owners of woodland and require co-operative effort, such as, for example, the destruction of vermin and the marketing of timber. From its inception in 1920 the English Committee has held thirty-five meetings. Drawn from very wide areas it has proved impracticable to have frequent meetings of these advisory committees, if they are to be well attended.

The organization of the Commission's work appears to be flexible, although all its committees are standing committees. Full reports of these committees are made to the full Commission, which co-ordinates their work at its monthly meetings. Commissioners are kept in touch with the work of various sub-committees by the circulation of reports through the post.

The chairman and the two assistant commissioners are the principal officers; in practice the power of the last two appears now to be greater than was foreshadowed in the Act of 1919. There is no evidence of any friction between the principal officers and the other commissioners. The frequent meetings of the Commission have probably prevented this by enabling work to be properly supervised. Certain other members of the Commission have shared various official duties with the principal officers. All communications between the officers and the Commission pass through the chief officer and are dealt with by the personnel sub-committee. Conferences of divisional officers are, however, organized from time to time to deal with administrative questions.

Each of the forest units is in charge of a forester. These units are grouped in the following seven divisions for England and Wales: (1) Northern England; (2) North Wales and West Midlands; (3) South Wales and South-West England; (4) East Midlands and South-East England; (5) East Anglia, Lincolnshire, and Nottinghamshire; (6) New Forest, Dorset, and the Isle of Wight; and (7) Forest of Dean and district. In Scotland the forests are divided into three main divisions for the North, North-East, and South-West, with a smaller division for the South-East. All the divisions are under the control of divisional officers who are responsible directly to the assistant commissioners. The divisions are subdivided into districts controlled by district officers, who supervise the foresters in their areas. Reports are submitted annually from all officers of the Commission to their superiors. Plans based on them are then drawn up and submitted by the principal officers to the Commission, which decides on the programme of work to be put in hand.

The administrative salaried staff of the Commission for 1936–37 totalled 513.[1] This included two paid commissioners, the two assistant-commissioners, one secretary, one estate officer, two finance officers, one education and publications officer, and one chief research officer. There were 62 clerks and 36 typists. Ten divisional officers administered the Commission's regions (those in the New Forest and Forest of Dean areas being called deputy surveyors). The subordinate districts were administered by 47 officers; to assist these were 180 foresters and 147 foremen who supervised the labour employed in planting and other forestry operations. The total number of manual workers[2] employed in the Commission's forests at the maximum period of employment in the winter of 1935–6 was 4,155, and in the summer of 1935 it was 3,280. A nucleus of a national forestry service has thus been created.

The Commission has to obtain approval from the Treasury as to the number of its administrative employees and the size of their salaries. Conditions of service resemble those in similar civil service posts. The divisional and district officers have received a university training in forestry, and the foresters and foremen have been trained in the Commission's schools. The wages paid to manual workers now amount to 35s. a week, or equal to the county agricultural wage, whichever is the highest; many of those employed on piecework receive more. The recruitment and training of staff and the settlement of grievances is dealt with by the personnel sub-committee of the Commission.

Salaried employees have the security of tenure and superannuation schemes usual in the civil service. Pro-

[1] *Civil Estimates*, 1936, Class VI, 118–23.   [2] *Sixteenth Annual Report*.

motion is frequent from the ranks, and is decided by merit
and seniority. Incapable officers are kept back. The principal officers usually possess both administrative and technical experience. The chairman is paid £1,953, the secretary
£1,058, the education and publications officer £1,011, and
the assistant commissioners £1,300 and £1,161 respectively.[1]
Divisional officers start at £738 a year, rising to £953;
district officers start at £277, rising to £634. Head foresters
begin at £215, rising to £277; foresters begin at £166 and
£126 according to whether they are in Grade I or II, and
they rise to £215 and £166 respectively. Foremen are paid
from 42s. to 45s. a week. All officers are given travelling
expenses and foresters and foremen are given free accommodation. No complaints have been made of interference
with the Commission's employees on the ground of their
political opinions. The manual workers frequently belong to
the Transport and General Workers' Union and the Agricultural Workers' Union, but there is no association for the
salaried staff. The Whitley Council machinery for dealing
with staff matters appears to work satisfactorily.

As has been shown earlier, Parliament exercises a very
extensive control over the Commission; the annual report
is sometimes debated in the House of Commons, but
Members exercise most influence through questions. Public
opinion, especially on the question of amenities, has exercised
considerable influence over the Commission. It has succeeded in drastically restricting the planting programme in
the Lake District, and has led the Commission to create
National Forest Parks.

Competition between timber grown by the Commission
and by private growers has not been of any importance so
far. The fact that so little private planting is being carried
out means that it is unlikely to become so. Recent figures
suggest a steady rise in the demand for timber. In preparing

[1] Actual salaries paid 1936-7. *Civil Estimates*, VI, 118-19. They rise with
the length of service.

a long-term planting programme a risk that some substitute may replace timber has to be taken. It seems very unlikely, however, that no use could be found for timber in this country once it has grown. At the moment the products of the Commission form a very small part of the timber consumption of the country. When it increases, some machinery will have to be created to co-ordinate the import of foreign timber and the marketing of home produced timber. The Commission carries out its own purchasing and markets its own products.

The Treasury's control over the Commission is very wide. It cannot borrow money and, although it was statutorily declared in 1919 that the Commission should receive £3,500,000 in ten years in instalments which Parliament should determine, no guarantee was given that any particular instalment would be voted. Actually the Commission received £3,500,000 by 1929, but in irregular instalments, with the unfortunate results mentioned earlier. In June 1928 it was proposed to pay the Commissioners £5,500,000 in the second decade; the next year it was decided to increase this to £9,000,000. After the crisis of 1931 this grant was reduced to £450,000 annually; this sum has been raised to £700,000 for 1936-7.

An analysis[1] of the Commission's main items of expenditure for its first fifteen years shows how it has attempted to carry out its work. Forestry operations of which the main items of expenditure are purchasing and planting land, claimed 81·7 per cent of its income. The creation and management of forest workers' holdings cost 8·6 per cent. Four per cent was used to make advances to landholders for afforestation purposes. Three and a half per cent was devoted to education, research, and experiment, and 2·2 per cent was claimed by miscellaneous services.

The total estimated expenditure of the Commission for 1936-7 was £884,790, of which £184,790 (21 per cent of

[1] *Fifteenth Annual Report*, p. 11.

its total income) was derived from receipts. This was obtained principally from the sale of forest products, although considerable sums came from rents for forest workers' holdings and unplantable land, mining royalties, the sale of rabbits, etc. The Commission pays rates, telephone charges, national health and unemployment insurance, etc. It has its own insurance scheme against fire.

The Forestry Commission differs widely from the more recently created public corporations in that it is more directly under parliamentary and Treasury control. Those critics of the public corporations who wish to bring them under stronger parliamentary control would do well to study the working of the Forestry Commission and the disadvantages, as well as the advantages, of its position. If any body of this kind is to work properly, it is essential that its financial resources should be not only planned, but also guaranteed ahead. The Forestry Commission has suffered from being in a peculiarly weak position *vis-à-vis* the Treasury. With returns on its expenditure so distant it was impracticable for its work to be financed by placing stock on the market or by borrowing. Had all the private woodlands been taken over when the Commission was established, it would have had considerable receipts at its disposal. Even in that case, however, it must have received a large grant-in-aid from the national exchequer. So long as it is financed primarily from national taxation, there will always be a temptation for needy chancellors to cut its grant in times of difficulty. Once the Commission is firmly established and the greater part of its income comes from receipts, its independence of the Treasury will grow. This is unlikely to occur before forestry is treated as a part of a national scheme for land development. When that happens, the constitution of the Forestry Commission and its relations with the Treasury will be drastically altered.

4

THE BRITISH
BROADCASTING CORPORATION

by

WILLIAM A. ROBSON

I

BROADCASTING in this country was at first operated through
a joint-stock company, the British Broadcasting Company,
Ltd., which was owned and controlled by the wireless firms.
The first phase lasted from late in 1922 until the end of
1926. On January 1, 1927, the British Broadcasting Corporation was created by Royal charter. This charter was
granted for a period of ten years in the first instance, so the
end of the second phase of British broadcasting was reached
towards the close of 1936. The public thereupon had to
consider the future policy of the country in regard to this
immensely important service. A departmental committee
presided over by Lord Ullswater was appointed in April
1935. Its report appeared in February 1936, and was the
subject of three lengthy debates in the House of Commons
and much public and private discussion outside. The
Government then made a statement declaring its policy on
the various questions in issue, and drafts of the new charter
and licence were laid before Parliament for approval. The
future position is therefore clear on most points relating to
the constitution of the B.B.C., although on some important
matters of practice the intentions of the Corporation have
not been clearly stated.

The B.B.C. is an outstanding example of a new and highly
significant type of organization: namely, the independent
public board operating a socialized service. A series of these
bodies has come into existence during the past fifteen years

*

or so, and several important specimens, such as the Central Electricity Board, the London Passenger Transport Board, and the Forestry Commission, form the subject-matter of detailed studies in this volume. But broadcasting differs from all the other services for two fundamental reasons. First, it is an engine of the mind, and carries with it cultural, moral, and political implications of the most formidable character. Second, it is a new service which came under stringent social control from the outset, and hence is not encumbered with large vested interests, requiring compensation or expropriation. In consequence, the broadcasting service is free from those stultifying financial conflicts and burdens which are so obstructive to progress in many other fields of public utility enterprise.[1]

II

Let us now consider the leading characteristics of the B.B.C. from an institutional point of view.

The B.B.C. is a publicly owned national organization possessing (in fact though not in law) an exclusive monopoly throughout Great Britain and Northern Ireland. It is non-commercial inasmuch as it is not permitted to distribute a profit. The preamble to the charter expressly declares that the service is to be developed and exploited to the best advantage and in the national interest in view of its great value as a means of information, education and entertainment; and the whole of its surplus revenue and other income must be applied solely to the promotion of this object. There are no shareholders or persons possessing proprietary rights of any kind whatever.

The most unusual feature of the B.B.C. is its relative independence both of Government control and parlia-

---

[1] The London Passenger Transport Board, for example, has an obligation to provide an excessively high rate of interest on an enormous volume of debt to the former shareholders in the various companies; and this burden will cripple the undertaking for decades.

mentary interference. The B.B.C. derives its powers from a charter supplemented by a licence granted by the Postmaster-General under the Telegraph Acts. The existing licence imposes certain obligations on the Corporation. Thus, it must transmit from its stations any matter which a Government department requires to be broadcast;[1] and it must refrain from broadcasting any matter which the Postmaster-General desires to exclude from the ether. In time of emergency the Government has the right to take over the stations and assume complete control of the undertaking. The Postmaster-General can revoke the licence in the event of the B.B.C. failing to observe any of the conditions contained in the charter or licence or neglecting "to send efficiently from the stations a programme of broadcast matter." And since the Post Office collects the licence fees from listeners, its ultimate control through finance is overwhelming. Moreover, since the first charter was granted for a period of only ten years, and the new charter is to run for a similar period, the Corporation's very existence is automatically liable to termination each decade, and is only likely to be renewed with Government support.

But although the Government possesses enormous contingent power over the B.B.C., it exercises in practice virtually no control over its day-to-day administration, nor does it even have the right to do so. People abroad sometimes allege that the B.B.C. is a State-run institution: witness the incident wherein the Polish ambassador delivered a Note to the Foreign Office protesting against the remarks on Poland made in a particular broadcast. And I have heard American broadcasting officials speaking of the B.B.C. as a State-run system. But this is far from the truth if it is intended to imply that the system is controlled by the Government. The Postmaster-General has stated in Parliament that he is responsible for questions of general policy but not for ques-

---

[1] Under the new licence the B.B.C. may at its discretion announce, when sending such matter, that it is sent at the request of a named department.

tions of detail and particular points of the service.[1] In the interpretation of this attitude there is a tendency to treat most matters as questions of detail; and it is exceedingly difficult to get a Parliamentary question on the subject of broadcasting past the Speaker's vigilant eye. For example, in February 1934, Brigadier-General Spears, M.P., attacked in the House of Commons Mr. Vernon Bartlett's broadcast on the subject of Germany leaving the League of Nations and his address on the Austrian situation. He was interrupted by the Speaker, who said, "I must remind the honourable and gallant member that the Government are not responsible for the B.B.C. organization, and that therefore it is hardly in order for the honourable and gallant member to raise the matter in this detail."[2] Another member (Mr. Boothby) then argued that since it is within the power of the Government to order the excision of any particular part of the B.B.C.'s programmes, it would be in order for General Spears to show why the Government should prohibit broadcast comments on foreign affairs. But the Speaker would not accept this suggestion. The Government's right of exclusion, he said, does not apply to general programmes, but only to particular items. And particular items, it can be seen from this incident, may not be discussed in Parliament. The whole question was debated at length in the House of Commons in February 1933, and a resolution was passed declaring that "It would be contrary to the public interest to subject the B.B.C. to any control by Government or by Parliament other than the control already provided for in the charter and in the licence of the Corporation." On a realistic view, therefore, the B.B.C. clearly enjoys a very high degree of autonomy. Whitehall and Downing Street undoubtedly exert a considerable degree of

---

[1] See the Postmaster-General's speech in the House of Commons, December 17, 1936; Hansard, vol. 318, col. 2748: "I have to discuss matters for which I am not responsible in detail and over which I have no control in detail."

[2] Hansard, 1933–4, vol. 285, cols. 1027–8.

influence in Broadcasting House—that is perhaps inevitable—
but the B.B.C. is in law and in practice substantially independent in its daily working both of the Government and
of Parliament. Nevertheless, the B.B.C. no doubt follows
attentively the clearly expressed views of Parliament on
any matter touching its affairs.

The relation of the B.B.C. to the Government was discussed at length in the report of the Ullswater Committee,
who recognized the high degree of independence which
the Corporation has exercised in practice.[1] In their view
the position of the Corporation is "one of independence in
the day-to-day management of its business, and of ultimate
control by His Majesty's Government. We find that this line
of demarcation has been observed in practice, and we are
convinced that no better can be found. We agree with those
who in recent years have examined the question that the
constitutional independence of the B.B.C. brings advantages
to the general public and to listeners which could not
otherwise be secured."[2] Curiously enough, although the
Committee approved strongly of the existing relationship,
and put forward proposals designed expressly "to make both
sides of this twofold position simpler and more evident," the
effect of their recommendations would have been to introduce a far-reaching change.

The Committee questioned whether the Post Office,
which exercises certain technical functions in relation to
broadcasting and also collects the licence fees, is necessarily
"the office most appropriate and best qualified to supervise
the policy of the service, to answer to Parliament for its
conduct, and to direct its destinies."[3] In answering this
question in the negative the Committee then went on to
recommend that "responsibility for the cultural side of
broadcasting" should be transferred to a Cabinet Minister
in the House of Commons unburdened by heavy departmental duties. Among other things this Minister would

[1] Par. 47.   [2] Cmd. 5091, 1936, par. 51.   [3] Ibid., par. 53.

exercise the powers of veto over programme items at present possessed by the Postmaster-General.

This proposal, if carried out, would have revolutionized the broadcasting service in this country. Once a Cabinet Minister was avowedly made responsible for "the cultural side" of transmission, the independence of the B.B.C. would have been destroyed at a single stroke, and it is impossible to believe that the Corporation would not have become a State-run organization. It would have assimilated the position of the B.B.C. in all essentials to that of the Government-dominated broadcasting organs of Italy and Germany. The Committee proposed this momentous change with apparently little realization of what it involved. They spoke about "transferring" a responsibility for the cultural side from the Postmaster-General which he does not either in fact or in law possess. They inquired into the fitness of the Post Office to "supervise the policy of the service, to answer to Parliament for its conduct, and to direct its destinies" regardless of the fact that the Post Office does not have to discharge these responsibilities.

Fortunately, these large changes, introduced by a side-wind without adequate analysis, were not accepted by the Government, which decided to continue as at present the existing functions of the Postmaster-General. The Postmaster rightly declared that "if a Minister 'free from heavy departmental responsibilities' were specially appointed to be 'responsible in respect of broad questions of policy and culture' he would find himself more and more obliged to exercise actual control. The Committee's recommendation is therefore felt to be inconsistent with the preservation of independent management by the Corporation."[1] No more need be said about this feature of the Report, therefore, except to remark that it is completely incompatible with the existing status of the B.B.C. which the Committee so highly praised.

[1] Cmd. 5207, 1936, par. 7.

The separateness of the B.B.C. as it now exists from the organs of the Central Government is shown by two other features of its structure. The staff of the B.B.C. does not consist of civil servants, and the Corporation has so far had an entirely free hand in regard to personnel without regard to civil service rules or standards. In regard to finance, again, the B.B.C. is self-contained. It makes a contribution to the Treasury each year, but the revenue and expenditure of the broadcasting service do not form part of the national finances under the control of the Chancellor of the Exchequer; nor do they find a place in the Budget.

An important aspect of the constitutional position of the broadcasting service concerns the relations between the B.B.C. and Parliament in regard to political talks over the microphone. These were for some time arranged in conjunction with the Parliamentary whips; but this arrangement broke down after the General Election of 1931, chiefly owing to the dissatisfaction of the Labour Party at the disproportionate amount of time allocated to pro-Government spokesmen as compared with the Opposition. The B.B.C. subsequently appointed a committee of back-bench Members to co-operate with it; but this method was not a success, and virtually broke down. Many complaints were made on this subject in a House of Commons debate in February 1933, but a satisfactory solution was not forthcoming. Many Parliamentarians desire that political talks should be entirely controlled by the party machines on the ground that only by so doing can Parliament remain the centre of the political life of the country. It is contended that to permit the B.B.C. to select what political topics shall be discussed over the wireless and to choose the speakers is opening the door to the creation of political power outside the Parliamentary arena. The present situation in this matter emphasizes the practical independence of the B.B.C. from Parliamentary control, to which I have referred above.

The Ullswater Committee emphasized the potential value

of broadcasting as an instrument for keeping Parliament before the minds of the people. For the very reason that the popular press tends to give a diminishing amount of attention to Parliamentary news it is important that the broadcasting service should look towards Parliament as "the focal point of political thought."[1] The Committee recommended that in general on the major political issues of the day there should be close co-operation and consultation between the B.B.C. and the authorized spokesmen of the recognized political parties; although they were careful to observe that it does not follow from this that all broadcast treatment of political questions must be controlled by the party organizations. "The B.B.C. must, of course, continue to be the judge of the amount of political broadcasting which the programme will stand, and while recognizing in the allotment of time, according to current Parliamentary practice, the preponderating position of the main political parties, should allow adequate expression to minority views, however unpopular."[2] In normal times it is recognized to be inevitable that more prominence must be given to members of the Government than to Opposition speakers. During a General Election the allocation of the total time determined by the B.B.C. for campaign speeches should be arranged by agreement between the parties; or in default of agreement, by the Speaker of the House of Commons.[3]

III

There is no doubt that this country is extremely fortunate in some ways to have evolved for broadcasting purposes the type of organization exemplified by the B.B.C. To have avoided the prostitution of broadcasting for commercial ends on the one hand and the exploitation of the radio for propaganda purposes on the other, is a great advantage which should be fully recognized. To have devised an institution

[1] Par. 90.   [2] Par. 92.   [3] Par. 93.

which secures disinterestedness and expertness in the operation of the service, possesses an area of operation which is technically satisfactory, an adequate financial basis,[1] and freedom from political interference in the management, while retaining ultimate public control, is an achievement of the first importance. The B.B.C. is an invention in the sphere of social science no less remarkable than the invention of radio transmission in the sphere of natural science. If we wish to appraise it at its proper value we have only to compare the general quality of broadcasting in this country with the general quality of the press and the films. One gets an impression of continuous effort towards an enlightened end in the case of the radio service which is entirely lacking in the case of the popular press and rarely encountered on the films.

But to recognize achievement is by no means the same thing as to rest content with the progress already made. The experience of the past ten years has disclosed numerous defects of a more or less serious character in the B.B.C.; and the amount of constructive criticism which can now be brought to bear on the undertaking may be regarded as a measure of the intelligent interest which it has evoked.

IV

The most serious question of all is whether the broadcasting service should remain a monopoly. As between a competitive system run on commercial lines and a socialized monopoly there can be no doubt whatever that the latter is infinitely to be preferred. But the dangers and difficulties of a monopoly in this new medium are formidable. An electricity undertaking can be established with the relatively simple task of supplying electricity on the cheapest and most efficient basis; and the success with which it achieves its purpose can be easily measured in terms of a standard unit. No such simple

[1] Subject to my later criticism concerning finance.

task can be assigned to a broadcasting service; nor can its achievements be easily tested. The officials who make the programmes must choose; all the time they must be selecting and rejecting. Sometimes their judgment will be good and sometimes bad, but most of the time it will be impossible to apply objective standards to their choice, save in a very broad manner. In regard to the choice of artistes, musicians, and talkers there is seldom an absolutely "right" or "wrong" choice—it is largely a matter of individual taste.

This is specially true in the field of music and entertainment; and it is illustrated by numerous instances where musicians and artistes who have broadcast for years have suddenly been dropped completely, as a result of a change of administrative personnel within the B.B.C. More serious than this, from a social point of view, are the cases where speakers who are believed to have offended the higher authorities in Broadcasting House have been suddenly denied all access to the microphone. I know personally of two cases where men of exceptional ability and high reputation have openly stated that they have been "black-listed" by the B.B.C. for reasons of a more or less personal nature. The case of Mr. Vernon Bartlett is a simpler one. Mr. Bartlett, as everyone knows, was a highly successful commentator on foreign affairs doing regular work for the B.B.C. He made some remarks over the wireless concerning Germany leaving the League of Nations and the situation in Austria which aroused much controversy in Parliament and elsewhere; and shortly afterwards it was announced that his contract with the B.B.C. had terminated. There was no doubt good ground for regarding Mr. Bartlett's observations as indiscreet or unwise on the particular occasions they were made. But is that good reason to wipe him off the map, metaphorically speaking, so far as an entire medium of communication is concerned? The question at issue is not merely one of the hardships caused to individuals but of the curtailment of free speech.

It is quite obvious that the B.B.C. must be free to choose its artistes, musicians, and speakers, and to reject them at its pleasure. No one can possibly be given any right to talk or to perform; nor would any system of appeal tribunals be of the slightest value. But the question does arise whether so immense a concentration of power and responsibility can safely be entrusted to any single organization possessing an exclusive monopoly.

A possible alternative is to make the regional organs independent bodies. It is claimed that the regional directors have great freedom at present. Be that as it may, they are certainly overshadowed and dominated by the central organization on all major questions.

My proposal is that the six provincial regions into which the country is divided should be made autonomous broadcasting authorities for regional purposes. Each of them would be transformed into a miniature B.B.C., with its own board of governors appointed by the Government as the responsible body. Each regional corporation would organize its own programmes, subject to interchange arrangements with the national programmes. Each region would be permitted to transmit on one wave-length only. A percentage of the licence fee would be allocated to each regional body, based possibly on the number of listeners in its area.

There are, of course, numerous objections which can be urged against a scheme of this kind. Some of them are very weighty. But I do not think any of them would counterbalance the immense advantage of having several potential avenues of employment for artistes and speakers, of introducing an element of rivalry among the programme-builders, of preventing as far as possible the exclusion from the ether of voices and views which ought not to be excluded. It cannot fairly be said that the B.B.C. is illiberal; but that does not meet the point. The *Manchester Guardian* is by universal agreement an exceptionally fair and liberal-minded newspaper, but would anyone be willing to make

the *Manchester Guardian* the only daily newspaper organization in the country? Would it be desirable, to take another
example, to place all the universities under a unified control,
so that if a teacher could not secure employment from the
central organ no other opportunity would be open to him?

It is to be regretted that the Ullswater Committee failed
to appreciate the key position which the regions might well
occupy as a brake upon monopoly. Their general attitude
towards the problem was one of helpless impotence. "There
is one class of persons to whom it seems impossible to give
any formal protection, that is, those who are engaged to
broadcast for remuneration. It is clear that the b.b.c. with
its monopoly of broadcasting is in a position to exclude
particular individuals from its programmes. It would, for
instance, be possible to exclude a critic of b.b.c. programmes
from ever obtaining an engagement to broadcast."[1] Having
stated the danger in this way, the Committee contented
themselves with expressing a hope that the b.b.c. would
welcome criticisms and not penalize those who indulged in
it by excluding them from the microphone.

The Committee's investigation of the position of the
regions was cursory in the extreme. Each region, they state
in their Report, is "controlled" by a regional director; and
the only limitations on his powers which are mentioned are
those of a financial kind. Then follow two almost meaning-
less sentences: "The limitations within which the regional
directors have sole authority within their regions have been
gradually relaxed during the existence of the Corporation.
The position of the regional directors in relation to Broadcasting House has just been strengthened by the appointment
of a Director of Regional Relations."[2] The first of these
statements presumably refers to the financial restrictions
placed on regional expenditure; and this is not the most
important point in issue. The Committee omitted entirely
to inquire as to the extent to which central control is

[1] Par. 40, Cmd. 5091, 1936.   [2] Ibid., par. 21.

exercised over the local choice of speakers and performers, or the strictness with which central prohibitions, tastes or prejudices are imposed on the local programmes. Again, the appointment of a central officer in charge of regional relations *might* mean a strengthening of headquarters control, since there is nothing necessarily conducive to regional freedom in such a step.

The Committee's conception of a region is, indeed, essentially parochial. They emphasize the importance of presenting in each locality the work of regional authors, performers, and speakers. But why should one assume that the inhabitants of Manchester specially desire to listen to the work of Lancashire musicians or comedians? One would have thought that just the contrary might be the case. But however that may be, it does appear to be a misunderstanding of the fundamental possibilities of the regions to regard them as breeding grounds of local talent rather than as alternative avenues of communication for talent which for one reason or another does not secure access to the national programme. It does not by any means follow that the regions would cultivate the "leave-overs" which Broadcasting House rejects for one reason or another. Indeed, one can well imagine many high reputations being made entirely on provincial work; just as many journalists and theatrical stars first made their names in the provinces. But such an approach does get away from the "Midland men for the Midland station" point of view; or, rather, insists on the regions serving a more fundamental purpose than the localization of talent.

V

The next matter to which attention should be directed is the board of governors. There are seven governors[1] (including

[1] The number has been increased from five in the new charter on the recommendation of the Ullswater Committee. There is something to be said for this change, but it is of secondary importance. The number may be from time to time increased or reduced by order in council.

the chairman) appointed normally for periods of five years each. The power of appointment lies with the Crown, and is exercised presumably by the Postmaster-General in consultation with the Prime Minister. Despite obvious fundamental differences, the board of governors occupies a position of responsibility towards the public and of authority over major policy not unlike that normally occupied by a minister in a Government department. The moral calibre, intellectual equipment, political opinions, social assumptions, and general capacity of the governors is therefore of crucial importance. They must not merely act as a buffer between the executive work of the B.B.C. and public opinion outside, but also be able to hold the balance between contending forces or influences inside the organization.

The criticism that may be made of the governors is that most of them are past the age at which they should be asked to direct the work of a new and growing service; and secondly, that most of them are and have been predominantly Conservative in outlook, consciously or unconsciously.

The first point is demonstrated by the death of the last two chairmen of the B.B.C. in rapid succession. The late Mr. Whitley was seventy years old when he died; Lord Bridgeman was seventy-two. One of the present governors is seventy years old, and the average age is very high. It is obviously desirable to appoint persons of established reputation and some experience of public affairs; it is equally obvious that the board of the B.B.C. ought not to be a retiring job for persons of advanced age or declining energies whose formative years occurred forty or fifty years ago.

The second point can also be revealed fairly conclusively from the record. The first chairman of the B.B.C. was Lord Clarendon, who had been chief Conservative whip in the House of Lords. The late Lord Bridgeman, the last chairman, was a Conservative politician all his life, and held ministerial office in successive Conservative Governments. On his death the vacancy on the board was filled by appointing his widow

a governor. She, too, had held office in the Conservative
party organization. During the whole existence of the B.B.C.
there has been a strong majority on the board of governors
of persons of pronounced Conservative or Conservative-
Liberal outlook. Only three members of the board (two of
them women holding office at separate times) are known to
have any sympathy with the philosophy of the Left. This
predominance makes the board highly unreflective of the
general outlook of the community.

The Ullswater Committee made a vague allusion to the
existing unsatisfactory state of affairs in language which
sacrificed frankness to politeness. "We think it important,"
they declared, "that any undue homogeneity of age or opinion
should be avoided. While new scientific developments are
constantly occurring, and changes of opinion and of practice
are so rapid that each successive generation is brought up
in a different world of experience, the board should be as
ready to entertain new ideas as it is to be guided by mature
judgment."[1] Mr. Attlee, a member of the committee, put
the matter more bluntly and forcibly in a dissenting reservation. It is undesirable, he said, that the governors should
be drawn solely from persons whose social experience and
background is that of the well-to-do classes. It is one of the
functions of the board to represent the general public for
whom the Corporation caters. If the governors represent the
general outlook of a minority only, this function will not
be properly fulfilled.[2]

There is, then, everything to be said for appointing
younger governors in the prime of life, and so composing
the board that Left opinion is more fairly reflected.[3] It
may be contended that we do not live in a totalitarian

---

[1] Cmd. 5091, 1936, pars. 12–13.

[2] Ibid., p. 48. Mr. Attlee proposed a retiring age of sixty for the governors,
but this was not adopted.

[3] The Committee recommended—and the new charter requires—the salary
of the governors to be increased from £700 to £1,000 a year, which should
raise their status *inside* the organization. (The chairman will continue to
receive £3,000.)

society, and that most of the questions which come before
the board are non-political; but the fact remains that the
complexion of the board will affect the whole trend of
administration in an organization such as the B.B.C., not by
virtue of their decisions on questions of policy, but by
reason of the feeling that executive officials will have as to
what line of approach is or is not likely to meet with approval
in the board room.

The composition of the board of governors and the
position it should occupy have never been fully understood.
The Sykes Committee in 1923 even went to the absurd
length of recommending a broadcasting board of twelve
members, representing such interests as the Association of
Municipal Corporations, the County Councils Association,
the Trades Union Congress, the press, and so forth! We have
got away from the notion of sectional representation but
have not yet arrived at a more constructive approach. For
example, it is not commonly recognized that the governors
should, among other things, possess some aesthetic taste.

We may consider now the official staff. The personnel of
the B.B.C., like that of most of the other independent public
utility bodies dealt with in this volume, does not consist of
civil servants. The Corporation has had complete freedom
in respect of its officials, and could pursue its own policy
without regard to the Civil Service Commission or the
Treasury. It would, of course, have been absurd to attempt
to man a ship of this kind, embarking on a new adventure
in uncharted seas, visiting strange lands of music, entertainment, information, and education, with men and women
who had merely passed through the regular Civil Service
channels or proved themselves efficient in an ordinary
Government department. A free hand to recruit new and
diverse types of experience and ability was and is absolutely
necessary.

But there is a good deal of evidence that the free hand has
been overdone, and that the best use has not been made of

it. It is highly important for the welfare of this country that civil servants shall not find themselves surrounded with organizations running socialized services whose officials are remunerated on a far more lavish scale than exists in the Civil Service, and who possess advantages unknown to the devoted priesthood in Whitehall. If we permit such a situation to develop, envy, discontent, disappointment, conflict, and deterioration will arise in the Civil Service; and once the rot has set in it will be very difficult to stop. The Civil Service is one of our most valuable national assets, and it is essential to preserve its morale. It would be perfectly possible to distinguish the purely administrative routine of the B.B.C. from the artistic or creative work, and to see that the officials in charge of the former are placed more or less on an equality with corresponding grades in the Civil Service.

The artistic, creative, news, and engineering positions present a much more difficult problem; and few people acquainted with the internal affairs of the B.B.C. consider it to have been satisfactorily solved. It would be invidious to mention particular instances, but some of the highest positions in the broadcasting service have been filled in an unusual manner.

The essence of the matter is to find a method of filling positions for which men or women with unique qualifications are required and yet guarantee the maintenance of standards. Universities have to face a similar problem, and the method they employ could, no doubt, usefully be followed by the B.B.C. That method is to set up an *ad hoc* committee to fill every important post consisting partly of persons drawn from inside the organization and partly of outside assessors with some knowledge of the field of work. This combines the free hand with an insistence that an appointment shall be capable of being justified to the outside world in terms of the candidate's record.

The Ullswater Committee observed that they had no evidence of undue influence in making appointments, but added that the existing methods of recruitment "leaves to its administrators the responsibility for avoiding patronage and prejudice." Those methods included (1) independent application, (2) recommendation by a friend, (3) recommendation by a university appointments board or some technical authority, (4) public advertisement—this was apparently not frequently used, (5) selection from the existing staff. The Committee recommended that recruitment should be "systemized"; and they advised that vacancies should in future be advertised and appointments (other than those of minor officials) made on the recommendation of a selection board composed of officials of the B.B.C., a Civil Service Commissioner, and possibly an independent additional member.

This proposal met with strong objection from the B.B.C. in the statement which the board issued on the Ullswater Report. Their resistance was based partly on the ground that only those who are occupied in the day-to-day administration of broadcasting can estimate the personnel needs of the service; partly on the ground that the existing methods of recruitment are satisfactory and impartial; and partly on the ground that the addition of a Civil Service Commissioner or an independent member to its appointment boards "would be incompatible with its independent status and productive of no good results."

When the matter came to be dealt with by the Government there is no doubt that public opinion had been much influenced by the debate which took place in the House of Commons on the Ullswater Report on April 29, 1936.[1] This debate turned largely on the question of personnel. The attention of the House of Commons was claimed for the grievances of the staff of the B.B.C. and the paternal and arbitrary methods of administration said to exist. The question of the right of the staff to form a staff association was debated at length in a House which always responds

[1] Hansard, vol. 311, No. 75, especially cols. 972 et seq.

readily to an appeal to its historic function of "the redress
of grievances"; and at the end of it members of all parties
were convinced that an improvement must be made in staff
conditions at Broadcasting House. Hence, when two months
later the Postmaster-General issued his statement of official
policy[1] on the future of the B.B.C., he stated explicitly that
the Government accepted the Committee's recommendation
of a selection board with outside members, and that the
B.B.C. had agreed to provide all necessary facilities for a
representative staff organization.

Shortly after this the case of Lambert *versus* Levita was
tried in the High Court, where it attracted widespread
public attention. The Prime Minister then set up a special
board of inquiry to investigate the statements made in the
course of that case affecting the B.B.C. The board took a
favourable view of the motives of the Corporation, but
made a number of criticisms of the actions of the chairman,
vice-chairman and some of the highest officials in their
dealings with Mr. Lambert's grievance; and they suggested
that, quite apart from the particular matter under inquiry,
the whole personnel side of the Corporation needed attention. There was a further debate in the Commons the day
following the publication of the report, in the course of
which the Postmaster-General (Major Tryon) announced
that in future "practically all" B.B.C. vacancies will be
advertised, except possibly in case of emergency; further,
that the Corporation "on its own initiative" had agreed to
invite the Civil Service Commission to send a representative
to the appropriate appointment board and, where special
qualifications are called for, it will also ask the help of
independent assessors.[2]

It is generally felt that the Lambert incident was a most
unpleasant affair and the outcome unsatisfactory. But it
had the effect of riveting public attention on the personnel

---

[1] Cmd. 5207, 1936, p. 9.
[2] Hansard, 1936, vol. 318, No. 34, col. 2753.

side of the B.B.C. in a way that no abstract discussion could have done. An improvement in staff conditions is almost certain to take place during the next few years. Mr. Lees Smith remarked in the Commons that although Parliament has agreed to leave the day-to-day management of the broadcasting service to the B.B.C. and to content itself with the control of general policy, the Corporation "cannot in the long run defeat the House of Commons."[1] Among the wishes expressed in Parliament by members of all parties was the desire to see established an adequate system of staff associations.

VI

It is sometimes alleged by disgruntled critics that the B.B.C. is an irresponsible body because it is not answerable to Parliament for its day-to-day administration. This accusation is by no means well founded. The B.B.C. is almost overburdened with a sense of responsibility. One sometimes has the impression that because it is not answerable to one particular body it feels itself to be answerable to everyone for all its actions. Its fits of excessive caution are doubtless due to a belief that nothing must be said or done which would give offence to powerful institutions or interests which may start a cry of "Down with the B.B.C. !" It is very probable that if a minister were made directly responsible to Parliament for broadcasting, the service would be conducted on lines less responsive to established and conventional opinion than is now the case. I believe, on the whole, that it would be a mistake to alter the existing relations with the Postmaster-General. The attitude of excessive caution, the tendency to steer a middle course at all costs, will, one hopes, disappear as the B.B.C. grows in prestige and status and self-confidence. It will perhaps acquire the strength to be different things to different men and resist the tempta-

[1] Hansard, 1936, vol. 318, No. 34, cols. 2737, 2739.

tion to be all things to a non-existent mass of average men. In any case, there would be nothing to gain and much to lose in attempting to strengthen the authority exercised by the Postmaster-General or by any other minister.

What does seem to be called for is a more satisfactory statement of the Corporation's activities than the singularly unilluminating document which the governors present each year to the Postmaster-General, and which he in turn dutifully hands on to Parliament. These reports are little more than catalogues of the year's activity in condensed form. They are undiscriminating and lifeless.

One feature of them which is specially objectionable is the remarkable absence of any detailed information concerning expenditure. There are only nine heads of expenditure shown, of which the most important is that on programmes (including payment of artistes, orchestras, news royalties, performing rights, and simultaneous broadcast telephone system, salaries, and expenses of programme staff) amounting to £915,025. Another heading is for administration salaries and expenses, the amount being £92,875. These un-itemized totals reveal nothing whatever of any significance, and it is pertinent to inquire on what theory of responsibility towards the public the B.B.C. maintains this refusal to reveal the allocation of its revenues. The very absence of Treasury control and ministerial responsibility should make the B.B.C. anxious to take the public into its fullest confidence rather than to imitate the most undesirable practices of commercial firms. The accounts should show precise details of the salary paid to every official; the sums spent on the various orchestras and bands; the amount paid respectively for talks, news service, the Empire broadcasts, the regional programmes, entertainers, operatic relays, crooners, and so forth.

The Ullswater Committee paid special attention to this question. Their view is that to ask the B.B.C. to give detailed information comparable to that furnished by a Govern-

ment department in the estimates would tend to impair
the independence enjoyed by the B.B.C. in the day-to-day
management of its affairs and would serve no useful purpose
unless Parliament desired to withdraw that independence.
The accountability towards the public of such an undertaking as the B.B.C., in their opinion, does not extend to the
disclosure of details which might prejudice its current
business operations, but is limited to the presentation of
"a clear and intelligible picture of its activities in broad
outline."[1] With this in view they recommend a specific
form of accounts for the annual report, which splits up the
undifferentiated block of expenditure on programmes
(mentioned above) into six separate items; and distinguishes
salaries and wages from other administrative expenses.

The attitude of the Committee is confused in more than
one respect. In the first place, neither the annual report
of the B.B.C. in its present form nor in the form recommended by the Committee gives "a clear and intelligible
picture of its activities in broad outline." So far as expenditure is concerned, they are both almost useless. In the second
place, detailed information concerning financial administration is essential if public criticism is to be informed and
intelligent. Unless it is desired to withdraw the B.B.C. from
serious criticism there is no justification whatever for with-
holding information concerning its financial policy. The
argument about embarrassing current business transactions
could apply equally well to the Post Office, local authorities
—and, indeed, to all other public bodies which are required
to publish full information about their accounts. Why is the
B.B.C. in a position requiring such special delicacy and high
degree of mystery? If it has, in fact, an exceptionally large
number of operations which would be adversely affected
by publicity, the Postmaster-General should be given power
to certify those items in the accounts which in the public
interest need not be particularized in any given year.

[1] Cmd. 5091, 1936, par. 76.

The illogical position adopted by the Ullswater Committee in this matter is illustrated by the recommendation made elsewhere in its report that the estimates for broadcasting should be presented separately from the Post Office estimates, of which they have hitherto formed part. The object of this excellent proposal is to enlarge the opportunities for Parliamentary discussion and control.[1] This suggestion has been accepted by the Government on the ground that it will give Parliament opportunities for "the specific purpose of discussing broad matters of policy."[2] It may be asked how members of Parliament—or anyone else for that matter—can criticize or debate even broad questions of policy without a proper idea of the financial background which forms the ultimate setting of all administration. How can one reasonably demand more of a certain kind of programme feature—orchestral music, for example—unless one has some idea of the cost of the existing supply compared with other programme features? How can one judge whether a region is receiving an adequate financial allowance without information of a detailed kind? The Ullswater Committee appears to have made a bad mistake in this direction, based apparently on the assumption that only Government departments should be required to publish complete accounts, whereas other kinds of public institutions should follow the thoroughly unsatisfactory tradition of secrecy adopted by private companies.

Apart from the presentation of adequate accounts and a much fuller and more illuminating annual report—the report of the L.P.T.B. offers a good example which might be followed—it is difficult to know exactly what one can expect from the B.B.C. itself in the way of promoting a high degree of public accountability. But it would appear that independent public service undertakings ought to be

[1] *Report*, pars. 55–6.
[2] Cmd. 5207, 1936, p. 7. See also the remarks of the Assistant Postmaster-General: Hansard, 1936, vol. 318, No. 34, col. 2784, from which it appears that a full day's debate will be given to broadcasting on each year's estimates.

investigated and reported on at regular intervals by outside
persons of keen insight and active imagination who could
draw public attention to inadequacies and achievements,
merits and defects. What is needed are visitors or auditors
who would inspect the broadcasting organization each year
from the widest point of view and report thereon to Parliament through the Postmaster-General. These visitors
would be appointed afresh every two or three years. They
should be few in number, and they should be drawn from
different fields of experience. Some of them might be
specialists in administration, engineering, the intellectual
and artistic professions, journalism, and the like; others
might have qualifications of a more general character.

If it be asked what good these visitors or inspectors might
be expected to do, the answer is that the public services
in this country owe an immense debt to inspectors and commissions of inquiry. Factory regulation, the police forces,
education, and other services have all been greatly developed
and improved by this means. The method varies, but the
basic idea is similar.

VII

The question of finance has not hitherto aroused the attention it deserves in connection with broadcasting. The listener
pays ten shillings for a licence, and apparently takes no
further interest in the matter.

Actually the financial situation has been far from satisfactory. During the period of the first charter (1926–36)
the arrangement was that the Post Office deducted 10 per
cent for collecting the licence fee and performing certain
other services for the B.B.C. In the year 1934–5 the Post
Office made a profit out of this charge of £26,360. In the
preceding year the profit was no less than £35,717.

The B.B.C. has been entitled to receive only a meagre part
of the remaining nine shillings, and a diminishing percentage

at that. The Treasury took 10 per cent of the revenue from the first million licences, 20 per cent of that from the second million, 30 per cent from the third million, and 40 per cent thereafter. Thus, as the success of broadcasting led to its increased popularity, so the share of the revenue from licences going to the B.B.C. has fallen. In 1934 the gross receipts from licences was £3,369,000; but the share of this received by the B.B.C. under the licence arrangement was only £1,897,785, the Treasury getting no less than £1,134,315. The B.B.C. did not, however, receive its full share, because under the stress of the so-called crisis of 1931 the Treasury exacted a further series of heavy "emergency contributions" from the B.B.C. In 1934 this amounted to £187,500. This reduced the net licence income of the B.B.C. to £1,710,285, out of which a further sum of £113,000 had to be paid to the Exchequer as income tax. The balance remaining to the B.B.C. for the broadcasting service was therefore only £1,597,282, or 47½ per cent of the gross licence revenue received from listeners. Thus, out of each ten shillings paid for a licence, only 4s. 9d. was available for broadcasting. During the eight calendar years 1927 to 1934 the total income collected from licences was £16,761,000, of which only £8,788,000 (52·43 per cent) went to the B.B.C., £1,836,000 (10·96 per cent) went to the Post Office, £4,963,000 (29·61 per cent) to the Exchequer under the scale allocation mentioned above, £575,000 (3·43 per cent) to the Treasury as "emergency contributions," £568,000 (3·39 per cent) to the Exchequer as income tax.

There is something substantially wrong in these arrangements whereby more than half of the listener's fee, paid for a specific purpose, is drained away in various forms of taxation and devoted to other purposes. It has for long been the policy of the Post Office that the revenue from telephone charges should go exclusively to benefit the telephone service; and this is undoubtedly the correct policy for a

D

socialized service. The Sykes Committee, indeed, expressly declared that the Government should not seek to make a profit out of broadcasting. The predatory raids of the Treasury on this new and growing enterprise are, however, the outcome of a confused and antiquated outlook. The Treasury regard every new source of income as fair game for taxation, regardless of the social issues involved. They are apparently unable to distinguish between the desirability of using taxation as an instrument for equalizing wealth and the undesirability of employing it to impede or cripple socialized services. They presumably regard every statutory monopoly as possessing a concession from the State for which tribute must be paid—a view which is quite unjustified where the undertaking is being carried on as a socialized service on a non-profit making basis.

The listeners of this country should not be required to pay any share of the licence fee to the Exchequer except perhaps a small sum equivalent to the entertainment tax on theatres and cinemas—and even that is doubtful. The Post Office should certainly not be permitted to retain any surplus from its percentage over and above the cost of the services it renders. And there is no good reason why the B.B.C. should pay income tax. The payment of "emergency contributions" in 1935 to relieve the financial stringency of 1931 was utterly absurd and should never have been tolerated.

The unfairness of the present position becomes manifest when it is remembered that the B.B.C. has no capital resources of any kind; that it has to provide for all capital expenditure out of revenue, and that large outlays for this purpose out of current income are continually necessary. Were it not for the substantial net revenue received from its publications (amounting to £347,707 in 1934), it is doubtful whether the technical development of recent years could possibly have been financed on the present basis.

The Ullswater Committee recognized to a certain extent the defects of the existing financial basis of the B.B.C., although their recommendations fell far short of what is desirable in this connection. In regard to the deduction made by the Post Office, they approved the principle of fixing the payment as a percentage of the gross revenue collected, but advised that the matter should be reviewed every two years in order that the percentage may be promptly adjusted to cover prospective costs.[1]

In regard to the much more important question of the division of the proceeds of the licence fee, the Committee declare it to be indefensible for the Exchequer to retain any part of the net revenue unless the Corporation has first received "an income thoroughly adequate to ensure the full and efficient maintenance and development of the service."[2] This principle, in the Committee's opinion, has not so far been observed in practice; and they place on record their considered opinion that the B.B.C. would have been able in the past to provide more varied programmes and a more rapid extension of service if its income had been larger. They accordingly recommended that in future "a substantially higher proportion of the sums paid by listeners should be allotted to the Corporation for the service."[3] The surplus retained by the Treasury has reached proportions which were never anticipated; and the Ullswater Report recommends that under the new charter the proportion of net revenue going to the B.B.C. should not fall below 75 per cent.

The Government accepted the view of the Committee that the B.B.C. should receive a larger share of the licence revenue. They decided to fix this at the 75 per cent proposed by the Committee, with the proviso that "if the Treasury should hereafter be satisfied that the income of the B.B.C. is insufficient to support their services, including

---

[1] The new charter provides for the Postmaster-General to deduct 9 per cent in 1937 and 1938, and thereafter sufficient to cover the expenses incurred by him on behalf of the B.B.C.

[2] This is a quotation from the Crawford Committee's report. Cmd. 2599, 1926.   [3] Par. 66.

television and Empire broadcasting, it should be open
to the Treasury to approve such increase as they may think
appropriate in the circumstances in the proportion of
receiving licence revenue payable to the B.B.C."[1]

This change will produce a substantial increase in the
revenue of the B.B.C. It is estimated that in 1937–8 it will
bring in an additional £400,000. The net licence revenue
will amount to £2,800,000, and on this basis about 6s. 5d.
out of the ten-shilling licence fee will be available for the
broadcasting service. It is, therefore, a step in the right
direction. But only a step. The proper course to pursue is
to press for the further allocation to the B.B.C. of the remaining share now going to the Treasury; and for the abolition
of the absurd levy of income tax which now falls on all
sums devoted by the B.B.C. to capital expenditure or set aside
for reserve.

VIII

One more question which remains to be discussed is the
relation between the B.B.C. and the public.

The B.B.C. has only the vaguest and most remote contact
with the world of listeners. It does not really know who
they are, to what they listen, or what their views are. Its
channels of communication are limited almost entirely to
the press on the one hand and the active letter-writing
correspondent on the other. The press is of little use for
this purpose, partly because it is jealous of the B.B.C. for
making large profits from journalistic publications; partly
because it is apprehensive of the extent to which broadcasting will compete with the newspaper's reporting
functions; partly because there are hardly any journalists
adequately equipped to deal with the subject; but chiefly
because the press is not in any closer touch with the listener
than is the B.B.C. itself.

[1] Memorandum by the Postmaster-General. Cmd. 5207, 1936, p. 4. Clause
20(3) of the new charter gives effect to this decision.

The letter-box as at present used is also an unsatisfactory instrument of contact. Most people do not write letters unasked in order to express their opinions to unknown officials; those who do write are seldom typical. "Fan-mail," when it does occur, is notoriously untrustworthy.

The intellectual, artistic, and social value of broadcasting will, however, largely depend on the extent to which the listener can be induced to co-operate more or less actively in the operation of the service. A new technique of communication will have to be devised, and one hopes the appointment of a public relations officer is the first step in this direction.

All kinds of suggestions occur to one. The listener could be asked to give specific replies to a questionnaire when applying for his licence—a solemn moment when his attention might be held. Prizes could be offered for the best criticisms of particular broadcasts and for suggestions for new ones. The *Radio Times* or *The Listener* might print blank spaces opposite to certain programme items and ask for opinions to be filled in and returned to headquarters. Statistical inquiries and random samples could be made to discover the composition of the listening public in terms of ages, sex, occupation, interests, and so forth.

This type of approach would, however, have to be linked up with a closer association between the layman who listens and the official who creates programmes. Nearly all the modern socialized services need to devise ways of introducing an element of consumer control or influence into their administration. In the case of broadcasting the need is especially insistent because wireless is a voluntary service, and it is difficult to secure an enthusiastic response from the public without integrating the listener at some point into the official machinery. This is scarcely the place to explore this subject at length; but it needs to be mentioned because of its essential importance and because, so far as one can see, the B.B.C. has not yet attempted to tackle it. All kinds of experiments might be made, such as the formation of "Critics Circles" in the large towns, or the election by certain types of listeners of persons to co-operate on their behalf with the B.B.C. in specified spheres of interest.

The efforts so far made by the B.B.C. have been mainly in the direction of establishing connections with professional workers, or organizations in particular fields of activity, rather than with the listener as such. There are several advisory committees (both central and local) on such subjects as religion, music, and charitable appeals. There is also the Spoken English Committee presided over by Mr. Bernard Shaw, the Central Council for School Broadcasting, and last but not least, the General Advisory Council set up last year to discuss questions of general policy. This body consists of about thirty Eminent Victorians leavened with a few Edwardians and presided over by the Archbishop of York.[1]

The B.B.C. is clearly making a laudable effort to build a series of bridges between itself and the outside world. One has the impression, however, that many of these committees are weakened by a tendency to overload them with *ex-officio* notables. There is a conspicuous lack of individuals possessing those qualities of taste, judgment, and imagination which would be most useful in assisting the B.B.C. to awaken and cultivate the public interest in particular fields.

The Central Music Advisory Committee is an outstanding example of this. Its membership consists of five Musical Knights, Colonel J. A. C. Somerville, C.M.G., C.B.E., Dr. Whittaker, and the President (*ex officio*) of the Incorporated Society of Musicians. At least three of the knights are heads of conservatories of music, and it would no doubt be impolitic for the B.B.C. to omit them. But such a predominance of administrative ability and such a paucity of creative or

[1] The Ullswater Committee recommended in each region an advisory committee of a similar character should be set up (par. 44).

critical talent cannot be a good thing. One looks in vain for the names of some of the outstanding critics and patrons of music, who, after all, are the people most experienced in leading and moulding the taste of the public. One looks in vain for the names of eminent musicologists and scholars of music, or of composers.

The Spoken English Committee is by far the best from the point of view of avoiding window-dressing. Only four or five members out of a total of twenty-three specifically represent official organizations such as the British Academy; most of the remainder are persons who have themselves helped to enrich the English language as writers, speakers, scholars or teachers. The result is that the work of this committee has aroused more public interest than that of all the others put together. At the other extreme is the Central Council for School Broadcasting, which has an overwhelming majority of representative members. The position of this council (and its Scottish sub-council) differs, however, from that of the advisory committees, for the B.B.C. apparently does not desire to be directly responsible for the material which is broadcast to the schools. In consequence, it is proposed to give the council an independent status, with power to determine the educational broadcasting programmes, which would then be carried out on their behalf by the B.B.C. acting in an executive capacity.[1]

In any case, quite apart from the membership of committees, there is the question of extending their number and scope. It would, I believe, be distinctly useful to set up advisory committees to deal with many varieties of subjects or spheres of interest, such as science, rural life, drama, news, literature, etc.

IX

From this rapid survey it can be seen that while we have much to be thankful for in the broadcasting system of this

[1] *Ullswater Report*, par. 102.

country, there is plenty of room for improvement and for the elimination of defects. Without doubt the b.b.c. is the right type of organization for the operation of broadcasting, and its officials are infused with a high degree of public spirit—of that there need be no mistake. Certain features of the organization appear to be based on mistaken ideas, but most of these could be altered with little difficulty if the b.b.c. and the Government, or at any rate Parliament, were convinced of the need for change. The actual constitution of the b.b.c. requires little, if any, alteration.

In conclusion, it may be said that no institution can expect to be able to criticize itself effectively, and there is at the present time a deplorable absence of serious criticism and intelligent information concerning broadcasting in this country. The general public, and indeed, even the listening public, is scarcely aware either of the achievements or the shortcomings of British broadcasting. Those who are responsible for the b.b.c. would do well to welcome a more searching and discriminating attitude towards their activities as an indication of an increased interest in the broadcasting service. Only by the awakening of such an attitude on the part of the public can the vitality and future progress of broadcasting be assured.

5

THE CENTRAL ELECTRICITY BOARD AND OTHER ELECTRICITY AUTHORITIES

by

GRAEME HALDANE

THE influence of the Central Electricity Board on the electricity supply industry has been profound; indeed the production and wholesale side of the industry has undergone a radical transformation during the last five years. The Board, which is a public body not making a divisible profit, came into being in 1927 following the passage of the Electricity Suppy Act, 1926. The first few years were wholly occupied in the actual construction of the Grid and it was not till about 1930–1 that the Board began trading operations. Full trading operations in the first two areas, namely Central Scotland and Mid-East England, did not commence till January 1, 1933. Since that date the remaining areas, South-East England, South-West England, North-West England, and Central England, with the exception only of North-East England and South Scotland, have commenced full trading operations. Full trading in the North-East England Area has been delayed pending the completion of the frequency standardization while the scheme for South Scotland is the most recent to be adopted. It is now difficult to imagine the industry without the Grid, and many of those who were opposed to the 1926 Act have accepted the present position and give the C.E.B. their full support.

THE GRID

The Grid itself is a network of some 4,000 miles of high-voltage transmission lines covering practically the whole

*

country and linking together all the large and efficient "selected" stations. This permits the generation of nearly the whole of the electrical requirements of the country in about 130 selected stations, of which fifteen provide over half the energy, thus greatly reducing the cost of production. It also permits very large savings in capital cost of generating plant because, by means of the Grid interconnection, each station can obtain support from the others in the event of breakdown, thus reducing greatly the amount of spare or "stand-by" plant required. In effect the Grid acts as an insurance scheme, spreading the risk over a large number of stations instead of each having to provide its own insurance fund. The Board does not own the selected stations, but it controls their operation, and the surplus over and above the requirements of the owners of the stations is carried over the Grid to numerous points at which supplies are tapped off to other supply authorities. Not only does the Board carry out for the industry the function of generation and main transmission, but in doing so its staff have co-operated with the staffs of the supply authorities both in improving engineering technique and in securing the transfer to the supply authorities' systems of large blocks of industrial power previously obtained from private generating plant.

SCOPE OF THE BOARD

Although the Board has exercised an influence on the whole industry, its direct control is limited to generation and transmission: that is, to the production and wholesale side of electricity supply. In terms of capital expenditure, generation and transmission represent about 40 per cent of the whole industry, the remaining 60 per cent being the capital invested in distribution; that is, in the retail side of the industry, which is still in the hands of a large number —about 630—authorized distributors, of whom more than half are local authorities, and the remainder companies. Although, therefore, less than half the industry is controlled by the Board, the absolute magnitude of that part is very considerable, representing, as it does, over £30,000,000 invested in the Grid, which is the property of the Board, and some £100,000,000 invested in the 130 selected power stations which are controlled by the c.e.b., although remaining under private or local authority ownership and administration. The c.e.b. is, in fact, a unique instance of the control by a public concern[1] of a large and very important section of the industry of the country.

COMPARISON WITH LONDON PASSENGER
TRANSPORT BOARD

The public concern which can best be compared to the c.e.b. is the l.p.t.b., which controls capital investments of approximately £112,000,000. The l.p.t.b. is, however, a regional body and is not subject to any transport competition within the area of its operations. It was formed by the taking over of existing organizations, and it was not, therefore, necessary to build up an entirely new organization from the beginning. On the other hand, in taking over the existing organizations, it became burdened with heavy capital expenditure on most of which there is a fixed rate of interest which must be met out of the earnings of the Board.[2] In contrast, the c.e.b. is a national organization and is subject to severe competition because it cannot sell to the existing supply authorities unless it can offer prices at least as low as the cost to these authorities of generating their own requirements or of buying in bulk from neighbouring authorities owning power stations. It is also affected by competition from the gas industry. This competitive

[1] A public concern may be defined as a body not making a divisible profit and engaged in commercial operation, which had previously been or at least might previously have been carried on by private enterprise.
[2] See infra, pages 187 et seq.

element has a very important effect on the Board's operations. A further difference is that the whole of the Board's organization had to be created *de novo*, and its business was something new which had not previously been undertaken by any other authority, with the exception of certain power companies which had been doing a somewhat similar business on a much smaller scale. The Board, like the L.P.T.B., has also very heavy capital commitments. On the other hand it has the right to suspend interest charges over a considerable number of years after construction is completed, a right not possessed by the L.P.T.B. It should be noted, however, that this power applies to expenditure on the Grid and not to capital invested in selected power stations which, though not under the ownership of the Board, are operated by the Board, who has to bear all operating costs including the capital charges.

It is interesting to inquire into the reasons why generation and transmission have been placed under unified public control, and why this has not occurred in the case of the larger section of the industry concerned with distribution, that is, with the retail side of the industry.

To do so, it is necessary to consider briefly the history of the industry, at least from the end of the war of 1914–18 onwards.

HISTORY OF ELECTRIC SUPPLY

Electric supply actually commenced between 1880 and 1890, but up to the end of the war of 1914–18 no serious effort had been made to introduce any measure of co-ordination. A considerable number of Acts were passed between 1880 and 1918 dealing with electric supply, but Parliament had failed fully to recognize the extent to which the supply of electricity is essential both for industrial and domestic purposes. Consequently the industry had been allowed to grow up in a haphazard manner, partly under private and partly under municipal control. During the war it became vitally necessary to expand industrial production at a very rapid rate in order to meet the necessities of a world war and virtually the whole economic life of the country was placed under public control. New industries had to be built up at high speed, and in many instances factories had to be erected in areas where either there was no supply of electric power available or the supply was inadequate. The difficulties created by this situation were very considerable, and the shortcomings of the electricity supply industry were forcibly brought to the attention of the Government.

COAL CONSERVATION AND ELECTRIC POWER SUPPLY COMMITTEES

In 1917 a Sub-Committee of the Coal Conservation Committee was appointed under the Chairmanship of Mr. C. H. Merz to report on measures which would improve the efficiency of the industry. As a result of the Interim Report of this Sub-Committee, a further Committee was appointed in 1918, under the Chairmanship of Sir Archibald Williamson, which finally reported in favour of a relatively drastic reorganization of generation and main transmission, which were to be placed under public ownership or control within about sixteen separate areas. The Williamson Committee Report and the previous Interim Report of the Sub-Committee dealt primarily with generation and main transmission, that is to say, with the production and wholesale side of the industry. It was in this field that there was the greatest need of reorganization since there were in 1918 some 600 independent generating stations, most of them small and inefficient.

The advantages of centralized generation were well known. In large power stations generating plant could be installed at a cost much less than the average cost of plant in small stations. Large power stations could also generate at much higher efficiencies, with consequent reductions in operating costs, and great savings could be made in the required amount of generating plant by inter-connecting power stations and so reducing the amount of spare or "stand-by" plant necessary. These facts, and also the fact that energy could be transmitted satisfactorily and economically at high voltage over long distances, had been demonstrated by the success of the one very large scale authority in existence in Great Britain in 1918, namely the Newcastle Electric Supply Company, which operated over a wide area in the north-eastern portion of England. Similar conclusions could be drawn from experience abroad, particularly in the United States.

The Williamson Committee therefore recommended that a body to be known as the Electricity Commissioners should be created who "should, after local inquiries, divide the United Kingdom into districts technically suitable for the economical generation and distribution[1] of electricity."

Although co-ordination of generation and main transmission were the first requirements, neither the Coal Conservation Sub-Committee nor the Williamson Committee overlooked the fact that the retail side of the industry could also be improved by co-ordination, as the following extracts from the two Reports indicate.

Coal Conservation Sub-Committee Paragraph 28

While it may be feasible for local concerns, whether municipal or company, to retain, as separate bodies, the ownership of mains and the business of supplying lighting and small power consumers, the generation and main transmission and distribution of electrical energy, and the business of supplying power to manufacturers, railways and other users, must in each industrial district be in the hands of one organization. . . . There can be no question, however, that if the criterion upon which this matter has to be settled is the price of electricity and the conservation of coal, the arguments in favour of handing over the whole business to the new authorities (i.e. the district authorities recommended by the Sub-Committee) predominate.

---

[1] The word distribution is used here to mean wholesale supply.

Electric Power Supply Committee Paragraph 56 E

With regard to distribution systems:—In the case of the local authorities the distribution system may be acquired on terms similar to those proposed in respect of generating stations, in cases where distributors wish to discontinue. In the case of electric lighting companies, distribution should either be transferred to the district electricity board on terms fixed by agreement or should remain in the hands of the company until the earliest date at which the concession may be terminated.

Electric Power Supply Committee Paragraph 65

We have already touched on the subject of distribution; but we think it well to state our opinion that, if the supply of electricity were being commenced *ab initio*, it would be found best for generation and distribution to be conducted by one and the same body.

Despite the above extracts from the Reports, the Committees tended to concentrate on generation and main transmission, where the most obvious improvements could be made and where existing interests would be least disturbed. Nevertheless, as will be shown later, both the Coal Conservation Sub-Committee and the Williamson Committee were prepared to interfere much more boldly with the industry than was the subsequent Weir Committee of 1925, which is described below. This is probably to be explained partly by the atmosphere which existed after the upheaval of the war and in which people were prepared to contemplate radical changes with comparative equanimity, and partly by the fact that interference with existing interests would have been less serious in 1918 than in 1925, between which dates the total capital invested in the industry had doubled.

THE 1919 BILL

The recommendations of the Williamson Committee were incorporated in a Bill presented to Parliament in 1919. This Bill in its original form was a very comprehensive measure which provided for the creation of the Electricity Commissioners with powers to create district electricity boards, which would acquire compulsorily the whole of the generating plant and main transmission lines in each area. There were also provisions in the Bill which would have resulted in the company distribution systems passing into the hands of the district boards in course of time. The boards would have been non-profit-making public concerns, the members of the boards being appointed under Special Orders made by the Electricity Commissioners, and the boards themselves subject to a certain measure of control by the Electricity Commissioners. As described later, the original Bill was drastically altered before being passed.

PUBLIC CONCERNS VERSUS COMPANIES

The Coal Conservation Sub-Committee report had left quite open the question of whether the proposed area boards should be public concerns or companies—that is to say, whether they were to make a divisible profit or not. As an appendix to the Report there was a description of the various possible types of body, and it would appear that there was a certain bias in favour of private enterprise, although, as already stated, the final conclusions left the matter entirely open.

The Williamson Report, on the other hand, proposed the creation of district electricity boards which could either:

(1) Operate the district themselves; or
(2) Operate by lease to a new or existing company.

The Report goes on to state that if the districts are actually operated by the boards, "it is essential that the district electricity board should make no divisible profit."

In the 1919 Bill (before it was altered by the House of

Lords) the district boards were allowed to delegate their powers to existing supply authorities, whether company or municipality (Clause 16). There can be little doubt, however, that had the 1919 Bill gone through as originally framed and had district boards been formed they would, in most instances, have operated the districts themselves and would not have delegated their powers. The most likely exception would have been a territory where a large power company was already operating an area approximately equivalent to a district as visualized by those who drafted the Bill. The reason why there probably would, in general, have been no delegation of powers to existing authorities was that in nearly all districts there would have been taken over a mixture of local authority and company generating stations and transmission lines, and the local authorities would almost certainly have objected to being supplied by a company. This difficulty is as great to-day as it was in 1919. It was, for instance, inevitable that the c.e.b. should be a public concern, because it had to interfere to a greater or lesser extent with every authority in the country and in particular had to operate selected generating stations belonging to both local authorities and company authorities.

A further argument for the public concern is that in the development of the electricity supply industry—and also in many other industries—it is essential to take a long view. Expenditure must be made, if the industry is to be developed rapidly and economically, on which there will be no return for a number of years, but which thereafter will be highly remunerative. It is not easy, particularly for small undertakings—whether company or municipal—to take a long view in this matter because it involves either suspension of dividends or payment of interest out of capital. Payment of interest out of capital, and also suspension of provision for depreciation, can readily be arranged in the case of a public concern. The difficulty in incurring temporarily unremunerative expenditure has probably been largely responsible for what many people feel to be the relatively slow progress in retail distribution, both as regards making supplies available and in bringing down prices and so increasing consumption, as indeed has been demonstrated in certain instances where a longer view has been taken.

Apart from the reasons given above for creating public concerns for the development of electricity supply, public opinion is inclined to demand that bodies set up by legislation and having more or less monopolistic powers should be non-profit making. It is interesting to note that the older—now probably obsolete—form of public concern such as the Post Office does contribute to the State what is in effect a monopoly rental and which is now fortunately fixed in amount. The general tendency is, however, to avoid monopoly rentals since they constitute a form of undesirable indirect taxation.

FATE OF 1919 BILL

Had the 1919 Bill been passed as originally drafted the whole subsequent history of electricity supply would have been entirely altered, but in the House of Lords the compulsory powers were struck out, and in this and other ways the whole Bill was radically altered. In this form it was finally passed and the Electricity Commissioners came into existence under the chairmanship of Sir John Snell, who had taken an active part in all the work leading up to the 1919 Bill and who was later to play a prominent part in the passing of the 1926 Act. The Commissioners lacked the essential compulsory powers to create Joint Electricity Authorities (which replaced the district electricity boards of the original Bill) and consequently were quite unable to co-ordinate the industry as had been intended; in fact up till 1925 only one Joint Electricity Authority was formed. It is impossible to estimate the financial loss to the nation resulting from the continuance of chaotic conditions in the industry from 1919 until at least 1926, but it certainly must have run into many millions of pounds. While the initial responsibility for this rested with the House of Lords, the Government was also responsible for not subsequently restoring the compulsory powers, particularly as they had promised to do so in the next Session.

THE WEIR COMMITTEE

After the Act of 1919 there was no further important development until in 1925, largely as the result of Sir John Snell's efforts, a Committee was appointed, under the chairmanship of Lord Weir, to inquire into the reorganization of the industry. The matter had actually been under consideration by the 1924 Labour Government, but the latter had not had time to take any active steps before it was succeeded by a Conservative Government under Mr. Baldwin. The Weir Committee confined itself almost entirely to generation and transmission, both for the reasons mentioned above in connection with the Williamson Committee, and also because, profiting by the difficulties experienced with the 1919 Bill, the Committee were aware that, under the circumstances then existing, interference with the industry should be limited to the minimum possible. In any event, improvements on the production and wholesale side were the more necessary.

The Weir Report followed generally the same lines as the Williamson Report, except that (a) it recommended a single new authority to control all generation and main transmission throughout the whole country, and (b) it avoided almost completely any reference to distribution. In the case of the Weir Report it is stated that "the detailed distribution of electrical energy—in other words its sale, transport, and delivery—is essentially a local matter and a suitable function for decentralization." The Report also states: "We do not desire to impair or interfere unnecessarily with existing rights. . . . We propose not a change of ownership but the subordination of vested interests in general to that of a new authority for the benefit of all, and this only under proper safeguards and in a manner which will preserve the value of private enterprise."

The Weir Report was, in fact, a good deal less ambitious than the Williamson Report, and with the help of the official Opposition the 1926 Bill, which was based on the Weir Report, passed safely on to the statute book despite a good deal of difficulty. As a result of the passage of the 1926 Act, the C.E.B. was appointed and commenced its labours in 1927. Since 1926 the only further legislation directly affecting the Board is the 1935 Act. This is a short measure the main purpose of which is to give the Board powers to supply railway companies direct instead of through the local supply authority as required by the 1926 Act, and to give supplies on special terms in certain circumstances. These powers can only be exercised with the approval of the Electricity Commissioners in each particular instance.

CONSTITUTION OF CENTRAL ELECTRICITY BOARD

The Board consists of a chairman and seven members appointed by the Minister of Transport after consultation with bodies representing local government, electricity, commerce, industry, transport, agriculture, and labour as laid down in the Act. Members of Parliament are not eligible for appointment to the Board, and no full-time member of the Board may hold shares in the industry, while part-time members must declare any such holdings. Apart from these negative qualifications there are no other qualifications laid down by the Act as regards membership of the Board. The following is a list of the present members of the Board (1936):

Chairman: Sir Archibald Page (electricity supply, previously general manager).
Members: Sir Andrew Duncan (finance and industry, late chairman).
R. P. Sloan (electricity supply).
Frank Hodges.
Alderman W. Walker (local government).
Sir Duncan Watson (electricity industry).
Sir Ralph Wedgwood (railways).
W. K. Whigham (finance and commerce).

The principal officers appointed by the Board are:
The General Manager.
The Chief Engineer.
The Commercial Manager.
The Chief Accountant.
The Secretary and Solicitor.
Eight District Managers in charge of the local organization in the nine areas into which the Grid is divided (two areas being operated as one).

The Act lays down that members of the Board shall be appointed for a period of not less than five years nor more than ten years, and empowers the Ministry of Transport to fix the amount of the remuneration, which in the last published accounts totals £11,617 per annum. The larger part of this sum represents the salary of the chairman who is a whole-time appointment, the other members of the Board being all part-time appointments. There is nothing in the Act to prevent members of the Board being re-appointed after their term of office expires, and when Sir Andrew Duncan resigned the chairmanship at the end of 1934, on his appointment as chairman of the Executive Committee of the Iron and Steel Federation, he became a member of the Board in the place of Lord Barnby; nor is there any provision in the Act for cancelling the appointment of members unless they be absent for six months or more, or become disqualified for the reasons given above. It would appear, therefore, that appointments could only be cancelled by a special Act of Parliament and in this respect the 1926 Act differs from the London Passenger

Transport Act, 1933, which contains provisions for removing members of the Transport Board from office for "inability or misbehaviour."

The Constitution of the C.E.B. has worked in practice, but this must be regarded as being in no small measure due to the appointment of Sir Andrew Duncan and subsequently Sir Archibald Page as chairman during the first and most difficult period of the Board's history. It is interesting to note that the actual constitution of the Board differs appreciably from that proposed in the Weir Report, which was as follows:

The Board to be composed as follows:

(a) To be nominated by the Minister of Transport after consultation with the Electricity Commissioners and such other bodies as he may think fit—
Chairman.
Two members experienced in Municipal or Local Government affairs.
Two members experienced in Electrical Company undertakings.
One member with Railway experience.

(b) To be nominated by the Minister of Transport after consultation with the Board of Trade—
One member representative of industry.

(c) To be nominated by the Minister of Transport after consultation with the Treasury—
A Government nominee.
In addition to the above there will be a whole-time Managing Director, to be appointed by the Board with the approval of the Minister, who will also be Vice-Chairman and will require to be paid a substantial salary.
The Chairman and other members to receive fees and expenses only.

INTERNAL ORGANIZATION

The Board is at liberty to determine its own internal organization, and has in fact done so. It is empowered by the Act to set up consultative committees, both national and district, representing the Board and the electricity supply authorities. A national consultative committee and eight district committees have been formed and have already proved of value although their function is purely consultative and they possess no executive powers. No bodies other than the electricity supply authorities are represented on the various consultative committees.

The Board itself meets about once a month, and these meetings are usually attended by certain of the principal officers of the Board's staff. Regular meetings of the principal officers also take place. In general the internal organization of the Board's staff is on the functional group system, but all communications to the Board themselves pass through the chief officers who attend the Board meetings. The individual members of the Board are not in any way responsible for particular departments of the work and, with the exception of the chairman, have little to do with the day-to-day working of the organization apart from attendance at the Board meetings.

OFFICE ORGANIZATION

The head office of the C.E.B. is in London (Trafalgar Buildings), where the managerial, engineering, accountancy, and legal staff are accommodated. There are seven district offices in Glasgow, Newcastle, Manchester, Leeds, Birmingham, London, and Bristol accommodating the district staffs responsible for operation and maintenance of the Grid in each of the nine areas in which the whole Grid is divided. In two cases—Central Scotland and South Scotland, South-East England and East England—two areas are operated from one office. Each district office is under a district manager who has a wide measure of authority as regards all matters affecting his area. All matters concerning general policy, finance, capital expenditure, placing of contracts, etc., and engineering problems, other than purely local problems, are, however, settled by the head office. Although the primary authority is therefore centralized, close contact is maintained between the head office and each district office and between the district offices themselves.

RELATIONSHIP WITH ELECTRICITY COMMISSIONERS

The Board is in no sense a Government Department, and is not under the direct control of Parliament. It is, however, indirectly under the control of the Minister of Transport in so far as the 1926 Act provides for a number of the Board's powers (particularly those relating to finance) being subject to the approval of the Electricity Commissioners, who are themselves directly under the Ministry of Transport. The Electricity Commissioners can call upon the Board to provide any information which they may require, and the Board has to submit to the Ministry of Transport an annual report and statement of accounts. Any of the Board's actions can, of course, be challenged in a Court of law, whose decision would be based on the Court's interpretation of the powers given by the 1926 and 1935 Acts. In actual practice the control exercised by the Ministry of Transport and the Electricity Commissioners does not result in difficulty because the Board works in close co-operation with the Electricity Commissioners on all matters with which the latter are concerned. Questions can be, and are, asked in Parliament about the Board's work, but the Minister of Transport is not bound to answer all these questions in view of the fact that the Board is not directly under his control. The annual report, to which reference has already been made, is submitted to the Minister of Transport and the 1926 Act also states that it is to be laid before Parliament. There is no special provision for a debate or discussion in Parliament on the policy of the Board, and this follows the general tenor of the 1926 Act in giving the Board definite powers subject to certain safeguards exercised mainly through the Electricity Commissioners, thus leaving the Board more or less independent of Parliament as regards its actual work. So far as the work of completing the Grid is concerned, this arrangement has worked admirably.

PERSONNEL

The Board is entirely free to appoint its own staff and does not require Treasury sanction or other outside approval. The total of the staff amounts now to about seven hundred, or approximately thirteen hundred including manual workers. The salary scales compare favourably with the Civil Service scales so far as the principal officers are concerned, but as regards the remainder of the staff the average is probably about equivalent to the Civil Service scale, taking account of the pension and insurance scheme recently introduced. The methods of recruiting the staff have not yet been standardized, as up to the present the whole organization has been largely in the process of creation. Generally speaking, the chief officers have made appointments from outside as required. In many instances members of the staffs of the consulting engineers and of the contractors engaged in the constructional work of the Grid have been absorbed into the Board's staff, and in the early period it was not difficult for the Board to find suitable applicants owing to the extent of unemployment in the professional grades. Promotion, up to the present, does not seem to have been wholly by seniority but has probably been influenced largely by merit. It will be appreciated that, in view of the Board's functions, a large proportion of the staff has technical qualifications, although there are also a considerable number holding legal, accountancy, administrative, or other qualifications.

FUNCTIONS AND POWERS

As already explained the Grid is a network, or gridiron, of high-voltage transmission lines covering practically the whole country and interconnecting the large and efficient selected stations, thus enabling generation to be concentrated in these stations and supplies to be tapped off at any point at which they are required. The Act, therefore, charges the Board with the duty of erecting and operating the Grid and of supplying electricity to distribution authorities, but it expressly prohibits the Board from itself building or owning power stations or supplying individual consumers except in special circumstances. The duties and powers of the Board are laid down in considerable detail in the Act, and although this may have been necessary because of the considerable initial hostility to the whole purpose of the Act, the somewhat detailed provisions have led to difficulties. The only modifications to the original 1926 Act are contained in the 1935 Act, the passage of which aroused considerable opposition. As already mentioned, this Act, while giving powers to the Board to supply railway companies direct under certain conditions, also enables the Board to make special arrangements for the supply of electricity at special prices subject to the approval of the Electricity Commissioners. Despite the limitations and difficulties which are referred to in more detail later, the purpose of the 1926 Act has been carried out and the Grid is now completed and practically in full operation.

The principal powers possessed by the Board are as follows:

1. Power to borrow up to £60,000,000[1] (with Treasury guarantee if the Board so wish and the Treasury agree) for the construction of the Grid and the standardization of frequency.
2. Power to suspend the sinking fund for a period of not more than five years and to pay interest out of capital for such period as the Electricity Commissioners may approve as being the period during which the expenditure is anticipated to be unremunerative.

[1] Originally £33,500,000, but later increased to £60,000,000.

3. Power of compulsory purchase of main transmission lines belonging to existing supply authorities.
4. Power to declare a uniform tariff (Grid tariff) at which supplies will be given to all authorities in each area other than owners of selected stations. The tariff is not the same for all areas. Supplies may also be given on special terms in certain instances subject to the Electricity Commissioners' approval.
5. Power to select efficient generating stations and to operate them as required, and to sell back to the owners the amounts required for their own purposes, that is, for use by the owners as distribution authorities. The price at which electricity is sold to the owners of such stations is either

> (a) "Adjusted station costs," which is the actual cost of generation at the station in question determined in accordance with the provisions of the 1926 Act, plus a proper proportion of the annual costs of the Grid, or, if this is disadvantageous to the owner,
> (b) The calculated and hypothetical cost of generation, had the Grid not been in existence, or
> (c) The Grid tariff.

6. Power (exercisable by the Electricity Commissioners) to close down inefficient stations subject to the cost of the Grid supply being less than the cost of generation at such stations.
7. Power to acquire compulsory wayleaves, to break up roads and to acquire land, similar to the powers held by local authorities who are authorized undertakers.
8. Power to standardize the generation frequency in areas which were non-standard, and power to recover the cost of this standardization by means of a levy made by the Electricity Commissioners on all electricity authorities in the country.

Certain of the above powers are subject to the approval of the Electricity Commissioners, who to this extent supervise the Board's operations on behalf of the Minister of Transport.

The Board's powers have not always been used to their

full extent. It has, for instance, been the Board's policy to avoid compulsory acquisition of wayleaves wherever possible, and, more important, they have raised all their loans without a Treasury guarantee. Nevertheless, the Board is now in a very real manner controlling the operation of selected stations. In each area there is a central control room from which instructions are being constantly given over a special communication system, the lines of which are hired from the Post Office, to all the stations in the area. Stations are told to take up load, to drop load, to close down, or to start up, as required. Instructions with regard to opening or closing switches connected to the Grid are also given from the central control rooms. The operating instructions issued to the stations are based on the rapidly growing data obtained by the Board from a scientific analysis of actual operating costs of each station. These instructions are resulting in a very marked reduction of generation costs.

Like all the electricity authorities, the Board has monopoly rights, but, as has already been pointed out, the Board is, to a large extent, in the position of having to compete with the existing supply authorities and therefore the monopoly rights are only partially effective.

FINANCE

The Board has raised all its loans, amounting in total to £50,000,000, without a Treasury guarantee. The argument for so doing was that the Board was thereby free of any restrictive influence arising from Treasury control. This argument no doubt carried particular weight in the early period of the Board's activities when Treasury control might quite easily have influenced the development of the organization. After the Board's organization had been established, the argument against the use of the guarantee would appear to have carried considerably less weight, but probably the

TABLE I

CENTRAL ELECTRICITY STOCKS

Amount Issued £	Interest Rate Per cent	Redemption Dates	Date of Issue	Issue Price	Proceeds £	ALLOCATED TO		INTEREST CHARGE		Interest Fundable till	Sinking Fund begins
						General Purposes £	Standardization of Frequency £	Total £	Of which borne by Grid £		
3,000,000	4	1959–89	May 1929	83	2,499,000	2,400,000	600,000	120,000	96,000	31.12.36	1935
7,000,000	5	1950–70	Jan. 1930 / Oct. 1930	97½	6,825,000	7,150,000	2,850,000	500,000	357,500	31.12.37	1936
3,000,000			Nov. 1931	*	2,817,500					31.12.38	1937
6,000,000	4½	1951–73	Nov. 1930	95½	5,730,000	4,620,000	1,380,000	270,000	207,900	31.12.38	1936
7,000,000	5	1955–75	Feb. 1932	95	6,650,000	4,725,000	2,275,000	350,000	236,250	31.12.39	1938
10,000,000	4½	1957–82	June 1932	96	9,600,000	7,600,000	3,000,000	450,000	315,000	31.12.39	1938
8,000,000	3½	1963–93	June 1933	93½	7,480,000	5,200,000	2,800,000	280,000	182,000	31.12.40	1939
6,000,000	3¼	1974–94	Oct. 1934	93	5,580,000	3,300,000	2,700,000	195,000	107,250	31.12.41	1940
3,500,000	3¼	1974–94	Feb. 1936	100	3,500,000	†1,750,000	†1,750,000	113,750	56,875	31.12.43	1942
53,500,000	—	—	—	—	50,672,500	36,145,000	17,355,000	2,278,750	1,558,775	—	—

* "Placed" in the market.

† Allocation not yet settled.

Treasury has not been particularly desirous of pledging the national credit in connection with an industry as prosperous as that of electricity supply. Table 1 gives the terms on which the various loans were raised.

Criticism has been directed against the Board because of the terms on which much of the money was raised, and the general trend of this is indicated by the following comment in the *Economist* (vol. 118, p. 1320):

As to the cost of borrowing, and the currency of Central Electricity Board stocks, it is a point of criticism, not infrequently made in the City, that the Board is handicapped by an excessive interest charge which, in the absence of early maturity dates, cannot be reduced for a long time ahead. There is substance in the criticism. The interest charge works out at just under $4\frac{3}{4}$[1] per cent on the actual sum raised, and the earliest optional redemption date is as far off as 1950. There is, therefore, no possibility (apart from payments by way of sinking funds) of scaling down the average interest rate for the next sixteen years. Whether blame may properly attach to the Board's financial advisers on this account is another matter. The whole scheme was settled as long ago as 1926. To maintain, therefore, that its financing should have been deferred until interest rates were near their present abnormally low level is to be wise long after the event. Whether the Board obtained the best terms available at the times when its money was required, it is, again, idle to dispute. The Board was certainly unfortunate in lighting upon June 1932—less than a month before the War Loan conversion and its attendant sharp drop in interest rates—as the appropriate moment to raise £10,000,000 at about $4\frac{1}{4}$ per cent. It may seem regrettable, also, in view of subsequent market tendencies, that the Board did not claim earlier options of redemption—which it could probably have done at the cost of little or no concession in issue prices. Without venturing to award either praise or censure, the investor can readily measure the dimensions of the resulting financial handicap resting on the Grid. If the expenditure on the Grid itself (leaving standardization out of account) had averaged only 4 per cent, instead of $4\frac{3}{4}$ per cent, the annual interest bill would have been reduced by about £225,000. This is an appreciable sum, but it is highly

[1] Now somewhat less.

unlikely that it will spell the difference between the failure and success of the scheme.

REVENUE

Several of the Grid areas have only recently come into operation, and during the temporary arrangement period, prior to 1934, no detailed accounts were published by the Board. The full accounts published with the annual reports of 1934 and 1935 are of very great interest.

These accounts show that sinking fund payments were suspended during the construction stage and that interest was paid out of capital as provided for in the Act. In accordance with regulations made by the Electricity Commissioners the interest charges will continue to be paid out of capital for a period of about seven and a half years from the date on which the money was spent, this being the anticipated period during which the expenditure will not be remunerative. From now onwards, however, sinking fund payments, which were only suspended for a period of five years, will start to appear in the Board's accounts, and, in fact, certain payments had to be provided for even in the 1934 accounts. Interest charges on the earliest loan will have to be paid out of revenue in 1937.

Excluding the three areas in which trading had not commenced, the Board's 1934 accounts showed a credit balance at December 31, 1934, of approximately £86,000 after payment of operating expenses and of certain sinking fund charges. Those for 1935 show a credit balance at December 31, 1935, of no less than £1,021,221, or over eleven times the balance at the end of 1934. This very great increase must be regarded as extremely satisfactory and as putting beyond reasonable doubt the Board's ability to pay the full interest and sinking fund charges out of revenue well within the period during which they can be charged to capital. The above figure of £1,021,221 does not include the North-East England and South Scotland areas, in which full trading has not commenced as yet.

The total capital expenditure on the Grid at the end of 1935 amounted to approximately £34,600,000. The interest and sinking fund charges on this sum will total about £2,500,000, so that the Board's present revenue, allowing for certain sinking fund payments already being made, is not far short of half the required total. Considering the comparatively short period during which full trading operations have been in progress, and the fact that the revenue figure does not include two areas where full trading has not commenced, the present position is very hopeful.

Apart from the rapidly increasing transfer of electricity over the Grid from the 130 selected stations to the 150 or so other points of Grid supplies, the operating costs of selected stations have been falling rapidly. In 1935 the average consumption of fuel per unit sent out from the selected stations was over 11 per cent less than the average consumption of the same stations in 1932, operating independently of the Grid. This represents a direct saving of about £920,000 in operating costs during 1935, of which part accrues to the Board and part to the owners of the stations.

SAVING IN CAPITAL EXPENDITURE

Although the Board's finances must be regarded as not yet completely established, there can be no question whatsoever as to the national saving which has been achieved through the creation of the Grid. The diagram opposite shows the probable extent of the capital saving, much of which accrues to the supply authorities.

The smooth curve represents the approximate average of the plant sanctioned year by year up to 1931, and the continuation of this curve (shown as a dotted line) represents a reasonable assumption as to the plant which would have been sanctioned during the period 1931 to 1935 in the absence of the Grid.

Although the Grid was not in full operation in 1931, it was partially completed, and had already markedly affected the sanctioning of additional generating plant. This was due not only to those portions of the Grid actually constructed, but to the fact that Grid connections could then be anticipated in the near future. As a consequence, the amount of plant sanctioned fell to very low figures during

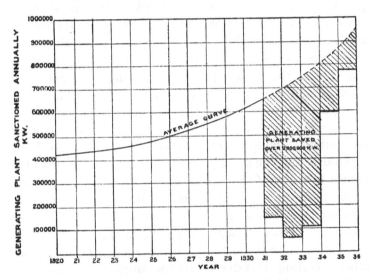

the three years from 1931 to 1934. This was due to the availability for commercial purposes of a large amount of the plant which under independent operation had to be kept as a reserve by each independent generating station. It will be noted that in 1934 and 1935 there was a big increase in plant sanctioned. This indicates that most of the spare plant set free by the Grid has now been absorbed, and that a regular annual increase in generating plant may be anticipated in future. It can, however, be confidently expected that the average curve from 1936 onwards will lie below the dotted curve and flatter, since the percentage of

E

spare plant required under Grid operation is much less than that under independent operation. It may be anticipated that the percentage of spare plant required under Grid operation will be round about 20, i.e. 20 per cent of the aggregate peak load, as compared with an average figure of nearer 80 before 1931. The total of the shaded area on the diagram represents the saving in generating plant up to date. If the value of this plant be estimated at £10 per kilowatt (a conservative figure), the total saving is over £20,000,000, which is nearly two-thirds of the total expenditure on the Grid. It should, however, be noted that although much of this saving has already accrued, the full amount will not accrue for another two years or so. The reason for this is that the area represents a saving in expenditure commitments and there may be a lag of two years or so between commitments and actual cash payments. Although the diagram does not presume to give an exact estimate of the national saving effected by the Grid, it can be fairly concluded that the saving already made (which is definitely known to exceed £11,000,000) is at least a large proportion of the total capital expenditure on the whole system. This conclusion does not take into account the fact that very substantial annual savings are also being made, and will be made even more in the future, by the reduction in coal and other operating costs due to the concentration of generation in the more efficient power stations.

GRID TARIFF

The 1926 Act requires the Board to declare a uniform tariff for each area, although the tariff may vary as between areas. This tariff represents the price at which the Board will provide supplies to any authorized undertaker in the area, although, as has already been explained, the owners of selected stations are entitled to receive supplies at a cheaper rate related to the cost of production in each selected station. The Grid tariffs are based on a sliding scale relating to the growth of load; thus, as the supply taken from the Grid increases, the charge per kilowatt decreases, the object of this being to encourage the distribution authorities to expand their business by putting them in a position to take on new loads at a decreasing price. As a further encouragement to the development of new areas or areas not previously developed energetically, a special adjustment of the maximum demand charges is offered for a limited period in cases where such a development is in progress. The kilowatt, or maximum demand, charges are assessed on the largest demand occurring in January, February, November, or December of each year, and thus supply authorities are placed in the position of being able to offer their consumers exceptionally low rates for supplies taken during the remaining eight months of the year. In the event of a large new load being taken on by a supply authority towards the end of the year, thereby substantially affecting the maximum demand for the year, the Board is prepared in such cases to make a reduction in the kilowatt charge for the new load during that year.

In this and other ways the Board is doing what it can to encourage supply authorities to pursue progressive policies. Perhaps the greatest encouragement of all is due to the fact that the Grid tariffs are calculated on budgetary periods of ten years, that is to say they are intended to balance revenue and expenditure only at the end of a considerable period. The framing of tariffs on such a basis is the *sine qua non* of a progressive policy in electric supply. Table II gives a comparison of the Grid tariffs and Table III shows the scale of increments of demand on which the kilowatt charges are reduced.

Supply authorities are entitled to only one supply from the Grid, but by a special arrangement, and usually by the payment of an additional service charge, further supplies may be given. It is only reasonable that additional payments

TABLE II

COMPARISON OF GRID TARIFFS

	Central Scotland	Mid East England	South-East and East England	North-West England and North Wales	Central England	South-West England and South Wales
	£ s. d.	£ s. d.	£ s. d.	£ s. d.	£ s. d.	£ s. d.
KILOWATT CHARGE:						
Basic demand, per kilowatt	3 10 0	3 10 0	3 10 0	3 7 6	3 10 0	3 10 0
First increment, per kilowatt	3 5 0	3 5 0	3 5 0	3 3 0	3 5 0	3 5 0
Second increment, per kilowatt	3 0 0	3 0 0	3 0 0	2 18 6	3 0 0	3 0 0
All in excess of above, per kilowatt	2 15 0	2 15 0	2 15 0	2 14 0	2 15 0	2 15 0
Variations of kilowatt charge:						
(a) For power factor:						
Increase of kilowatt charge per 0·1 below 0·85 lagging	0 4 6	0 4 6	0 4 6	0 4 6	0 4 6	0 4 6
(b) For rates:						
Basic rates per kilowatt of plant installed at selected stations	0 6 0	0 5 3	0 4 3	0 4 0	0 4 0	0 4 6
Variation of kilowatt charge per 1s. variation from basic rates	0 1 10	0 1 10	0 1 10	0 1 10	0 1 10	0 2 0
RUNNING CHARGE:						
Per unit	0·2d.	0·186d.	0·21d.	0·2d.	0·196d.	0·225d.
Variation of running charge:						
For fuel:						
Basic cost of fuel per ton	0 13 6	0 13 0	0 16 0	0 15 0	0 12 0	0 14 6
Basic calorific value of fuel (B.T.U.s per lb.)	11,000	11,500	11,500	11,600	10,000	12,700
Variation of running charge, per 1d. variation from basic cost of fuel at basic calorific value	0·001d.	0·001d.	0·0008d.	0·0009d.	0·001d.	0·0008d.

Each tariff enables the Board to make a service charge for each point of supply beyond the first.

should be made for multiple supplies, since in effect by taking a supply at a second or third point, the supply authority is avoiding the cost of distribution mains by means

TABLE III

SCALE OF INCREMENTS OF DEMAND ON WHICH THE KILOWATT CHARGES PAYABLE UNDER THE TARIFF ARE REDUCED

	Basic Demand Kilowatts	Standard Increment of Demand Kilowatts
Not exceeding	3,000 ..	.. 3,000
Exceeding 3,000 but not exceeding	4,000 ..	.. 2,900
,, 4,000 ,, ,, ,,	5,000 ..	.. 2,800
,, 5,000 ,, ,, ,,	6,000 ..	.. 2,700
,, 6,000 ,, ,, ,,	7,000 ..	.. 2,600
,, 7,000 ,, ,, ,,	8,000 ..	.. 2,500
,, 8,000 ,, ,, ,,	9,000 ..	.. 2,400
,, 9,000 ,, ,, ,,	10,000 ..	.. 2,300
,, 10,000 ,, ,, ,,	11,000 ..	.. 2,200
,, 11,000 ,, ,, ,,	12,000 ..	.. 2,100
,, 12,000 ,, ,, ,,	13,000 ..	.. 2,000
,, 13,000 ,, ,, ,,	14,000 ..	.. 1,900
,, 14,000 ,, ,, ,,	15,000 ..	.. 1,800
,, 15,000 ,, ,, ,,	16,000 ..	.. 1,700
,, 16,000 ,, ,, ,,	17,000 ..	.. 1,600
,, 17,000 ,, ,, ,,	18,000 ..	.. 1,500
,, 18,000 ,, ,, ,,	19,000 ..	.. 1,400
,, 19,000 ,, ,, ,,	20,000 ..	.. 1,300
,, 20,000 ,, ,, ,,	21,000 ..	.. 1,200
,, 21,000 ,, ,, ,,	22,000 ..	.. 1,100
,, 22,000 ,, ,, ,,	— ..	.. 1,000

"Basic demand" means the maximum demand of the undertaking in the calendar year 1932, or 2,000 kilowatts, whichever is the greater.

of Grid transmission. Since the Grid tariff is uniform throughout the whole area, there is no attempt (except in special instances) to relate the prices of each supply to the actual cost of giving it, and indeed this would be impossible since the Grid is really a single entity, the cost of which it would be difficult or impossible to allocate geographically. Even allocation of cost to each area is somewhat artificial.

OTHER TARIFFS

Supplies given by the Board to supply authorities are charged at either:

(1) Grid tariff—this applies primarily to supplies given at points other than selected stations.

(2) Adjusted station cost—this applies to supplies given to the owners of certain selected stations.

(3) Calculated cost of generation had the station in question been operated independently of the Grid—this is in accordance with Section 13 of the 1926 Act, which safeguards the owners of selected stations against any loss in taking supplies at adjusted station cost. Thus under no circumstances can such owners be penalized.

(4) Special terms—this applies to a number of non-selected generating stations with the owners of which the Board has, by agreement, made special arrangements to operate the stations for the time being. It also applies to special agreements made under other circumstances where the ordinary Grid tariff could not be applied. These special arrangements are entered into voluntarily by the Board and the undertaker in question and are subject to the approval of the Electricity Commissioners in accordance with Section 1 of the 1935 Act. The Commissioners have to be satisfied that the arrangements will not result in a financial loss to the Board nor in any "substantial prejudice" to other supply authorities.

SELECTED STATIONS

A large proportion of the owners of selected stations are receiving supplies in accordance with (3) above. The principal reason why "adjusted station cost" could not be applied to these cases is that the 1926 Act defines the

"adjusted station cost" as being the actual cost of generation at the station in question plus a "proper proportion"
of the annual costs of the Grid. This "proper proportion"
amounts roughly to about 0·06 pence per unit. "Adjusted
station cost" is divided into two components, namely, a
kilowatt charge of so much per kilowatt of maximum
demand and a running charge of so much per unit, say, for
example, 0·15d. per unit. If to the 0·15d. per unit is added
a further 0·06d., representing the proper proportion of the
annual costs of the Grid, there must be a substantial saving
on the kilowatt charge to the owner of the station to balance
the increase in the running charge. When the 1926 Act
was drafted it was assumed that generation would be concentrated in about 50 selected stations and that at these
stations the Board would bear a large proportion of the
kilowatt charges because of its use of the selected stations
for sales to non-selected authorities elsewhere. This reduction in the kilowatt charges would suffice, it was thought,
to compensate, or more than compensate, for the addition
to the running charge on account of the annual costs of the
Grid. This did not prove to be so in practice, particularly
at some of the largest and most efficient stations, and consequently the alternative of selling to the owners of the station
at the calculated cost of independent operation had to be
adopted.

Although the calculations on which the 1926 Act was
based were more or less correct in total, it has been found
in practice that the reduction in the kilowatt charge varies
greatly from one station to another. At many stations,
especially those where the owners are themselves buying
from the station nearly up to its maximum output, the
saving on the kilowatt charge is too small to offset the
addition to the unit charge on account of the Grid costs.
At these stations it has therefore been necessary to apply
Section 13, but this in turn has affected all the original
estimates. The real difficulty is that the benefits of the Grid

cannot, as things are, be equitably distributed between all the supply authorities concerned.[1]

The actual position to-day is that there are about 130 stations selected instead of 50 as originally contemplated. In addition, special arrangements, sanctioned by the 1935 Act, have been made with a number of non-selected stations to give supplies at prices below Grid tariff subject to the Board using their generating plant at times of maximum load. Additional stations have been selected, or supplied on special terms, partly because, by doing so, the Board is able to get them connected to and supplied from the Grid, whereas it might have been impossible to frame a Grid tariff sufficiently low to enable the stations to be shut down, and partly because it was found economic to utilize these stations for generating purposes to a limited extent. It is often cheaper to use existing plant, even though comparatively old and inefficient, for generation during a limited period when the system load is at its maximum, rather than to instal new and efficient plant elsewhere. Obviously high operating costs do not matter very much if a machine is only run for a small proportion of the year. On the other hand, if new generating plant were to be installed and run under the same conditions, its higher efficiency would not balance the additional capital charges.

OWNERSHIP OF POWER STATIONS

The whole position with regard to the charges made by the Board for supplies given from the Grid is somewhat complicated. The difficulties arise mainly from the fact that the Board does not own the power stations which it has to operate. If the Board owned all power stations, it might eventually be possible to give supplies to all authorities

[1] Discussion with the Consultative Committee for North-West England has resulted in an agreement between the Board and the owners of selected stations in this area for the pooling and equitable distribution of the savings due to the Grid.

at one uniform Grid tariff in each area, thus wiping out all the complications of "adjusted station cost" and "calculated cost under independent operation." Such an arrangement would also permit a lower Grid tariff than at present. The reason for this is that the owners of the large and efficient selected stations—who are usually also the owners of the largest distribution systems—obtain their supplies at the low price related in one way or another to the actual cost of generation at these large selected stations. If sales were made to all authorities at the same price, a small increase in the price of the large sales to the owners of the big selected stations would enable a substantial reduction to be made in the existing Grid tariff and yet result in the same total revenue.

Such an arrangement is not practicable under existing conditions, but in principle there does not seem to be any good reason why consumers who happen to be situated in a certain area supplied from a large selected station should benefit compared to consumers who happen to be situated elsewhere. Moreover, supply authorities who did not possess large and efficient stations at the time the Act was passed, can reasonably argue that they might have built such stations later if they had been allowed to do so, and that consequently it is unfair that they should be permanently required to buy at a price considerably higher than that paid by the owners of the selected stations.

The present arrangement works despite the complications, and it has the advantage of avoiding any possibility of penalizing the owners of selected stations who are fully protected under Section 13 of the 1926 Act. This clause states that the cost of supplies given to the owners of selected stations must not be greater than would have been the cost under independent operation. It would, however, appear desirable at least to provide for sales to the owners of selected stations to be at Grid tariff as soon as the Grid tariff has fallen below the calculated cost of production at

*

the selected station under independent operation, and to abolish entirely sales at "adjusted station cost." If this alteration to the 1926 Act were made, all authorities would in course of time receive supplies at a uniform Grid tariff within each area.

STANDARDIZATION OF FREQUENCY

Of the £53,500,000 already raised, about £17,000,000 have been allocated to the cost of standardizing frequency. The areas in which this standardization was necessary were Glasgow (25 cycles), North-East Coast (40 cycles), Birmingham (25 cycles), and South Wales (25 cycles), the standard for the country as a whole being 50 cycles. The total expenditure incurred up to December 31, 1935, was just over £16,000,000, and it seems probable that the final cost will be about £19,000,000 gross,[1] the work being now very nearly completed. The original estimate of the cost was about £10,500,000 gross, but this estimate was based on a survey made for the Weir Committee in 1924, and the main reason why the actual cost is considerably higher than the original estimate is that the work of changing over was not started until some five years after the preparation of the estimates, and has been spread over a longer period than originally contemplated. In the meantime the amount of apparatus to be converted had greatly increased, particularly consumers' apparatus, the growth of which could not be restricted. The delay in commencing the changeover was unfortunate, but was probably inevitable. The Act creating the Board and sanctioning the changeover was not passed until the end of 1926, and subsequently complicated negotiations and arrangements had to be made with the supply authorities involved in the changeover.

---

[1] Part of the gross cost represents expenditure which would have been incurred in any event, at a later date, by the authorities concerned. This ante-dated expenditure will be repaid in due course.

Despite the heavy cost it is probable that the ultimate benefit to the country of standardization will be very great, particularly in view of the rapid rate of growth of the industry. In effect the higher cost involved by the delay has only postponed the date by which the savings due to standardization will balance the annual charges on expenditure involved. This, however, must be to some extent a matter of opinion since the actual saving cannot be calculated with even approximate accuracy, involving as it does not only the advantage of Grid interconnection of all areas, but also savings in the manufacturing costs of plant and equipment and other benefits not readily assessable. It may be noted, however, that 50-cycle generating plant is about 8 per cent cheaper than 25-cycle plant, and that 50-cycle transformers are some 30 per cent cheaper than 25-cycle transformers.

The actual cost of standardization does not affect the Board's finances because it is borne by a levy on the whole industry, each authority paying in proportion to gross revenue. The annual burden on the industry represents approximately 1 per cent of the gross revenue. Part of the cost has, however, been met by unemployment grants made by the Ministry of Labour in connection with frequency standardization work carried out in the depressed North-East Coast area. In 1935 these grants totalled approximately £330,000 apart from a further £104,000 for expenditure in connection with the Grid itself.

ELECTRICITY COMMISSIONERS

The relationship of the Electricity Commissioners and the c.e.b. is both complicated and confusing. It must be remembered that the origin of the Electricity Commission was the 1919 Act and that the original intention was that the Commissioners, through their control of the district electricity boards, which they were to create, would become in effect the central authority for generation and main transmission. Had the Bill gone through in its original form, it would not have been necessary to create the C.E.B., for the Electricity Commissioners working through the district boards would have performed not only the functions now performed by the C.E.B., but would probably also in course of time have become largely responsible for distribution. Since, however, the essential compulsory powers were struck out of the 1919 Bill, the Electricity Commissioners were unable to perform the functions originally intended and have become to a large extent a licensing, judicial, and supervisory body.

The powers of the Electricity Commissioners were obtained largely through delegation by the Minister of Transport, the Minister who, in succession to the President of the Board of Trade, was made responsible for these matters under the 1919 Act. Although under the Ministry of Transport the Electricity Commission is not a Government department, its expenses being met by a levy on the supply industry amounting at present to 0·0012d. per unit sold. The first of its functions is that of granting statutory powers to supply electricity. These powers take the form of Special Orders (to be subsequently confirmed by the Minister of Transport and approved by Parliament) superseding the Provisional Orders granted by the Board of Trade. Under the 1919 Act the power of local authority undertakings to borrow money for electricity purposes is made subject to the Commissioners' consent. The consent of the Commissioners must also be obtained before new generating stations or main transmission lines can be established or existing ones extended; their approval is necessary for bulk supply agreements between undertakings, for systems of supply or for alterations in such systems, and for types of meters; they deal on behalf of the Minister of Transport with questions regarding the erection of overhead lines and regarding the maximum price which undertakings may charge; they have powers to collect financial and technical statistics from all undertakings, and they make regulations for the safety of the public and for insuring a proper and sufficient supply of electrical energy.

In addition to the above the Commissioners have power to hold inquiries for any purpose such as settling disputes between authorities or adjudicating on complaints made by consumers with regard to prices or other matters, but in all such adjudications the Commissioners' powers are limited by the various applicable Acts and Orders. Not the least of the Commissioners' functions is the publication of statistical information with regard to the industry, which has been of very great value although often criticized on the ground that the information published is several years out of date. All the above mentioned judicial and administrative functions have been of great importance and value to the industry.

It was probably because the Commissioners had become in practice largely a judicial authority that the promoters of the 1926 Act decided to create a new body—the c.e.b.— to carry out the executive functions of building and operating the Grid. The relationship of the Electricity Commissioners to the c.e.b. was, therefore, made more or less judicial. That is to say, the Commissioners are responsible for seeing that the Board does not exceed its powers under the 1926 Act, and the exercise of a number of these powers is made definitely subject to approval by the Commissioners. On the other hand, Parliament was evidently not too clear as to the desired relationship between the two bodies because an alteration was made during the committee stage of the 1926 Bill resulting in the Commissioners, instead of the Board, being made responsible for the preparation in the first instance of the Grid Area Schemes. After the schemes have been initially prepared by the Commissioners they are transmitted to the Board, which may modify them extensively before adopting them. It would have seemed more logical if the Board had prepared the schemes and had adopted them after obtaining the approval of the Commissioners. The fact is that when the 1926 Act was passing through committee there was undoubtedly much uncertainty in the minds of the committee as to the real functions of the two bodies. Had legislation been based on proper planning of the industry, it is probable that only one of the two bodies would have been created.

The Electricity Commissioners consist of the chairman, Sir John Snell, who as already mentioned has played a prominent part in the history of the supply industry, and the following three members:

> Sir John R. Brooke (Vice-Chairman).
> J. M. Kennedy.
> C. G. Morley New.

The total staff of the Commission is somewhat under one hundred.

JOINT ELECTRICITY AUTHORITIES

The Electricity Supply Acts of 1919 and 1922 empowered the Electricity Commissioners to determine electricity districts. If it appeared to the Commissioners that the existing organization for the supply of electricity in any district should be improved, the Commissioners were further empowered to hold an enquiry to consider schemes for such improvement, including proposals for the formation of a Joint Electricity Authority. In the event of no satisfactory scheme being proposed, the Commissioners could themselves formulate a scheme for the creation of such an Authority. This procedure has been somewhat modified by the 1926 Act and now Joint Electricity Authorities must be established if and when the Electricity Commissioners determine an electricity district. The actual creation of the Joint Electricity Authority is effected by an order made by the Commissioners and laid before each House of Parliament.

Although the procedure for creating Joint Electricity Authorities has been somewhat modified by the 1926 Act, there has been no restoration of the vital compulsory powers necessary to ensure the effective functioning of such Authorities, and in consequence of this only four Joint Electricity Authorities have as yet been created. These are as follows:

North Wales and South Cheshire Joint Electricity Authority.
  Created in 1923

The powers of this Authority have been delegated to and are exercised by the North Wales Power Company.

London and Home Counties Joint Electricity Authority.
  Created in 1925

This Authority is now distributing electricity in certain parts of the district. A description of the Authority is given below.

West Midlands Joint Electricity Authority.
  Created in 1925

This Authority has acquired the generating stations of the principal authorized undertakers within the district, the area of which is approximately 1,000 square miles, and has also acquired or constructed certain main transmission lines. It has constructed a new generating station (Ironbridge Station) and is distributing electricity in parts of the district. All this has been done by agreement between the principal authorized undertakers within the district. The total capital expenditure by the Authority is about £3,250,000 and the number of consumers in the distribution areas is about 2,500.

North-West Midlands Joint Electricity Authority.
  Created in 1928

This Authority has acquired certain power stations and has acquired or built some main transmission lines, the total capital expenditure being about £1,000,000. It is also carrying out a limited amount of retail distribution, the total number of consumers supplied amounting to approximately 3,000.

As indicated above there are only three of the four Joint Electricity Authorities in active operation, but in all three cases it is interesting to note that these Authorities are not only carrying out generation and wholesale transmission, but are also carrying out some retail distribution. The difficulty in forming Joint Electricity Authorities has, of course, been due to the absence of compulsory powers in the 1919 Act, but in this connection the case of the London and Home Counties Joint Electricity Authority is of special interest and is described below. So far as generation and main transmission are concerned the functions of Joint Electricity Authorities overlap very largely with those of the C.E.B., and the latter is now performing the principal duties which it was originally intended should be carried out by the Joint Electricity Authorities. The future of the Authorities lies, therefore, mainly in the development of the relatively small amount of retail distribution which they are at present carrying out.

LONDON AND HOME COUNTIES JOINT ELECTRICITY AUTHORITY

The London and Home Counties Joint Electricity Authority was created by an order made by the Electricity Commissioners in 1925 following on the passage of the two London Supply Acts of 1925. The special circumstance attending the formation of this Joint Electricity Authority was that the tenure of the London supply companies was due to expire in 1931, on which date they were, therefore, liable to compulsory purchase by the London County Council. This enabled the L.C.C. to enforce certain measures of reorganization under the two London Electricity Acts of 1925 as the price of postponing the date of compulsory purchase to 1971, and to vest this in a London and Home Counties Joint Electricity Authority to be formed on the passage of the two Acts in question.

The London and Home Counties Joint Electricity Authority consists of 36 members, and has a most unwieldy constitution. Its members are appointed as follows:

By Whom Appointed or Elected	*Number of Members Appointed or Elected*
Local authority undertakers inside the County of London (jointly)	8
Local authority undertakers outside the County of London (West Ham Corporation one member, the remaining five elected jointly by the other authorities)	6
London Power Company	1
The four East London companies	1
The following companies jointly—Kent Electric Power Company, Metropolitan Electric Supply Company, North Metropolitan Electric Power Supply Company, West Kent Electric Company	1
Other companies within the London district (jointly)	2
London County Council	6
Middlesex County Council	1
Other county councils (jointly)	2
City of London	1
Workers in the industry (jointly)	2
Railway Companies' Association	2
Local authorities in the Thames Valley distribution Area	1
Local authorities in the Mid-Surrey distribution area	2
TOTAL	36

The reorganization effected by the 1925 Acts was not very drastic. The four East London companies undertook to enter into certain working agreements with regard to co-ordination of generation and main transmission, subject to the approval of the Electricity Commissioners. They also agreed to accept a sliding scale of dividends related to the charges made by the companies for the sale of electricity. The first of these obligations did not result in any very definite action and was largely superseded by the formation of the C.E.B., which in effect amalgamated the generation, and to some extent the main transmission of the four companies. The provision in the 1926 Act with regard to the sliding scale of dividends has, however, had an appreciable effect on prices, although it does not apply to those portions of the companies' areas which lie outside the London district.

Similar undertakings were accepted by the ten West End London companies, who gave effect to the first undertaking by the formation of the London Power Company, which carries out the whole of the generation and main transmission for the ten companies in question. Although this has probably resulted in a very considerable reduction in the production costs of electricity in the west of London, the functions of the London Power Company now overlap those of the C.E.B.

So far as generation and main transmission are concerned the Joint Electricity Authority has few duties, although it has entered into special agreements with the C.E.B. on behalf of various local authorities within the London district for the operation of their non-selected generating stations and the taking of bulk supplies from the Grid. It has, however, acquired distribution areas in the southern part of the outer London district including Dorking, Leatherhead, Surbiton, Sutton, Twickenham, and Weybridge. The Authority commenced distribution in 1931 in certain of these areas, and now supplies about 100,000 consumers. The total number of units sold in 1935–6 amounted to approximately 100 million, and the total capital expenditure was over £4,000,000, much of which represented the purchase price of the undertakings acquired. These acquired undertakings were certain extra-London company undertakings whose tenures were approaching expiration and which were, therefore, liable to compulsory purchase. The stocks issued by the Joint Electricity Authority are as follows :

Date of Issue	Description	Issue Price
December 1930 ..	£1,000,000 4½ per cent 1955–75	95·5 per cent
March 1932 ..	*£1,500,000 5 per cent 1955–75	101·5 per cent
December 1934 ..	*£1,000,000 3¼ per cent 1955–75	97·5 per cent

* Compare with C.E.B. borrowings (see Table 1).

Date of Issue	Description	Issue Price
February 1932 ..	£7,000,000 5 per cent 1955–75	at 95 per cent
October 1934 ..	£6,000,000 3¼ per cent 1974–94	at 93 per cent

Although the London and Home Counties Joint Electricity Authority now carries out quite a considerable amount of retail distribution, this represents a very small proportion of the total of the London district, the area of which is approximately 1,850 square miles, whereas the area actually belonging to the Authority is only 190 square miles, mostly on the outskirts of the district.

The Joint Electricity Authority has taken over the publication of the annual statistics relating to electricity supply within the London district formerly published by the l.c.c. Those published in 1936 show that the number of units generated per head of population in the London district, excluding railway and transport supplies, was 485 during 1934–5. Including railway and transport supplies, this figure increases to 598 units per head. The latter figure is very considerably above the average for the whole country. Of the total supplies in the London district 42·7 per cent are given by local authorities, including the Joint Electricity Authority itself, and 57·3 per cent by companies. The total number of units sold in 1934–5 was over 3,300 million, of which some 46 per cent represents domestic supplies. The number of distributing authorities in the London district was 82, of whom 30 (16 local authorities and 14 companies) are within the County of London, but an amalgamation of half a dozen of the West End companies has now been carried out. Nearly half of the Joint Electricity Authorities' *Statistical Review No. 9*, published in 1936, is devoted to a comparison of the very large number of tariffs in operation within the district.

ELECTRICITY BOARD FOR NORTHERN IRELAND

The functions of the British C.E.B. are, as already pointed out, limited to the production and wholesale side of electric supply. In Northern Ireland a somewhat similar non-profit making Board has been formed under the 1931 Act of the Northern Ireland Parliament, but the functions of this Board cover both the wholesale and retail side of the industry. The Northern Ireland Electricity Board is therefore of very special interest. The Board, consisting of a chairman and three members, has much the same powers as the British Board plus power to generate electricity, to acquire existing distribution undertakings and to sell direct to individual consumers.

The area in which the Board operates covers about 3,000 square miles and a population of about 500,000. The average density of population is therefore low—only about 167 per square mile—which is not much greater than the density in average rural areas of England. Within this area a large number of existing supply undertakings have been taken over, and the Board now supplies over 26,000 consumers. Bulk supplies are at present taken from the Belfast Corporation and the Londonderry Corporation power stations, the latter being a selected station whose operation is controlled by the Board. Very rapid development is at present in progress which is being assisted by the comparatively low prices charged by the Board and by schemes of hire and hire-purchase of wiring installations and apparatus. The main tariff is a two-part tariff which for domestic consumers consists of a moderate fixed charge based on floor area plus a unit charge of $\frac{1}{2}$d. for all units above 500 per quarter, the latter being charged at $\frac{3}{4}$d. In view of the comparatively sparse population such rates can be regarded as low.

The total capital expenditure is about £1,600,000, the interest on borrowings being guaranteed by the Ministry of Finance. Gross revenue for 1935 was £171,000 and expenditure £104,000, leaving a net revenue of £67,000, which is already sufficient to pay interest on capital plus a contribution to the sinking fund. The net revenue is rising rapidly, and in 1935 the increase was over 50 per cent. Generally the results of the Board's operations seem to have been very satisfactory, particularly in view of the short time it has been in existence—only about five years, of which the early period was largely occupied in construction of lines, etc., and the acquisition of existing supply authorities.

The further progress of this interesting public concern will be watched with considerable interest.

CONCLUSIONS

The c.e.b. represents one of the most interesting of recent developments in public concerns. The older type of public body run on the lines of a Government department—of which the Post Office in its original form was perhaps an example—has become obsolete because the organization of such bodies was unsuitable for the management of important industries. Rapid development of the public concern has, however, taken place during the last ten years or so because of the increasing extent of public ownership in various spheres of industry and the consequent demand for an organization combining business efficiency and initiative with the elimination of divisible profits. This development is still continuing, and it is probable that there will be considerable variation in the constitution of future

public concerns both to meet the particular circumstances
of each application and because of experience gained from
existing bodies. The old bogey of bureaucracy and lack of
initiative has, however, already been exorcised. Certainly
there is no more red tape or bureaucracy in such a concern
as the C.E.B. than is to be found in most joint stock companies. On the other hand, capacity to plan development
over a long period not seeking immediate financial return
has been marked, and this is combined with a very real
sense of public duty and responsibility. Equally important
is the fact that the Board's organization has been able to
acquire first-rate men who have probably been attracted
quite as much by the importance of the work and the
relative security of employment, as by the salaries offered.
In consequence the technical standard of the work has been
remarkably high, and this in turn has influenced the technical standard of the whole industry. Much valuable
research or experimental work has been, and is being, done
on a large scale, and this is accelerating the progress of
electrical engineering particularly in the field of high voltage.
A few years ago critics of the Board's work, both technical
and non-technical, were numerous, but to-day the Board's
key position in the industry is generally recognized and
criticism has largely disappeared. A very important advantage which the Board has, as a public concern, is the greater
confidence inspired when negotiating their bulk supply
agreements. Such negotiations are always difficult, but the
fact that they are made with a body making no divisible
profit undoubtedly renders it easier to reach agreement.

Fears have been expressed in the past that large public
concerns might impede progress because they would tend
to uniformity and would not give sufficient scope for
variety of individual ideas and effort. No doubt there are
industries, particularly those which are in the very early
stages of development, where variety of small-scale experiment is of prime importance, but as industries get larger

and more established the need for some degree of central planning and control becomes increasingly important and, moreover, technical progress depends on large-scale and costly experiment which cannot readily be carried out by numerous smaller bodies. Undoubtedly the electricity supply industry passed beyond the early stage of development some considerable time ago, and by 1926 had reached the point where central planning and co-ordination were considerably overdue.

There might, however, remain the danger that, with the removal of the profit motive, a public concern would tend to atrophy in course of time. This danger can be, and in practice is, to a considerable extent guarded against by the expression of public opinion. The more instructed and enlightened public opinion is the more it will act as a stimulus—annoying though this stimulus may be at times to those operating a public concern. Of course, the effectiveness of public opinion in the capacity of stimulant must largely depend on the degree to which the particular public concern directly affects the general public. In the case of the British Broadcasting Corporation it is extremely effective; in the case of the C.E.B. less so. If public opinion does not form a satisfactory stimulant there might be a need for some independent supervisory body acting in lieu of public opinion. However, it is unlikely that any such special measures will be necessary provided the executives and experts within the organization of a public concern are able freely to put into effect their specialized knowledge and to make improvements. The fatal condition is if, due to lack of financial resources or other reasons, administrative and technical developments are restricted and executives and experts are denied freedom of enterprise. Then, indeed, there is a grave danger of atrophy. Such conditions have actually arisen in certain industries with very unfortunate results, but the more important instances have not been public concerns.

If in the future the present tendency to place more and more of the industries of this country under the control of public concerns continues, the correlation of the various concerns must become an increasingly important problem. This problem does already exist, and up to the present no special provision has been made for relating the activities of one public concern with another. For instance, the Post Office, the l.p.t.b. and the c.e.b. come in contact with each other in various spheres. No serious difficulty has arisen so far and collaboration on mutual problems has been satisfactory, but clearly issues may arise in the future involving important matters of principle which would require decision by some independent authority. It therefore seems that sooner or later an independent authority, superior to all public concerns, will be required, more especially if the number of public concerns continues to increase.

The future progress of all the existing public concerns, and perhaps particularly that of the c.e.b., which is operating an industry on a national scale, is bound to be watched with increasing interest by all those concerned with administration or organization. No doubt there will be many changes to make in the future as a result of experience. In the case of the c.e.b. the fact of having at last brought some measure of organization into the electric supply industry has made very evident the previous wastage of national resources arising from the haphazard legislation with which the industry had been afflicted during the whole of its earlier history. A legacy of this older legislation is the existence of various other bodies whose functions overlap with those of the Board, so resulting in considerable loss of economy. The anomalous position with regard to selected stations, the operation of which is controlled and paid for by the Board, although owned by other authorities, has already been mentioned, but the further organization of the industry, particularly in the field of retail distribution, has not been dealt with because it does not fall within the scope of this survey. Nevertheless, any improvement in the retail organization leading to increased availability of supplies, lower prices, and greater consumption would increase the economy of the Board's operations in regard to production and main transmission, and so further benefit the general public. The need for such improvement has long been recognized and has been confirmed by the recent report of the Committee on Electricity Distribution under the chairmanship of Sir Harry McGowan, whose terms of reference were:

To bring under review the organization of the distribution of electricity in Great Britain, including the control of statutory electricity companies by other companies, to advise on methods by which improvements can be effected with a view to ensuring and expediting the standardization of systems, pressures, and methods of charge, further extending facilities (including supplies in rural areas), and reducing costs, and to make recommendations.

In their Report the Committee state:

In all the circumstances and having regard to the evidence placed before us there can, in our opinion, be no question that an improvement in the present organization can and must be effected.

The Report contains an analysis of the history and present organization of the retail distribution of electricity and reveals its very unsatisfactory condition. It also makes many valuable recommendations, but for reasons which are very briefly stated it rejects a complete and permanent reorganization under public ownership, and instead recommends schemes of amalgamation both under company and local authority ownership, with provision for financial control of the companies and their ultimate transfer to public ownership. The preparation of such schemes of amalgamation are to be left to temporary District Commissioners to settle, but certain principles such as the necessity of compulsory powers to bring about the amalgamations and the importance of creating authorities supplying large areas of a mixed urban and rural character are laid down. If the scheme is to be carried out early legislation will be desirable, but the preparation and passing of the necessary Bill may, under the circumstances, be a matter of great difficulty.

6

THE LONDON PASSENGER
TRANSPORT BOARD

by

ERNEST DAVIES

THE London Passenger Transport Board is the accepted model of the Labour Party and the trade unions for the organization of socialized industry. Based more on the structure of the capitalist units it superseded than on the municipal undertakings also absorbed, the L.P.T.B. arose out of the embryo of the planned capitalist monopoly which was aiming to control London's transport. The L.P.T.B. has retained many capitalist characteristics, at the same time incorporating some of the essentials of successful public ownership. As a result, in the operation and control of London transport there is being carried on an experiment in public ownership of particular interest and importance. Its creation constituted the largest transfer from private and municipal to public ownership that has taken place at any one time in this country. Apart from the Post Office, it is the largest publicly owned undertaking having direct relationship with the consuming public, and it was the first Board to be created that was modelled on the capitalist public company with financial autonomy and with no direct responsibility to the central government.

It was largely an accident of politics that the L.P.T.B. came into being. A change of political fortune on the eve of the passage of a London County Council Bill to cede control of its tramways to the traffic combine as a step towards the co-ordination of London transport prevented the crystallizing of a private monopoly subject both to a measure of public control and to limitation of profits. It provided an opportunity for public ownership. When

Herbert Morrison, leader of the Labour Party on the London County Council and secretary of the London Labour Party, who had been in charge of London Labour's fight against this Bill, both on the Council and in Parliament itself, became Minister of Transport the Bill was abandoned. To him can be traced not only the eventual creation of the L.P.T.B., but also the particular type of public corporation which emerged. It was ironical, but not surprising, that the Board created should incorporate many of the features of the combine proposed in the Bill against which Mr. Morrison and his colleagues had been fighting, but it was unavoidable that it should be based on the capitalist units the Board was created to supersede. In principle Morrison's Board differs fundamentally from a private monopoly, but in practice those who are in charge of London's publicly owned transport are justifiably largely the same as those who would have controlled it as a private monopoly, while the original shareholders are entitled to receive a greater return on their investment than they ever received from the combine. The former was as it should be. Lord Ashfield, who was chairman of the combine and who became chairman of the Board, had been responsible for building up as efficient and competent a traffic system as was possible within the limits of the sections over which he had been able to obtain control. He had realized that co-ordination was essential to an efficient system, and he had concentrated his efforts to that end. No doubt he and his chief assistant, Mr. Frank Pick, were better acquainted than anyone with London transport, and better able to carry out its reorganization. As regards the shareholders, however, the high level of possible return was due to subsequent events outside the Minister of Transport's control, the inescapable political situation in which the Labour minority Government found itself, and the working out of the business cycle. But to be entitled to a large revenue and to obtain it are very different things, as the shareholders to date are aware.

Fundamental differences between the private monopoly proposed and the public monopoly created included the removal of the principle of operation for private profit together with that of shareholder control, and the appointment by an extraneous body of a Board ultimately, though indefinitely, responsible to the Government and Parliament. Public responsibility took the place of capitalist independence. Nevertheless, the necessity of earning profits to provide a return on the capital invested by the original shareholders remains.

When on July 1, 1933, the L.P.T.B. took over control of London's transport a determined and practical attempt was made to solve the problem of London transport which had been worrying the metropolis for seventy years. The first committee to investigate London's problem had been appointed by the House of Lords as early as 1863,[1] and this had been followed at varying intervals by inquiries by no fewer than two Royal Commissions,[2] two Select Committees,[3] various Advisory Committees,[4] and a Court of Inquiry.[5] Little had been done through Government instigation, and the unplanned competitive development of London's transport could but lead to chaotic conditions. The unco-ordinated development of trams, buses, tubes, and suburban railways led to waste and overlapping, and had added to the confusion of the traffic on the streets.

The consolidation of the underground system started with the acquisition of the Metropolitan District Railway and the London Electric Railway by the Underground Electric Railways in 1907. Five years later the London General Omnibus Company was brought into the same group and the Central London Railway a year later. The next step in

[1] Select Committee of the House of Lords on Metropolitan Railway Communication. [2] 1905, Cd. 2597, and 1923, Cmd. 1830.
[3] H.C. 278 of 1913; H.C. 147 of 1919.
[4] The chief were in 1920 and 1927.
[5] Ministry of Labour Court of Inquiry into London Passenger Transport Strike, 1924.

this attempt to bring order out of chaos was the passage of
the Common Fund Act in 1915. Between then and 1924
there developed this combine controlled by Lord Ashfield,
consisting of the tubes, the bulk of the omnibuses, and a
certain number of tramways. The operation by this combine
of a common fund had enabled the less profitable forms of
transport and the unpaying routes to be supported by the
more remunerative ones. This group controlled the greater
proportion of transport in central London apart from that
carried by the four main-line railways and the Metropolitan
Railway. Although at the time of the changeover the combine controlled approximately 60 per cent of London
passenger transport, the competitive manner in which the
tubes and underground railways had been built made co-
ordination difficult, and required capital expenditure far
greater than private enterprise could easily obtain or cheaply
raise. The problem became greater as the need for extensions
outwards arose with London's continuous geographical
growth.

In addition to the combine, other forms of transport,
carrying passengers in many cases to the suburbs, included
the municipal tramways, of which the L.C.C. operated the
largest system, as well as a number of independent omnibus
and coach owners. Up to about 1922 the London General
Omnibus Company, which was part of the combine, had a
virtual monopoly of the bus traffic, both through the
operation of its own large fleet and in its working agreements with the other companies. Thereafter economic conditions made competition with the L.G.O.C. by independent
owners profitable, and within two years a great number
of small companies were formed. They succeeded to some
extent in skimming the cream of the combine's surface
traffic. This not only made traffic conditions worse, but
reduced the profits on the combine's buses which were being
used to subsidize the tubes. Indeed, had it not been for the
combine's revenue from its surface traffic the extension and

modernization of the tubes would have been impossible and their continued operation doubtful. At the same time, the unco-ordinated traffic arrangements, the rapid development of the outer ring of London, and the prohibitive capital sums which were required to provide the necessary transport drew attention to the necessity for action.

It was not until the Minister of Labour appointed a Court of Inquiry into the London passenger transport strike in 1924 that action was finally taken. A settlement of the strike, which started on the trams but spread to the omnibuses, was only arrived at after the Labour Prime Minister had arranged with the L.C.C. and the combine to control London's traffic by restricting omnibus operation. The London Traffic Act, 1924, resulted. This conferred powers on the Minister of Transport to control the number of buses in the City and Metropolitan Police districts, and to limit the number of journeys they might make, after consultation with the London and Home Counties Traffic Advisory Committee which the Act created. Although this Act was the product of a Labour Government, it was supported by the Tory L.C.C., by the London traffic combine, and the Transport and General Workers' Union, but it was opposed by the London Labour Party. Herbert Morrison opposed the Bill mainly because it gave the L.G.O.C. a virtual monopoly by preventing an increase in independent buses, and so providing the necessary protection against competition which made the buying out of the existing independent bus proprietors worth-while. Nor was the Bill a step towards the public ownership which was the Labour Party's aim. On the contrary, the way was paved for a private monopoly without any extension of public financial control; but as it turned out it helped in the creation of the L.P.T.B. by limiting the number of bus companies running in the London district, thereby making the task of absorption easier.

The London and Home Counties Traffic Advisory Committee created by the Act held inquiries into London's travelling facilities, and in its reports stated that only in the unified management of the various transport agencies could a solution be found. The Minister of Transport accordingly in 1926 authorized this Committee to enter into discussion with the companies and municipalities concerned to advise how combined action could be obtained if found desirable. The result of this was a "scheme for the co-ordination of passenger transport facilities in the London traffic area," published as a report in 1927.[1] This provided for the creation of a common fund and for common management, but, except in the case of the smallest bus companies, left the ownership with existing proprietors. It was also suggested that the co-operation of the main line railways, as far as their suburban traffic was concerned, should be sought, and if possible power be given for the pooling of receipts received from carrying suburban passengers to London. In effect this report suggested the creation of a monopoly for London's transport under joint private ownership. These recommendations had the support of the trade unions concerned, but through the Labour Party Herbert Morrison opposed this measure. The Government did not take the initiative, but in preference to implementing this report gave facilities to two Bills, one introduced by the L.C.C. and the other by the combine,[2] for the co-ordination of passenger traffic. These are known as the Traffic Co-ordination Bills of 1928-9. Both sought authority to enter into agreements to provide for the joint working of the traffic combine and the L.C.C. tramways system through common management, the apportionment of traffic, and the establishment of a common fund. Power was also sought to extend these arrangements to other transport undertakings within the London traffic area. But for the sustained opposition to the

[1] Known as the *Blue Report*.
[2] London County Council (Co-ordination of Passenger Traffic) Bill and London Electric Railway Companies (Co-ordination of Passenger Traffic) Bill.

Bills on the part of the Labour Party on the L.C.C., and the London Labour Members of Parliament in the House of Commons, the Bills would almost certainly have become law before the fall of the Conservative Government in 1929. The Bills had reached so advanced a stage in the House of Commons that it was only by chance that on a parliamentary technicality it was necessary for them to be submitted to the new House of Commons, assembled after the General Election. When the Bills were introduced for a further third reading, the House of Commons accepted the advice of Herbert Morrison, the chief opponent of the Bills, who was now the Minister of Transport, and rejected them. He undertook to produce alternative proposals, and these were finally submitted in the London Passenger Transport Bill in 1931.

With this background, Herbert Morrison, the Minister of Transport in office, had to be consistent with Herbert Morrison, the leader of the London Labour Party in opposition. To be so, he had to solve London's transport problem by securing unification under public control of passenger transport, thereby eliminating uneconomic and unnecessary competition. The Labour Government being in the minority, there could be no question of compulsorily taking over the transport undertaking on any terms but those that the existing owners could be persuaded voluntarily to accept. Any measure which would fulfil these requirements and at the same time be assured of becoming law would be a result of compromise with the existing owners. As soon, therefore, as the Government's policy of public ownership had been announced, much exploratory work had to be done before any definite scheme could be devised. In his investigations Herbert Morrison was soon persuaded that the only solution was to be found in a public board.[1] In

[1] For the evolution of the London Passenger Transport Bill and the story of the negotiations and its parliamentary passage see Morrison's *Socialization and Transport*, 1933.

F

the autumn of 1930 he announced in Parliament his intention of introducing a Bill "to create a new statutory public body embracing the railway, omnibus, and tramway undertakings controlled by the Underground Electric Railway Company of London Limited, the Metropolitan Railway, the tramway undertakings owned by the local authorities in the London area, and other omnibus undertakings operating within the London area." From the lengthy and difficult negotiations that followed with the traffic combine, the Metropolitan Railway and municipalities operating the tramways and other bodies concerned, a scheme was eventually devised for the transfer of the existing undertakings to the L.P.T.B.

The Bill that finally emerged from the Select Committee, which examined it for thirty-five days with the assistance of counsel after its second reading in Parliament, included the details of the terms of transfer of ownership of most of the undertakings to the new Board, and provided machinery for the determination of compensation for other bodies to be taken over. The L.P.T.B. was to be operated as a commercial concern, by which was meant its income had to balance its expenditure and enable a pre-determined rate of interest to be received by stockholders of the new concern. The Board was to be treated as a commercial concern in that it would pay taxes, rates, etc., and have no special financial privileges. The ordinary shareholder ceased to be the owner and became as it were a creditor with a very limited right to enforce his claim in event of default.

Before the Bill was passed through all these stages the Labour Government fell, the Labour Minister of Transport was succeeded by a Liberal member of the National Coalition Government who in turn was superseded by another Minister of Transport, also a Liberal. The parliamentary history of the creation of the L.P.T.B. must be unique. The Bill was launched by a Labour Government, and by pure chance was carried over to a "National" Government, where it was piloted farther by a Liberal, eventually to become law through the hands of a third Minister of Transport who was a Conservative.[1] With so much handling it might well have become an unrecognizable hybrid, but apart from the removal of the responsibility for the appointment of the Board from the Minister of Transport to a body of appointing trustees, and transfer of certain powers from the Minister to the Railway Rates Tribunal, the final Act which received the Royal assent in April 1933 differed hardly at all either in principle or in practice from that originally introduced two years earlier. The fundamental differences between the Board and a capitalist merger were the manner of the Board's appointment, and the indefinite but implied responsibility to the Minister of Transport, but mainly in the vesting of the ownership of London's transport in the public instead of in bodies of shareholders.

July 1, 1933, was fixed as the appointed day on which the L.P.T.B. was to become responsible for the traffic in the London traffic area created under the Act. On the appointed day there were to be transferred to the Board the undertakings of the traffic combine, including the underground railways and tubes, the combine's tramway system, the L.G.O.C., the Green Line and other coach companies, the Metropolitan Railway, the tramways of the Hertfordshire, Middlesex, and London County Councils, of the County Boroughs of West Ham, East Ham, and Croydon, of the Boroughs of Barking, Ilford, Leyton, and Walthamstow, of the Urban District Councils of Bexley, Dartford, and Erith, as well as the trams of the City of London and the London omnibus undertaking of Tilling & British Automobile Traction, Limited. Also to be acquired were the London omnibus undertaking of Thomas Tilling, Limited, and the independent omnibus undertakings. Terms of

---

[1] Sir J. Pybus, Liberal National, succeeded Herbert Morrison as Minister of Transport in August 1931. In February 1933 he resigned, and the Hon. Oliver Stanley, a Conservative, took his place.

transfer were specified in the Act for the majority of these undertakings, but where this was not done, or where an agreement could not be reached, provision was made for the approval or settlement of terms by an arbitration tribune set up under the Act.

In effect the scheme was similar to a merger of capitalist companies, and the difficulty lay in the apportionment of interest in the amalgamated concern to the constituent units it was absorbing. The similarity to a capitalist merger was carried farther by the retention of Lord Ashfield, the chairman of the traffic combine, as the chairman of the new Board. While the Bill was passing through Parliament, it was frequently suggested both inside and outside Parliament that the heads of the combine would control the new board, but it was denied that there was any understanding on this matter. As it happened the removal of the appointment of the Board from the Minister to the independent trustees (by the National Government's amendment to the Bill) indicated that freedom of appointment still remained after the passage of the Act.

The L.P.T.B. consists of a chairman and six other members. Three members constitute a quorum. The qualifications defined by the Act were experience and capacity in transport, industrial, commercial, or financial matters or in the conduct of public affairs. Two members must have had not less than six years' experience in local government within the London Passenger Transport area. Members of Parliament were disqualified from being members of the Board. The original Bill provided for the appointment of this Board by the Minister of Transport. The National Government substituted for the Minister of Transport appointing trustees to consist of the chairman of the L.C.C., a representative of the London and Home Counties Traffic Advisory Committee, the chairman of the Committee of London Clearing Bankers, the president of the Law Society, and the president of the Institute of Chartered Accountants in

England and Wales. Now that the Board is constituted, the chairman of the Board is included. The appointing trustees are responsible for filling any vacancies that occur. In forming such a group of appointing trustees the Minister of Transport desired to remove the appointments as far as possible from politics and thus eliminate the possibility of choice being made according to a particular political colour.[1] It is difficult, however, to justify such an ill-assorted collection of trustees whose knowledge of persons capable of administering London's transport might be nil. In practice it was of not such great importance as common sense ruled that both Lord Ashfield and Mr. Frank Pick would be among the members of the Board. The chairman of the Board is appointed by the appointing trustees, whilst the vice-chairman is appointed by the Board from among its members.

The appointing trustees selected Lord Ashfield as chairman for seven years. Other members of the board appointed were Mr. Frank Pick for seven years, Mr. John Cliff and Mr. Patrick Ashley Cooper for five years, Sir John Gilbert, Sir Edward J. Holland, and Brig.-General Sir Henry P. Maybury for three years.[2] Lord Ashfield and Mr. Pick were full-time appointments, and the others part-time. The chairman's annual salary was agreed with the Treasury at £12,500, the vice-chairman's at £10,000, and that of the other part-time members at £750 each. The Board subsequently appointed Mr. Frank Pick as vice-chairman and chief executive officer, and also entrusted Mr. John Cliff with certain special duties relating to the staff. The chairman and Mr. Pick had been associated with the traffic combine, the former as chairman and the latter as managing director. Mr. Cliff was an official of the Transport and General Workers. Mr. Ashley Cooper was a director of the Bank of

---

[1] "Risk of political interference in constituting a business body" were the words of a Government White Paper on the matter. Cmd. 4133 (1932).

[2] These last two were reappointed for a further three years in 1936.

England and of several companies, while Sir John Gilbert
had been chairman of the l.c.c., and on his death was
succeeded by Mr. Charles Latham, also of the l.c.c. Sir
Edward Holland was also experienced in municipal affairs,
while Sir Henry Maybury was a former director-general of
roads at the Ministry of Transport and chairman of the
London and Home Counties Traffic Advisory Committee.
On the Board thus constituted, the concerns taken over
were represented by two members, the municipalities by
two members, the trade union movement by one, banking
interests and industry by another, while the seventh member
was experienced in transport matters.

The Act provided also for the appointment of an arbitration tribunal which played a very important part in the
transition period. To this body was remitted not only
the task of agreeing the terms of transfer of the undertakings
to be acquired after the appointed day, but also such
matters as agreeing the terms of a pooling scheme with the
suburban railways.

The London Passenger Transport Arbitration Tribunal
consisted of three commissioners appointed by the Lord
Chancellor. One had to be a lawyer, one experienced in
business, and the other in finance. Their term of office
expired when all matters referred to them under the Act
had been settled. The Act laid down detailed principles on
which terms of transfer were to be arrived at, but gave the
tribunal a large measure of independence. Its decision was
to be final, but the tribunal could state a case on a question
of law for the Court of Appeal, and had to do so if required
by the Court of Appeal. The main task of the tribunal was
settling terms of transfer of the acquired concerns where
disputes arose or of approving terms where amicably agreed
upon. For this purpose public hearings were held. The
tribunal, consisting of Mr. Joshua Scholefield, k.c., Sir
James Martin, and Sir Philip Nash, had a number of cases
to settle, including the transfer of the various independent

omnibus concerns and the Thomas Tilling undertaking. It held over a hundred public sittings.

Within the London Passenger Transport area the Board's duties consist of providing an adequate and properly co-ordinated system of passenger transport. This area comprises 1,986 square miles. The whole of the administrative county of London and the county of Middlesex is within the area, while parts of the counties of Bedford, Buckingham, Essex, Hertford, Kent, Surrey, and Sussex are included. Approximately 9½ million persons are estimated to live in this area, in which the Board must provide all the necessary travelling facilities, avoid the provision of unnecessary and wasteful competitive services, and where necessary extend and improve the passenger transport services. The Board must run its various services as one undertaking, and fix fares and charges so as to bring in sufficient income to cover all expenditure and liabilities, which includes the payment of interest on the interest-bearing stocks of the Board. The insistence on one unit enables services which are run at a loss to be paid for by the more profitable ones, a system as essential to a comprehensive transport service as it is to the Post Office.

Of the Board's area, 1,550 square miles is known as the "Special Area," and within it the Board has a monopoly, alone having the right to run road services. No other concern can carry bus or coach passengers solely between two points within the area, except with the written consent of the Board, which is meant to apply mainly to special journeys, such as sports meetings. Long-distance services to or from places outside the London Passenger Transport Area can, of course, start or end inside it. The "Special Area" excludes certain districts on the borders of the London Passenger Transport Area, where the Board can operate its vehicles but does not have a monopoly, and is subject to the rulings of the Traffic Commissioners. In its "Special Area" it is exempt from the sections of the Road Traffic Act, which limit the number of vehicles operated, but the Minister has similar powers, being authorized to regulate the number and frequency of journeys made. Before doing so, however, he has to place his proposals before the Advisory Committee, and if any representation concerning them is made, a public inquiry has to be held. In any case, the Minister's regulations have to be laid before both Houses of Parliament, who can in effect veto them by presenting an address to the King. The routes over which the Board's vehicles run have to be approved by the Metropolitan Traffic Commissioner, whose powers under the Act were extended to include those previously exercised by the Commissioner of Metropolitan Police, and thus covered the whole London transport area. In the other areas the Board has to obtain road service licences from the Traffic Commissioner.

In the 1927 Traffic Report it had been stated that no solution to London's transport problem could be complete unless the suburban services of the railways were co-ordinated with the competing services of the tubes and buses. Permissive powers to create a traffic pool were sought in the Co-ordination Bills of 1928-9. These services are an integral part of the main railway system, and cannot be entirely divorced from it. Some working arrangement between the Board and the railways was necessary to eliminate competition and overlapping. This was desired by the railways, who feared the competition of the proposed Board, and only when they were satisfied that the Bill unequivocally compelled the closest possible co-operation did they give it their support. The Act therefore provided for the setting up of a common pool for the traffic receipts (after the deduction of operating and additional allowances) of the Board and of the main line railways from traffic which both originated and terminated within the London Passenger Transport Area. To establish this pool, allocate its receipts, and co-ordinate the activities of the Board and the railways was the work of a Standing Joint Committee, consisting of eight members, four appointed by the Board and one each by the four main line railways. Its composition is Lord Ashfield, Mr. Frank Pick, Mr. Ashley Cooper, Sir Henry Maybury, and the chairman of the London, Midland & Scottish Railway, and the general managers of the London & North-Eastern, the Great Western, and the Southern Railways. The Act required the preparation within a year of the pooling scheme and, if agreed on, its submission to the arbitration tribunal for its approval. Once the Act was law the railways had no alternative to co-operation, but that was unimportant as the railways themselves desired to have a pooling scheme. If the Standing Joint Committee failed to arrive at a satisfactory pooling scheme, the arbitration tribunal was empowered to draw up such a scheme which would become operative. Actually the work involved in devising a basis for allocating the pool receipts was so great that no agreement was arrived at during the stipulated time. The Minister extended this period, however, and the scheme was ultimately approved by the arbitration tribunal in June 1935. Under it the adjusted net passenger receipts are pooled and allocated according to the standard proportions based on the income of 1932. The proportions agreed upon were 62 per cent to the Board and 38 per cent to the main railway lines. Provision was made for a revision where efficient services were not maintained, where new facilities were provided, or where changed circumstances required it.

In some ways the greatest advantage of the Act as far as the travelling public is concerned has come from co-operation of the Board and the privately owned railways. This was desired by the railways, but co-operation had been impracticable as long as London traffic was divided between a number of different companies. A co-operative examination of traffic requirements by the Standing Joint Committee now became possible, and this resulted in Government aid in the raising of capital to undertake extensive improve-

*

ments and extensions on the suburban lines and on the
Board's system. It is pointed out in the second Report of
the Board[1] that the transport undertakings themselves could
not venture upon these major additions and improvements
in the competitive conditions which existed before the Board
was created. The substitution of co-operation for competition
made it possible, but even so the amount involved was so
large that it was not expected that the return from this
investment would be sufficient to cover the rate of interest
that would have to be paid to raise the money. The Government was approached, and agreed with the Board and the
Great Western and the London & North-Eastern Railways
to guarantee the principal and interest of a loan not exceeding £40,000,000. This money was to be expended on the
electrification of certain suburban lines of the London &
North-Eastern Railway, and the provision of additional
tracks on the Great Western Railway, and the construction
of additional tubes and other works on the Board's system,
as well as the substitution of trolley-buses for trams.

Owing to the division of ownership among the Board and
the companies concerned, a new device was evolved by the
Treasury for the raising of the necessary money. A company
to act as go-between in the form of the London Electric
Transport Finance Corporation was formed. This obviated
the danger of direct Treasury interference, and saved the
various companies from the delays and difficulties of raising
the money themselves. The finance company created solely
for raising the money has four unpaid directors: Mr. W. K.
Whigham, director of both the Bank of England and the
London and North-Eastern Railway, Mr. Ashley Cooper,
director of the Bank of England and a member of the
L.P.T.B., Mr. E. Holland-Martin, director of the Bank of
England, and Mr. K. O. Peppiatt, chief cashier of the Bank
of England. It has borrowing powers up to £40,000,000,
and its *modus operandi* is to lend the money to the Board and

---

[1] L.P.T.B. Report for year ended June 30, 1935.

the companies as they need it at the same rate as the finance company borrows the money from the public.

The finance company issued in July 1935 £32,000,000 of Guaranteed Debenture Stock, 1950–5, at 97 per cent. In view of the Treasury guarantee of the principal and interest the rate of interest of 2½ per cent was substantially lower than that at which either the Board or the main line railways could have borrowed, and it was anticipated to be low enough to enable the works to become remunerative. The period of loan is limited to twenty years. The ultimate repayment of the money to the finance company can take place as far as the Board is concerned by the issuing of further London Transport stock. From the public's point of view the increased facilities will be one of the most concrete results of the Board's creation.

In other directions the Board is also strictly prevented from competing with private enterprise. Its activities are confined to the carrying of passengers within the London Passenger Transport Area; the carriage of goods by road vehicles is forbidden to it, subject to certain exceptions. Care was taken to prevent the Board from becoming a vertical trust. Where previous activities of the combine were not directly confined to the carrying of passengers, they were not acquired by the Board. This necessitated a division of the assets of the combine between the Board and the old shareholders.

The Board cannot accordingly manufacture for its own requirements either rolling stock for its railways, or buses for its surface traffic. Manufacture must be confined to experimental research, although there is an exception made in the manufacture of omnibus bodies; but the number manufactured is limited to the annual average which the L.G.O.C. manufactured at its Chiswick works during the five years preceding January 1, 1932. Competition with vehicle manufacturers is therefore ruled out. The Board's powers are less than the traffic combine's, for that body controlled an associated company, the Associated Equipment Company, which manufactured buses, spare parts, and other equipment. Its transfer with the other assets of the combine need have caused no difficulty, but under the Act it was segregated from the other assets and in the liquidation of the old underground companies its shares were distributed to the underground shareholders. To protect the equipment company provision was made that it should suffer no loss through its segregation. It was made lawful for the Board to contract with the equipment company to supply its vehicles and spare parts, and if this was not done within six months the company was entitled to claim compensation as if a contract had been repudiated. In December 1933 an agreement was entered into with the Associated Equipment Company for the supply of omnibus chassis and spare parts for a large part of its fleet for ten years.

Another sphere where competition with private enterprise is expressly forbidden is in catering for the motoring public. The Board cannot run garages, which is an accessory business which might well fit in with its surface transport activities. Exceptionally it is allowed to continue the operation of the Morden Garage which was owned by the Underground, and it can provide parking spaces for passengers using its services. Apart from this it cannot provide for the motorist. The Board is strictly prohibited by the Act from going into the taxi business, nor is any provision made for the future acquisition of that important transport service.

In another sphere, that of generating electric current for its own use, its powers are circumscribed by the Act, while where local authorities were providing current to their own tramways, the Board is compelled to continue to take current for their future operation. If this is not done, and an agreement to discontinue is not arrived at with the local authority, it can only take place with the consent of the Electricity Commissioners, or in certain cases on the directions of the Central Electricity Board. Where the taking of a supply ceases, either the plant has to be taken over by the Board or payment made sufficient to enable the authority to meet any liabilities or obligations attached to the undertaking.

In these ways the Board is carefully prevented from entering into competition with private enterprise. It is prejudiced because it is a public corporation, for the railways can manufacture their own rolling stock and bus companies their own buses. This may well prove a handicap by placing the Board at the mercy of any manufacturers' ring. On the other hand, provision is made for the creation of the Board's own insurance fund if desired. This fund can cover all risks, including workmen's compensation and third party claims, fire and accident. The building of such a fund out of revenue could result in substantial saving to the Board on the cost of insuring with commercial concerns. A similar practice has been followed by some municipalities, notably the L.C.C.

The L.P.T.B. started operations on July 1, 1933, with its functions clearly defined, its powers strictly limited, and its relations with Parliament undefined. When the terms of the transfer were represented to the shareholders of the combine by Lord Ashfield he informed them that "there could be no question of political interference."[1] This statement referred to Morrison's original Bill, and as the responsibility of the Minister was lessened by removing the appointment of the Board from the Minister to the appointing trustees, this statement can be applied more strongly to the ultimate Act than to the original Bill. Mr. Pick was even more uncertain whether the Board had any responsibility to anyone. He stated that "the Minister of Transport has almost faded from the Act, and the Board is neither respon-

[1] At a meeting of stock- and share-holders of the constituent companies of the combine, May 2, 1931.

sible to the Minister of Transport nor to the Railway Rates
Tribunal. It may be responsible to Parliament, but Parlia-
ment must undo its work to re-establish its sovereignty. . . .
In the escape from capitalist control we have almost fallen
into a dictatorship."[1] In the Bill originally proposed by
Mr. Morrison, the Minister was to appoint the Board and
on him some responsibility would have rested. The National
Government changed this, and if in the Act the Minister of
Transport survives as the link between the Board and
Parliament, he is a very weak link indeed. True, to him and
to Parliament the Board has to go when it desires to borrow
by issuing further stock in excess of that provided for in the
Act, but any legislation that results is not sponsored by the
Minister. For its annual parliamentary Bills the Board has
to find its own backers. Such Bills are not Government Bills
and differ in no way from similar Bills introduced by the
privately owned railway companies. The usual procedure
of private Bill legislation is followed. The Minister of Transport has to approve the manner in which the accounts are
issued, and has to be consulted concerning the appointment
by the Board of its auditors. The Board is subject to no
greater ministerial or parliamentary control than any other
public utility. In theory questions can be asked in Parliament; in practice the questioner is referred to the Board,
and members representing constituencies in the Board's
area are now more inclined to approach the Board direct.
Parliamentary control has been reduced in the case of the
L.P.T.B. to the absolute minimum. The activities of the
Board cannot be a drag on parliamentary time, nor has
Parliament the right to interfere with the detailed operation
of the Board.[2] The present independence of the Board
cannot be overstressed. The Act provided no machinery for

[1] In a lecture at the London School of Economics, February 26, 1934.
[2] It was originally thought the Board could be discussed on appropriate
occasions in Parliament, such as when the supply vote for Minister of Transport
was before the House. This has not been done, and if raised would be a matter
for the Speaker to decide.

control of policy, and with a chairman jealous of the Board's separate identity nothing in the way of Government interference has been read into the Act that was not there.

As a substitute for direct parliamentary control other means had to be provided to prevent the Board's power being abused. The public has to be protected from excessive charges, the staff from exploitation, and the authorities with whom the Board may come into contact from unfair treatment. In the case of fares the Railway Rates Tribunal is made the arbiter. The Board assumed as initial charges those previously ruling, and remained bound by the various Acts which governed such fares. These Acts fixed maximum fares for the Tubes, Underground and Metropolitan Railways. The Board can reduce these charges withoutreference to the Tribunal, but before it can raise them application has to be made to the Railway Rates Tribunal and their permission obtained. Similarly the trams were governed by separate Acts, and this accounts for differences between fares and conditions on the trams and buses, such as the provision of workmen's fares on the former and not on the latter. As the buses and coaches operating solely within the Board's Special Area are subject to no special Act the Board can in their case determine its own charges. Outside the Special Area the Board is subject to the Road Traffic Act, 1930. The only way in which outside bodies can bring about changes in fares is through the local authorities, who can apply to the Railway Rates Tribunal, as can the Board itself where it has not the power to make changes. To enable this Tribunal also to deal with the Board, the Act provided that its membership should be increased by two, both of whom were to be appointed by the Minister of Transport. One had to be experienced in local government, and the London and Home Counties Traffic Advisory Committee had to be consulted, while the other had to be experienced in finance and appointed directly by the Minister. The Rates Tribunal has to report to Parliament annually on its activities in connection with the Board. The Board is not autonomous in regard to all the charges it makes, but it is expressly provided by the Act that the Rates Tribunal must always have regard to the necessity of the Board to pay its fixed charges and to meet all its obligations. This in effect ties the hands of the Tribunal as long as no surplus over the standard rate on the "C" Stock is earned. The Railway Rates Tribunal is also the arbiter of the fares charged by the amalgamated main line railways.

In connection with the provision of services, in the case of the amalgamated main line railways the local authorities can apply to the Railway Rates Tribunal when dissatisfied with the facilities provided. This body can compel the railways to provide certain services if it thinks fit, but must always pay regard to the financial position of the railways and cannot make orders which would require the raising of fresh capital. In the case of the Board, local authorities can appeal to the Minister when dissatisfied, but he must refer it to the London and Home Counties Traffic Advisory Committee. This committee represents, as it were, the consumer interest, and was reconstituted under the Act. It now consists of forty representatives, of whom twenty-three are appointed by the various municipalities in whose areas the Board operates, others by varying interests concerned, such as the Home Secretary, the Minister of Transport, and the police. The Board itself also has two representatives, as have the amalgamated railway companies, while the Minister of Labour has to appoint five to represent the interests of labour; others concerned in sections of London transport not controlled by the Board are also represented. The powers of this Advisory Committee under the Act are considerably increased and outside Parliament it provides a channel for public contact with the Board. It has no power to compel any action on the part of the Board, but it has a duty to make representations to the Board concerning services or facilities which it thinks ought to be considered. In other words, if it thinks the Board is failing in providing necessary services, it can make its protest and as it has the power to bring to the Minister's notice any matters relating to traffic, where the Board does not satisfy it, it can go to the Minister. Joint meetings of the Board and the Advisory Committee have to take place at least three times a year, unless it is agreed that they are not necessary. Under the London Traffic Act, 1924, it can hold public inquiries. The powers relating to these were extended under the 1933 Act to include the taking of evidence under oath.

The consumer interest is provided for only in these two ways—through the local authorities and the London and Home Counties Advisory Committee. This voice in control is inadequate. The local authorities can request improved facilities, and an investigation has to be undertaken. The Advisory Committee can undertake any inquiry on transport matters, and would undoubtedly do so when it was stimulated to act by the public. This is the limited extent to which consumer control can function, and as long as the consumer remains quiescent it is difficult to conceive any useful purpose in the creation of consumer bodies with a more direct voice in the Board's operation except on his own initiative. The Board's answer to any consumer demands can always be that the Act requires the operation of the Board so that all charges are met up to the standard rate on the "C" Stock, and in consequence they cannot be afforded. But there is much that can be done and many facilities provided without a material effect on earnings being realized, while reduced fares at times may well increase travel. Further, sufficient public protest could no doubt be effective in preventing the payment of the additional interest on the "C" stock and eventually in compelling Parliament to amend the Act in order to allow a reduction in the standard rate. But at present the standard rate is sacrosanct. In this direction municipal ownership has an

advantage over the public corporation. A municipal undertaking, serving as it does its own community, is more
directly under the control of the consumer who through
democratic representation can exercise control far more
directly. Modern economic units, however, make municipal
ownership of transport undertakings more difficult, and
in London, with its multiplicity of local authorities, it was
impossible. Only the extension of the L.C.C.'s boundaries to
the whole London Transport Area would have made this
practicable.

The London and Home Counties Advisory Committee
has far too many functions for an unpaid body to carry out
efficiently. Its main concern has been with traffic control
and road construction, which are largely outside the scope
of the Board. It concerns itself with questions of safety,
the layout of the roads, and road traffic improvements,
control signs, and similar matters. One of the appointing
trustees is a representative of the Advisory Committee, and
two of its members are appointed by the Board, namely
Mr. Pick and Sir Henry Maybury. One of its sub-committees is concerned with passenger transport facilities, and
its duties include the examination of complaints from local
authorities and other bodies regarding facilities, proposals
for the development of passenger transport facilities, proposals affecting conditions under which passengers are
carried, and proposals for restricting the number of vehicles
on certain streets.[1] No doubt, if the matters arising from
these duties became burdensome, some way of coping with
the increased work would be found, but for the present
it is clear that the Advisory Committee does not concern
itself overmuch with the Board's affairs.

In its first report[2] issued since its reconstitution after the
creation of the Board, the only matters mentioned which
arose directly from this duty were in regard to special

[1] Ninth Annual Report of London and Home Counties Traffic Advisory
Committee.   [2] Report for the year 1933–4.

facilities for old age pensioners and blind persons, and a request for the renaming of Enfield West station. The request of West Ham for the old persons was turned down after consultation with the Board; facilities for blind persons were partially granted; while those who wished Enfield West named Oakwood had the satisfaction of having the name added to the signboards but not substituted. Little use of this machinery for consumer complaint was therefore made in the early days of the Board. In some directions, however, where the community has been dissatisfied with the travelling facilities provided, steps have been taken to make representations to the Board and other authorities concerned. In the Gravesend area, for instance, protests for certain services were made and through various mediums, including the local Press, a permanent committee was set up to pursue the matter. Action was also taken in the Romford area. The Board, desirous of keeping contact with the public, appointed a public relations officer and set up a public relations department. This department has succeeded in co-operating amicably with committees where they have been created, and is itself desirous of developing the public interest in this way in the operations of the Board. All public criticism is conscientiously considered.

On the matter of publicity of accounts ample provision is made in the Act, which declares: "The Board shall furnish to the Minister such financial and statistical returns as may be agreed between the Minister and the Board or, in default of agreement, as may be determined by the Rates Tribunal." Annual accounts must be kept, and an annual audited statement must be sent to the Minister and placed on sale at a reasonable price. The Minister of Transport can prescribe the manner in which the accounts are compiled, and has to be consulted concerning the auditor's appointment. In compliance with the Act detailed accounts of the Board are issued at 1s. a copy. These are a model of clarity and detail, being far more informative than those generally issued by public companies. The accounts are published for the general public as much as for the stockholder's information. The stockholders do not receive copies by right as do stockholders in public companies.

The London Passenger Transport Bill being introduced by a Labour Government, particular interest attached at the time to the question of workers' control and relations with employers. In the original transfer Herbert Morrison made no provision for workers' representation, maintaining that it was far better for the Board to be appointed on merit than as a body representing various interests. His attitude became the bone of contention at annual conferences of the Trades Union Congress and the Labour Party, but apart from minor alterations in the wording as to the qualifications for membership of the Board, the Act was no different from that of Morrison's original Bill. Labour became represented on the Board by the appointment of Mr. John Cliff as a part-time member, and to him was allocated the responsibility of dealing with labour matters. With so small a Board as that provided for in the case of London Transport, it would have been difficult, if not impossible, for all interests to be represented, and would have meant a departure from the main principle of the public corporation as conceived by the framers of the Act. It is essential for an autonomous body to be controlled by the most experienced and most highly capable persons available. To limit the choice by attaching qualifications other than ability not only makes this more difficult, but would tend to establish a Board lacking in unity and divided between opposing interests. The members of the Board can more nearly approximate to the traditions of the Civil Service in representing the public as a whole than they can in representing the interests of a class.[1] Labour's policy is

[1] On the other hand, without either workers' or shareholder control and with such indefinite Ministerial responsibility the Board could become something of an autocracy.

now to include by statute workers' representatives on every board, but whether this can be done on the model of the L.P.T.B. without materially altering the whole set-up is questionable. It is difficult to conceive this compromise between the capitalist model of the Board and a democratic institution being workable. Either there must be an organization controlled by a fully qualified and experienced board or one provided with the proper appointment of workers as controllers with the ample checks and balances of democratic control. Herbert Morrison chose the former, and within the capitalist society it works well. Within the framework of a socialist commonwealth it would require drastic alteration. But while in the initial stage it may be possible to obtain the services of experienced capitalists, the training of others to replace them on death or retirement is highly important. The success or failure of an industrial concern or transport undertaking of the size required for economic operation in this mechanical age depends to a very great extent on the abilities of the directive heads. Neither amateur politicians nor trade union officials are likely to possess the necessary training for the job. If industry is to be efficiently run and services adequately and economically provided only those possessing the specialized training and proved abilities must be in charge. It is necessary for a public concern to provide the most capable with an opportunity of attaining the highest positions. Systematized recruitment combined with careful grading and selective promotion must ultimately be part of the internal organization of every public concern. In this respect London Transport is deficient. The platform and outside staffs have very little scope for promotion, while lack of provision for recruitment in the Act leaves the way open for the Board to recruit for superior jobs any particular class it favours. London Transport has not yet satisfactorily worked out this problem. No greater part is accordingly played by the staff in the administration of London Transport than in any other concern. As in capitalist undertakings, it is limited to a system of monetary rewards for suggestions made.

Similarly, the manner in which the relations between staff and management are handled is derived from the practices in force when the Board came into existence. Both the railwaymen and the tramwaymen are subject to national agreements. The Underground and Metropolitan Railway staffs were subject to the Railway Wages Board, and the Act accordingly sets up similar machinery. Where disputes arise and the trade unions and the Board are unable to settle them, they have to be referred to a negotiating committee. If this committee fails to settle the matter, a wages board has to take up the dispute. To the negotiating committee the Board appoints six of its representatives and the employees six, two of whom have to be appointed by each of the Society of Locomotive Engineers, the National Union of Railwaymen, and the Railway Clerks' Association. To the wages board the Minister of Labour appoints an independent chairman, the Board six representatives, and the employees six, of whom two are appointed by each of the trade unions, while the General Council of the Trades Union Congress, the Co-operative Union, the Association of the British Chambers of Commerce, and the National Confederation of Employers' Organizations appoint one each. In this way on the negotiating committee which first discusses the dispute there are equal representatives of the Board and the employees, while the same applies to the wages board, with the addition of two outside labour representatives and two outside employers' representatives, but they are presided over by an independent chairman. The constitution of both the committee and the wages board can be changed by agreement through a committee appointed by both sides. In the case of the busmen, represented by the Transport and General Workers' Union, a system of direct negotiation had always been preferred. When the Act was being framed and throughout its passage, the union opposed any form of negotiating machinery, and accordingly none was created. In practice, however, there is a busman's council at every garage, from which delegates are sent to a busmen's delegate conference which meets regularly. This provides the necessary machinery for dealing with all matters of wages and conditions. Frequent contact between the union's representatives and the management is necessary owing to the complicated nature of traffic schedules and conditions. These are generally local matters settled by the local organizations, but this leads to sporadic strikes which mainly arise over changes in schedules including running times. Here attempts by the strikers to dictate policy arise. Nevertheless, the highly organized London busmen maintain an efficient and effective organization, with which as a rule the Board maintains the best relations.

Agreements have been arrived at between the unions responsible, the Transport and General Workers' Union, the Railway Clerks' Association, the Society of Locomotive Engineers, and the National Union of Railwaymen. Provision was made in the Act for the setting up of Councils of Officers of the Board, and representatives of the employees, which has been done. Within two years of the creation of the Board negotiating machinery for the whole of the staff had been set up and the Board was able to state in its annual report:

With a view to securing adequate consideration and a fair settlement of all matters arising out of the application and interpretation of agreements governing rates of pay and conditions of employment, practically the whole of the Board's staff are now covered by negotiating machinery through Trade Union representation or their elected staff councils or committees.[1]

Concerning the transfer of staff, the Act provides that no employees transferred shall be in any worse position as regards conditions of service than before the transfer took

[1] Second Annual Report of the L.P.T.B.

place. This includes such matters as remuneration, superannuation, etc. Where disputes arise the matter has to be
referred to the standing arbitrator appointed by the Lord
Chancellor in accordance with the Act. Where the creation
of the Board made officers or servants redundant and
dismissal takes place or remuneration is reduced, that is
to say where pecuniary loss results as a consequence of the
Act, compensation has to be given. In the same way, where
officers and servants were not transferred to the Board
compensation has to be paid. Protection is also provided in
the case of superannuation for officers and servants. To
certain members of the staff sums were paid in compensation after the Board's creation, but although the transfer
involved 75,000 officers and men, only a very few were
displaced. Where compensation was given in other cases
it was generally on the technical ground of change of
status. In effect the main displacements were of directors,
who were compensated liberally by the companies and not
by the Board.

Lord Ashfield and Mr. Frank Pick are beyond dispute
the controllers of the L.P.T.B. The rest of the Board is part-
time, and apart from the fact that Mr. Cliff has certain
staff matters assigned to him, no member of the Board is
responsible for any particular aspect of the concern's
operations. From time to time, however, they have special
duties deputed to them. The Board meets twice monthly,
and when matters come before it they have already been
sifted, and as a rule the attitude of the chairman and vice-
chairman thereon will govern the decision. Any member of
the Board can, of course, raise any matter at its meetings,
but where the experience of the chairman and vice-chairman
is of so much greater length, and where their judgment and
ability have already been proved, psychologically the other
members must find it difficult not to defer to them. By the
time the matters reach the Board they have already gone
through the hands of the various departments concerned,

been considered by a committee of officers meeting under the guidance of the vice-chairman, and probably have been further reviewed by a meeting of a special chairman's committee. This committee consists of the Board's chairman and vice-chairman and the senior officers who attend the vice-chairman's committees. It meets about once a fortnight. It is on these lines that the Board has been organized internally. Each function is organized into a committee of officers which meets the vice-chairman who reviews with them the activities of the particular department. Any officers concerned in the matter under discussion are present. If when the matter under discussion leaves the committee it requires the confirmation or decision of the Board, it goes next to a meeting to be presided over by the chairman, and only when it has emerged from this meeting will the Board consider it.[1]

The departmentalization of the Board does not correspond to the committee system of local authorities nor to the civil service administration. It is far less formal than the former and much less bureaucratic than the latter. London Transport, having no precedent, has to evolve its own organization, and not being bound by tradition or fearful of too great a measure of public accountability, need not become entangled in red tape. It is tending, however, to develop a series of precedents and organizational regulations which may add to the complexity of the organization as it grows.

The L.P.T.B., although its operation is subject to a series of controls, has a large measure of financial autonomy. The principle underlying its finance is that income must balance expenditure and leave sufficient surplus to meet the fixed charges and other obligations on the capital outstanding. The joint stock company having been taken as the model, the public corporation has to operate commercially and

[1] Second Annual Report of the Board.

remain a financial entity capable of standing on its own feet. There being no direct Government control, it remains entirely independent of Treasury control, and as long as the provisions of the Act are adhered to no interference can be exercised. The Act requires the establishment of a Transport Fund from which all payments have to be made.

In the case of the L.P.T.B., its commercial operation is reasonably simple. It mainly operates on a cash basis; after an unprofitable development period the operation of much of London's transport system had proved profitable in the years immediately preceding the introduction of the Bill proposing the creation of the L.P.T.B., and in view of the growth of population of Greater London and the Home Counties and the increase in travel, appeared to be capable of remaining profitable when the Board was created. The tendency of London's population to migrate from the centre outwards and the tremendous growth in private ownership of motor cars was not foreseen.[1] To meet interest payments on stocks, charges to the consumer can be adjusted in the way already described, which makes the payment of interest a first charge, taking precedence over other considerations.

In this connection it must be borne in mind that the raising of charges does not necessarily lead to an increase of revenue. The volume of passenger transport is very sensitive to changes in facilities and fares as well as to weather conditions. A rise in fares might easily so decrease the traffic that the total revenue might decline. London Transport's profitable operation depends on there being a reasonable volume of extra travelling above the daily necessary travel to and from work; any changes in fares or facilities which substantially reduce that volume might change a surplus into a deficit. Put in another way, the earnings of fixed charges and the interest on the "C" stock is dependent on a small margin of traffic, which might disappear with unsound raising of fares. For this reason, although in the

[1] See Third Report of the Board.

fixing of fares, etc., the Rates Tribunal has to have regard
to the meeting of all the Board's obligations, including
the payment of the standard rate on the "C" stock, the
earning of that rate cannot simply be determined by their
ordering an automatic raising of fare charges. Any change
in business conditions, or any substantial rise in costs, might
easily prevent the standard rate being earned and the
arbitrary raising of fares would be no guarantee that
earnings would improve.

The amount of London Transport stock which can be
issued was limited under the 1933 Act to the amount
necessary to replace the stock taken over, and to the discharging of any liabilities imposed by the Act. Any further
borrowing was limited to £10,000,000 plus certain powers
taken over from the acquired concerns. In excess of this,
permission to borrow must be obtained from the Minister
and through Parliament, as has already been done.

To enable the existing undertakings to be transferred or
acquired the capital of the Board was divided into five
classes of stock—5 per cent and 4½ per cent "A" Stock,
redeemable at par at earliest December 31, 1985, and at
latest June 30, 2023. Four and a half per cent "T.F.A."
Stock, 1942–72, Local Authorities Stock, 1975–2023, 5 per
cent "B" Stock, 1965–2023, and "C" Stock. The interest
on all but the "C" Stock is fixed, and all the stocks are
redeemable on three months' notice at earliest on the first
date and at latest on the latter, at par. In the case of the
"C" Stock issued, redemption is on six months' notice on
or after June 30, 1956. There is no final redemption date.
The standard dividend on the "C" Stock was for the first
two years 5 per cent and thereafter 5½ per cent. It also has
the right to participate after 1935 equally in surplus profits
with the Reserve Fund up to an additional ½ per cent,
making the maximum dividend 6 per cent. The "T.F.A."
Stock carries the guarantee of the Government and was
given solely in exchange for stocks already guaranteed under

the Trade Facilities Act. In this case the position of the owners remained unchanged. Local Authorities Stock was given to certain local authorities whose tramway undertakings were taken over. In the main the basis was the substitution of sufficient "L.A." Stock to meet the service of loans created by the authorities on account of the undertakings.

The "A" Stock is divided into 5 per cent and $4\frac{1}{2}$ per cent Stock, the former being given mainly in exchange for debentures which paid 6 per cent or 5 per cent per annum, on the basis of £100 of "A" Stock for each £100 of existing 5 per cent stock and £120 for each £100 6 per cent Stock. The $4\frac{1}{2}$ per cent was given mainly in exchange for debentures on which interest of less than 5 per cent was paid. Existing $4\frac{1}{2}$ per cent Stock received the same amount of "A" Stock, 4 per cent Stock £88 17s. 9d. per £100, $3\frac{1}{2}$ per cent Stock £77 15s. 0d. for each £100, and 3 per cent Stock £66 13s. 4d. for each £100. The basis of exchange was to give sufficient new stock to assure the continuance of the same income. In the case of the tramways only was this principle departed from, and where the interest was not secure "B" and "C" Stocks were substituted. The "A," "T.F.A.," "L.A.," and "B" Stocks are all full trustee securities ranking in this order both as regards capital and charge on revenue. The "C" Stock ranks last, but corresponds to an equity stock inasmuch as interest can vary within the standard rate and to the extent of an additional $\frac{1}{2}$ per cent according to earnings. It resembles a debenture inasmuch as its interest ranks before the sinking funds applicable to the other stocks, and because holders have the right to ask for the appointment of a receiver if interest at the standard rate is not paid in each of any three consecutive years after June 30, 1935. The importance of this is not so much in the likelihood of an appointment of a receiver, but because it concedes the principle that all holders of Transport Stock have the right to a certain rate of interest or dividend, and thereby have not only prior claim on the earned profits, but are entitled to insist that charges be so adjusted as to allow sufficient profits to be earned to meet their claim. As mentioned earlier, however, changes in fares will not necessarily increase takings. There can be no compulsion on the public to travel. Those who held bonds, debentures, preference shares, or ordinary shares in any of the constituent companies of the Underground or the Metropolitan Railway received stocks in the L.P.T.B. bearing a fixed rate of interest, or entitled to a standard rate at least equal to their 1930 income. The London Transport Stocks (with the exception of the Local Authorities Stock) became negotiable on the London Stock Exchange, the Bank of England acting as the registrar for it. The "L.A." Stock cannot be dealt in without the permission of the Board.

The success of the public corporation from the community's point of view turns on the extent of the capital burden it inherits from the companies it supplants. If from the outset the corporation is overcapitalized and has difficulty in meeting the fixed or other interest charges on its capital, it is handicapped from the beginning. If, on the other hand, capital charges are low it will be able to make concessions the more easily both to the consumer and to the worker in the industry. The danger is that the terms on which the corporation's stock is substituted for the companies' capital may be such that the financial interest of the original shareholder is perpetuated on too generous a scale. If this is the case, it is conceivable that in order to pay the stockholder's interest a capitalist value of efficiency has to be put above all else. Consumers' and workers' interests may easily be sacrificed to efficiency. This may even influence the selection of the Board, the best capitalists being employed at what may appear to be extravagant salaries.

The amount of compensation is, therefore, of the greatest importance in the formation of the public corporation. The difficulty lies in deciding on what basis the concerns taken

over are to be valued, and what is a fair income return to
grant. In the case of the L.P.T.B. the formula of "net maintainable reasonable revenue" was proposed. It became
interpreted on the basis of the average earnings of the years
1928, 1929, and 1930, and the outcome was that the taking
over of the combine's undertakings and the Metropolitan
Railway resulted in the necessity of providing an income
within £200,000 of that received by the stockholders of that
group in 1930. That year, however, proved to have been a
more prosperous year for London Transport than those
which immediately followed, and had 1932—the year preceding the appointment of the Board—been taken the basis
would have been less favourable to the shareholders and
more favourable to the Board. The income of the shareholders between 1930 and 1932 fell by practically £600,000,
which means that the increased income ultimately receivable
by the stockholders of the Board will be greater by more
than £700,000, if and when earned, than was the income
received from the combine by its shareholders in 1932. The
following table gives these details, the standard rate of
5½ per cent, which, of course, has not yet been paid, being
taken on the "C" Stock.

Class of Holding in Acquired Concerns of Combine	1930 £	1932 £	Income Payable on Transport Stocks Received £	Increase Over 1930		Over 1932	
				£	%	£	%
Debentures	2,686,725	2,686,725	2,686,712				
Preference & Ordinary	1,936,613	1,356,169	2,129,621	193,008	9·9	773,452	57·0
Total	4,623,338	4,042,894	4,816,333	193,008	4·1	773,452	19·1

The improved position of the stockholders is even better
than that indicated. Before the Board came into being the
average net return from operations on the total capital of
the underground and tube railways was 3¼ per cent, on the
whole tramway system about 4 per cent, while 25 per cent

of the bus miles did not earn sufficient revenue to meet in full the costs of their provision and the sum required to meet the depreciation of their equipment.[1] This latter is still the case because with the population of the area served, increasing and new residential areas being developed, a large amount of unprofitable development has always to be undertaken. The income which can be received if earned from the stocks substituted exceeds $4\frac{3}{4}$ per cent on the nominal capital of the combine and Metropolitan undertakings acquired, and provides for capital repayment to begin after ten years. Lord Ashfield made a good deal for his stockholders, and this sorry tale he told after the Act was passed. On the other hand, gain from further expansion is definitely limited, as at meetings of the stockholders of the combine held May 2, 1931, Lord Ashfield pointed out:

In fact I have assured you not once but several times at the annual general meetings that I thought your position was a stable one and that you still had prospects of advancement, but I could not foretell how far you would be able to advance or how quickly. Now under the terms which I have put before you, except for the gap of two years immediately following upon the transfer, you should have an assured position at least as good as that which you have now, and your future prospects, while they are definitely limited, represent something more than you are now obtaining by way of return.

Turning to the tramway companies, I need hardly argue the position, for at the present time, as far as the tramway undertakings proper are concerned, you are without any return upon your investments except in so far as those investments are debenture stocks. Under the terms of the memorandum you will immediately begin to receive some small rate of interest from the stocks of the Board.

It would ill become me to depreciate your prospects, but when

[1] In London School of Economics speech, March 5, 1934, quoted in *Financial Times*, March 6, 1934, Lord Ashfield gave these figures. More precise calculations are as follows: the Common Fund Railways, after operation of Common Fund, and with the Metropolitan Railway, earned in 1930 $4\frac{1}{4}$ per cent, in 1931 4 per cent, and in 1932 $3\frac{5}{8}$ per cent. The 4 per cent for the tramways appears incorrect. The actual earnings of the London and Suburban Traction Company for 1930, 1931, and 1932 were only 2 per cent.

I compare the basis upon which they must now depend with the basis offered by the Board I feel bound to point out to you that the Board is to have a monopoly of provision of passenger transport services within the London traffic area; is to be placed in a position to control to a large extent the terms and conditions under which its operations are to be conducted; is to secure its income from a much wider basis, in that all local passenger transport undertakings within the area are to be brought under one ownership; and is expressly directed in the Bill so to conduct its undertaking and to fix its fares and charges as to secure that its revenues shall be sufficient to defray all the obligations falling upon it under the provisions of the Bill, amended to cover the terms of the memorandum which you have before you. I cannot, therefore, but think that your prospects are improved by the proposals of the Bill and that if, in the future, you may not obtain quite such a large return as you had a chance of obtaining under the present management, yet the increased return which we anticipate you are to receive will be more surely secured and will be more certain to continue.

In addition, since the maintenance of the income was made in the Act a main consideration, shareholders of the acquired concerns received in effect a bonus on conversion. No allowance had been made for the fact that a public corporation enjoying a statutory monopoly and having the right to fix its charges to meet its obligations would enjoy better credit than that of privately owned companies, subject to the vagaries of competition and with its potentialities dependent to some extent on the statutory curbing of competition. Had this been taken into account, somewhat less compensation might have been given and the capital burden imposed on the Board from the outset could have been less. Another advantage to shareholders was the failure to provide for optional redemption of the stock on the part of the Board should interest rates move favourably to it. The redemption periods are long, and no action can be taken by the Board. A heavy burden over an extensive period irrespective of the rates of money is thereby imposed. The difficulty here was the fact that certain debentures of the concerns to be acquired were irredeemable and others long dated. Interest rates had already started to fall when acquisition took place, and they fell steadily for two years more. The result was that what might have appeared reasonable interest when negotiations started became over-generous after the Board had been in operation for a short while. The result was naturally an appreciation in the value of the stocks. The combination of high income and long life, plus the improved credit of the public corporation, has led to a rise in the value of the stocks of the Board far greater than the general market rise of similar securities. A comparison made of the value of the marketable capital prior to the announcement of the terms of acquisition in 1931 and its value in 1934 shows a very large appreciation. This, of course, makes no actual difference to the Board itself, but is only an indication of how terms less favour-able to the shareholders and more favourable to the Board might have been devised, and how this determining of the terms of compensation must always refer to a great many factors other than the past income interpreted as "net reasonable maintainable revenue." The following tables give this comparison in the case of the stocks of the Under-ground combine and the Metropolitan Railways:

COMPARISON OF CAPITAL VALUES

	Debentures £	Preference £	Ordinary £	Total £
Nominal capital original companies	61,421,994	17,366,900	23,619,973	102,408,867
Value April 24, 1931 (before acquisition)	57,269,316	11,897,999	19,242,820	88,410,135
Transport Stock received (nominal)	57,134,642	13,773,145	22,143,956*	93,051,743
Value April 24, 1934	68,134,699	16,119,797	21,282,236	105,536,732
Increase in value April 24, 1931–4	10,865,383	4,221,798	2,039,416†	17,126,597
Value December 31, 1934	71,385,130	17,115,690	26,664,318	115,165,138
Increase in value April 24, 1931, to December 31, 1934	14,115,814	5,217,691	7,421,498†	26,755,003

* Shares in North Metropolitan and A.E.C. and cash distributed to share-holders not included.

† Including value of distributed assets received by shareholders, but excluding cash distributions.

The percentage increase in values over April 24, 1931, is as follows:

	At April 24, 1934 Per cent	At December 31, 1934 Per cent
Debentures	18·9	24·65
Preference	35·4	43·85
Ordinary	10·6	38·57
Total	19·4	30·26

On capital value there was a total net gain to stock-holders in the Underground group and Metropolitan Railway between April 1931 and 1934 of £17,126,597, which equals 19·4 per cent on the April 1931 value of the stocks analysed, and between April 1931 and December 1934 of £26,755,003 or 30·3 per cent. During that period there was a general rise in the value of Stock Exchange securities, but that is to some extent irrelevant as different terms of exchange particularly as regards redemption dates might have prevented transport stocks participating in the general rise. The high interest bearing "A" and "B" Stocks would not, for example, have stood at these dates 20 to 30 points over par if they could have been redeemed. Were they redeemable, a lower interest-bearing stock, say 3 per cent to $3\frac{1}{2}$ per cent, could have been offered stockholders and considerable saving to the Board effected.

But even if this argument is unacceptable, the over-generous nature of the compensation is evident from a comparison of the gain to stockholders and the general rise in security values taken on the basis of the *Bankers' Magazine* index of prices of 365 securities divided into 87 fixed-interest stocks and 278 variable-dividend securities. With December 1921 as 100, the April 1931 index was 111·9, the April 1934 figure 123·8, a rise of 10·63 per cent, while the December 1934 figure was 126·5, a rise of 13·05 per cent over April 1931. These compare with rises of 19·4 per cent on the value of the stocks of the acquired concerns analysed above by April 1934, and of no less than 30·26 per cent by December 1934. If the rises in the fixed interest and variable

dividend stocks are taken separately, the rise in the *Bankers'*
Magazine index is from 111·3 in April 1931 to 126·9 for
April 1934 and 132·7 for December 1934, or 14·01 per
cent and 19·23 per cent for the two different months
respectively in the case of fixed-interest, and from 113·3
in April 1931 to 117·3 for April 1934 and 113·5 for December 1934, or 3·53 per cent and 0·18 of 1 per cent for the
two months respectively in the variable-dividend securities
index.

The reason for taking the two dates of April 1934 and
December 1934 is that the former was three years after the
announcement of the scheme but was before any substantial
improvement in the takings of the transport system had been
realized. In other words, the rise that took place during
those three years can be considered as due to a normal
market rise up to the point where it reaches the rise in the
general index of market prices. Thereafter it is due to
appreciation by investors of the more favourable status of
stocks of a public board and of their greater merits as investments when compared with stocks of public companies. From April to December 1934 the rise was due
more to the rapid recovery in the traffics of the Board, as
shown in the weekly published figures and over-optimistic
forecasts by the Stock Exchange as to the future earnings of
the system and to the rate of dividend which the "C" Stock
would receive. In other words, stocks having been previously valued on depression results jumped as soon as recovery
set in, the fruits of the returned prosperity being applicable
to the stockholders. Had acquisition taken place on the
basis of depression earnings and not on the assumption that
prosperity earnings would continue, stockholders would
benefit less from recovery, and the public—and perhaps
the worker—more. In other words, until the level of the
peak earnings of 1930 is reached and surpassed, any real
benefits from returning prosperity will go to the original
owners of the London passenger transport system and no

concessions that cost money can be made to the consumer
or to the worker. To the extent that economies through
monopoly operation are effected, the stockholder gains until
the 1930 net earnings have been realized.

The following table shows the rises referred to:

PERCENTAGE RISE APRIL 1931 TO APRIL 1934 AND
TO DECEMBER 1934

	"Bankers' Magazine" Index		Acquired Concerns	
	April 1934	December 1934	April 1934	December 1934
Fixed Interest Stocks ..	14·01	19·23	21·8	27·95
Variable Dividend Stocks	3·53	0·18	10·7	38·57
Total	10·6	13·05	19·4	30·26

If the stocks of the acquired concerns had risen only as
much as the *Bankers' Magazine* index, the gain in the capital
value would have been £10,855,338 at April 1934 instead
of £17,166,597 and £13,364,355 at December 1934 instead
of £26,755,003, which is nearly double the amount. This
indicates that on the assumption that the *Bankers' Magazine*
index is representative, the minimum amount of the additional gain accruing to the stockholders of the Underground and Metropolitan Railway groups through the
transfer of the London transport system to the L.P.T.B. under
the London Passenger Transport Act was by December 1934
£13,390,648, which is the difference between the rise of the
Bankers' Magazine index and the actual gain to stockholders.

This burden of interest which the Board has to shoulder
might well have proved too burdensome but for the fact
that the stockholder has no right to take action if the standard
dividend of 5½ per cent has been paid in any one of the
three years ending June 30, 1938. Only if the standard rate
is not paid at all in three consecutive years has the stockholder the right to apply for the appointment of a receiver.
This would permit wide fluctuations in earnings and payments without complications arising with the stockholders.

As, however, it is an obligation on the Board to fix its charges with a view to paying the standard rate, where the immediate outlook is not one of increasing income, any wide fluctuations in revenue could lead to rapid demands for changes in charges, etc. The three-year provision further provides an opportunity for manipulation in the event of the Board desiring to pay out a minimum amount of interest. The dividend being non-cumulative, expenses, as well as allocations to renewals, could be so adjusted that a very low rate of interest could be paid for two years and the standard rate only every third year. Such a policy may become necessary owing to the rapid rise in expenses, but it would damage the credit of the Board. Further, it is made more difficult by the necessity of creating a reserve fund out of the balance of revenue available, but only after meeting all charges, including interest, and, after ten years, the sinking fund. This reserve fund must be drawn upon to pay the standard rate, but any funds taken from it must later be refunded. Such manipulation would probably be distasteful to the Board, the more so as the Act requires that of the amount of stock issued not more than one-third can be "A" Stock and not less than one-third must be "C" Stock unless the permission of the Minister has been obtained. At the present time excluding the "T.F.A." and "L.A." Stock, "A" Stock represents 45 per cent, "B" Stock 26 per cent, and "C" Stock only 29 per cent of the total of these three stocks. Any further borrowing is therefore likely to conform to the proportions fixed by the Act and be partly of "C" Stock. In view of the necessity of raising further capital, the Board's credit must be maintained and the price of the "C" Stock kept as near par as possible. Mr. Pick confirmed this when he said:

The Board cannot raise any capital until the "C" Stock has received such a return that it has a market value not far below parity at the worst, otherwise there must be excessive expense attached to the raising of capital.

By this provision, too, the financial stability or the maintenance of the rate of return on the Board's "C" Stock assumes an additional importance. For the Board must always be wanting fresh capital. So long as London grows the transport facilities must grow too. Indeed, they must grow appreciably in advance of demand by way of encouragement. It is the interest of everyone that the Board should flourish.[1]

Under the Act all stocks other than "C" Stock has to be repaid in ninety years. Where stock is redeemed out of fresh borrowing, that stock must be redeemed within ninety years of the date of issue of the stock redeemed. A sinking fund must accordingly be established, but conscious of the difficulty of doing this out of revenue, the framers of the Act put off its compulsory commencement for ten years, except in the case of the Tramway Debt Liquidation Fund. To this fund the Board must charge such sums as are payable to local authorities by way of capital payment in respect of loans raised for the purpose of the transferred undertakings, and must transfer from revenue sufficient to liquidate these payments in ninety years. When the sinking fund has to be started something like £250,000 a year additional net revenue will be necessary. Contributions to this stock redemption fund come after payment of the standard rate on the "C" Stock but before the payment of the additional ½ per cent. This is an innovation. It places upon the consumer a burden of repaying the capital cost of much of the transport system within ninety years. Should the life of the undertaking exceed that period the removal of the capital charge would be of great benefit to the travelling public of 2023 onwards, the more so as renewals are in addition provided out of revenue. Let those, therefore, who complain of high fares to-day take comfort that their sacrifice is in the interests of posterity. In this connection Mr. Pick in the speech already referred to said:

---

[1] London School of Economics speech, February 26, 1934, quoted in *Financial News*, February 27, 1934. The alternative is, of course, to raise such capital by Government aid, as has been done. See page 170.

On the other hand, the capital of the Board is always wasting (I speak in a technical sense). To a major extent this waste is met by appropriations to reserves for renewal, but these are never adequate to deal with some complete revolution in transport which makes that which exists obsolete. The Act has therefore made provision against it by requiring the Board, after ten years in which to establish itself, to set aside sinking funds to redeem the capital outstanding over a period not exceeding ninety years, and as a result of this the Act has introduced a new feature in capitalization of local passenger transport in London by making all the stocks and shares out of which the Board's stocks have been constituted, redeemable and not perpetual.

This is a prudent move, though it throws a heavier burden upon transport.

. The fares of the passengers must yield not only the cost of the service, the depreciation charge, the interest charge, but over and above all these, the redemption charge. It remains to be seen whether the passengers will accept the burden and willingly bear it.[1]

The result of the Board's operation during the first two years indicated that on the basis of current charges and with an indicated increase in takings, plus the economies resulting from consolidation, there was a possibility of the standard rate of $5\frac{1}{2}$ per cent being earned before the three year period expired. But as expenses rose in 1936 more than the increase in traffics, it is only as yet a remote possibility. In announcing the 1936 interim payment the Board stated that there had been a substantial increase in working expenses, and this was confirmed by the full accounts for the year. This was mainly due to the restoration of the percentage deduction from salaries and wages made in 1931, to other adjustments in rates of pay and conditions of service, and to an increase in the cost of fuel. The increase in expenses shattered hopes of an early payment of the standard rate. The income has fallen short of that estimated by Sir William

[1] School of Economics speech, February 26, 1934. Mr. Pick was not entirely correct, as loans raised by Local Authorities had always been redeemable.

McLintock when the Bill was passing through its final stages.[1]
He estimated a balance available for interest on "C" Stock
and Reserve Fund of £1,620,020 for the first two years.
The actual earnings available for the "C" Stock were
£874,664 for the first year, £1,015,192 for the second year,
and £1,058,591 for the third year.

Owing to the delay experienced in completing the pooling
scheme and to the complexity of the transfer of certain
undertakings where terms of acquisition had not been
agreed upon by the Arbitration Tribunal, with Parliament's
permission the first two years' accounts were issued together
in October 1935. After paying the interest on the stocks
ranking before the "C" Stock, income was sufficient to pay
$3\frac{1}{2}$ per cent on the "C" Stock for the first year. For the
second year income enabled 4 per cent to be paid. The
standard rate for these two years was 5 per cent, but as
the provisions covering non-payment of the standard rate
only apply to the three years after 1935, the stockholders
could do nothing. On account of 1936 the same interim
of $1\frac{1}{2}$ per cent paid in 1935 was distributed, followed by a
final distribution of $2\frac{1}{2}$ per cent, making 4 per cent for the
year. The position of the Board at June 30, 1936, was that
London Transport Stock had been issued to the extent of
£111,935,454, of which £25,698,802 was in "C" Stock.
The capital expenditure of the Board stood at £118,088,715,
but of this £8,315,461 is designated as "balance of consideration for undertakings transferred or acquired under
the provisions of the London Passenger Transport Act,
1933," which means that the Board considers this amount
has been paid out in excess of the value of assets acquired.
In a public company it would be designated as "goodwill."
Generous provision appears to be made in the accounts for
renewals, the sum of £2,020,500 being allocated in 1934,
£2,526,000 in 1935, and in 1936 £2,300,000. To date only
£437,083 has been charged against this fund. Apparently

[1] Cmd. 4204 of 1932.

this item could fluctuate according to the wishes of the Board in such a way that it could materially influence the amount of interest payable on the "C" stock, but no doubt the auditors would consider it their duty to comment on any excessive or inadequate allocations here.

The total receipts of the Board for the year ended June 30, 1936, were £29,724,723, of which all but approximately £200,000 came from passengers under the pooling scheme. Working expenses, including the allocation to renewals, amounted to £25,815,821, leaving net traffic receipts of £3,908,902. Other receipts, less miscellaneous charges, brought the total net revenue to £5,472,116. The Tramway Debt Liquidation Fund and Annual Payments to Local Authorities in respect of interest on loans raised in connection with their transferred tramway undertakings absorbed £20,337. Interest paid, including the 4 per cent paid on the "C" Stock, amounted to £5,172,032. The equivalent of 4,214,955,963 passengers were carried during the year in the London Passenger Transport Area on the pooled system, of which all but 566,993,330 originated on the Board's system. The average receipt per journey was only 2·312d.[1]

The result of the creation of the L.P.T.B. is that whereas prior to its creation facilities in what is now the Board's Special Area were provided by five railway companies, exclusive of the main line railways, fourteen municipally owned tramways, three company owned tramways, and sixty-one companies, firms, or individuals operating bus services, to-day transport facilities are provided by one Board and four main line railways operating in co-operation. The transfer of these undertakings to the Board and the establishment of co-operation with the railways through a pooling scheme entailed a vast amount of work, the bulk of which was spread over the five years 1931-6 falling into

[1] L.P.T.B. Third Annual Reports and Accounts, in which many other interesting statistics are given.

*

two periods: the work involved in negotiation and in Parliament prior to the passage of the Act, and the transfer after the establishment of the Board on July 1, 1933. The capital involved, apart from that of the main line railways, exceeded £110,000,000, and the staff was in excess of 75,000. The creation of the pool required a vast amount of detailed examination. That the transfer was achieved without any interference with the facilities provided, or any inconvenience to the travelling public, without any financial loss to stockholders, or any serious dispute arising with the staff, is a feat for which credit is due both to the framers of the Act and to those responsible for carrying it into effect.

It is perhaps early yet to judge the final result of the creation of the Board. Unquestionably the creation of a monopoly has made possible the co-ordination of London transport and its orderly development and efficient and economic operation. Wasteful competition and unnecessary overlapping have been abolished and extensions undertaken with Government aid which otherwise would have been difficult to provide. To conceive the benefit that results from this requires a vision of how much more chaotic London transport must have become without the co-ordination of services and the provision for development that the Board makes possible. The initial work of the Board being mainly in the direction of co-ordinating services and standardizing equipment, no spectacular achievements are discernible. Of the benefits that arise from monopolistic operation, clearly thus far the economies and increased efficiency largely benefit the stockholders. Since so much of the Board's initial activity was directed to the removal of the evils of haphazard development, which was necessary before the best could be obtained from existing facilities and future developments most advantageously considered, the result will be better judged five years hence. As regards the railways, the chief task undertaken was the bringing of the Metropolitan Railway into the underground and tube system, thereby increasing its usefulness and enabling more extensive through services to be run to the districts it serves.

It was on the roads that the greatest confusion existed, not so much in Central London as in the outer circle. Out of a mass of unrelated and overlapping services the Board has been busy building co-ordinated and regulated services. From the point of view of efficiency and economy, the main work has been the standardization of equipment, a task of no small magnitude in view of the diversity of vehicles taken over. The maintenance and overhaul of buses has been centralized and a systematized garage system instituted. In these directions considerable saving must eventually result.[1]

The machinery has been set up or kept in existence for the regulation of conditions of service of the staff. Working conditions have been in some cases improved where they were prejudiced through the competitive conditions that previously existed. The raising to a common standard of similar grades of employees and the removing of anomalies has been achieved only in part. There still exists a great variation in salaries for similar work, the indoor staff having been taken over for five years at the old rate of pay. Despite increased wages the tram men still receive less than the bus and railway men and the great difference in pay of these three sections remains. Already labour costs have risen and must rise further.

In the way of facilities, despite the withdrawal of a few minor concessions exceptionally made by some of the local authorities, and a reduction in some motor coaches and country bus services, new facilities have been introduced in the way of cheaper evening travel where it arises on the suburban lines; greater co-ordination of services has been achieved and more through traffic made possible. No less than 6,500 railway fares were revised in a downward

[1] L.P.T.B. Second Annual Report and Accounts.

direction in the first three years of the Board. On the other hand, adjustments in the coach and country bus services led to increases in 1,390 fares.

The travelling public has not consciously benefited to a great extent as yet from the Board's creation. The regular fare paid is the public's greatest concern, and there has been no change in the majority of regular fares. Nor is there any prospect of this coming about. And this is the chief criticism that can be levelled against the Board's constitution. As described above, the terms of transfer were such that heavy interest charges have to be met before concessions that increase costs can be made to the travelling public. Such were the terms granted to shareholders that benefits arising from the economies resulting from co-ordination and from the increased revenue will go to meet their claims. Net revenue must rise somewhere in the neighbourhood of 7 per cent before any surplus will be available for others than the stockholders. While the majority of wage earners cannot point to any improvement in their condition as a result of the Board's creation, those who were assimilated have been brought up to the general level prevailing among the combine's workers. The combine employed the largest proportion of those transferred, and while, except in the case of the tramwaymen, their conditions are no different than they would have been had the combine remained under its old control, it must not be overlooked that the combine could always be classed as a good employer, and many of the employees were enjoying working conditions superior to the general standard. Nor does the consumer, that is the travelling public, feel that he has any greater say in the operation of London passenger transport than he had before. Only exceptionally is he conscious of any power to complain or suggest or advise as to its operation. Nevertheless, the Board keeps a close watch on public criticism, and is considerably influenced by it, believing perhaps that by meeting it any demand for greater public control can be kept off.

Why is it that so drastic a change in control should result in so few spectacular changes? The answer is probably to be found in the fact that the Board resembles mostly a capitalist monopoly. It has abolished the evils of competition as does the capitalist trust, it is subject to control over charges to the public no more than are the privately owned railways. To all intents and purposes London transport is still run in order to earn sufficient to pay its upkeep and the interest on the capital put up to build it. The fault, if it be a fault, lies not in this, as in a capitalist State every undertaking must operate at least at cost unless subsidy through taxes or rates be sought. Industry has for the most part been organized under private enterprise, so it is inevitable that those put in charge of public corporations will have received their training in a capitalist environment, and more often than not it will be those who have proved the most successful in that field who will be selected for the highest positions in the public corporation. Once the Board is created, opportunity should be provided for the most capable to be rewarded with rapid promotion. In addition, only specialized technical training combined with practical experience within the State education system can create that new outlook and spirit of public service without which the full opportunities and advantages of community ownership cannot be enjoyed.

In detail certain changes in the structure of the L.P.T.B. are necessary and criticisms can be made. In conception it is State capitalism highly developed, and in practice it works. In general it can be criticized mainly for lack of democratic control, and in detail for the limitation of its powers to the actual operation of passenger transport and for its failure to give the staff any improved status, except in the security of keeping the job, as compared with that of any capitalist concern ranking as a good employer.

To the socialist who looks for something more in a publicly controlled concern than efficiency and limited

profits the Board is deficient in many particulars. Apart
from the question of too heavy interest charges which arose
from the circumstances of its creation, the fault lies not in
its constitution, but in the interpretation of that constitution. There has been no conscious change in the operation
of the London system on the part of the public, staff, or
management. The transport system of London is still to
the ordinary member of the travelling public a monopoly
which he feels has him at his mercy. Here the public is
partly to blame. It could play its share through using every
channel open for the airing of criticisms and the demanding
of facilities; the staff perhaps would find it more difficult
to share in the expression of its views, but action is possible
through those on the Board and on the London and Home
Counties Traffic Advisory Committee who hold Labour
views.

For the present there are two directions in which change
is called for: increased facilities and reduced financial
burdens. The former should be demanded by the public,
taken up by the Labour Party and the trade unions, and
persisted in. As regards finance, only if a Government were
willing to upset statutory bargains could action be taken.
Then additional parliamentary measures could enable
change to be made and steps could be taken to reduce the
burden of compensation. The first would be the making of
the "A," "B," and "C" Stocks of the Board redeemable
forthwith instead of at the earliest in twenty-three years in
the case of the "C" Stock, thirty-two for the "B," and fifty-
two for the "A" after their creation. With the current low
interest rates ruling, conversion from 5 per cent and $4\frac{1}{2}$ per
cent to 3 per cent or $3\frac{1}{2}$ per cent would effect considerable
savings which would enable fares to be lowered and working
conditions to be improved. The original stockholders would
have no just cause on financial grounds for complaint as
the large premium at which their stocks stand above parity
has come about since the transfer took place and the option

to convert into a lower interest-bearing security or to receive cash would cause no hardship. In the same way the standard rate on the "C" Stock which is fixed by the Act at $5\frac{1}{2}$ per cent, plus a further $\frac{1}{2}$ per cent when earned should be reduced by parliamentary action. At 4 per cent the stock would probably stand at or near par. This financial burden is the Board's greatest handicap, and a Board or a Minister of Transport who was bent on putting the interests of the consumer before those of the stockholder would be compelled to take action in this way before he was able to do so.

Another difficulty is the lack of elasticity in the creation of reserves. The fact that the L.P.T.B. has to take each year's operation entirely separately as regards its finances makes its operation extremely difficult. Normal commercial practice is publicly or secretly to create reserves which can be drawn upon when needed, and in this way results can to some extent be levelled out. Transport, like all other industries, is subject to the business cycle, and if in good years large reserves could be created to be drawn upon in bad years, not only could the fluctuations in the stockholders' income be made less violent, but the necessity of changing fares might be avoided. Since a reserve fund can be created only if the high standard rate of $5\frac{1}{2}$ per cent has been paid, and then further net receipts have to be shared with the "C" Stock to the extent of an additional $\frac{1}{2}$ per cent, the creation of a large fund is unlikely, especially as in 1943 a sinking fund has to be started. The only elasticity lies in the renewals fund, but as the auditors have to be approved by the Minister of Transport, they are unlikely to allow such excessive contributions to this fund as in effect to constitute a secret reserve. One financial lesson London transport is likely to teach is the necessity of public concerns in future being given the power to build up a reserve fund before more than a low rate of interest is paid on what corresponds to its equity stocks.

The faults of the Board are by no means insurmountable. The public corporation provides the framework for a model which can be experimented with and improved upon. It successfully provides the manner in which the operation of an industry or a service can be made independent of Treasury control, and so dealt with as to occupy the minimum of parliamentary and ministerial time. It takes the best from capitalism and introduces public ownership and control. Criticisms raised can be overcome within the framework of the public corporation, and for these reasons the experiment of the L.P.T.B. is likely to be the forerunner of many similar public concerns.

7

THE COAL MINES REORGANIZATION COMMISSION

by

IVOR THOMAS

THE Coal Mines Reorganization[1] Commission differs from the other bodies described in this volume inasmuch as it has no powers of ownership or control. It is endowed with compulsory powers for the reorganization of the coal-mining industry, but so far they have proved incapable of exercise. In the present state of the law it does not appear that those compulsory powers can be given effect; and an attempt by the Government to change the law so as to give the Commission such effective powers as Parliament intended it to possess has been abandoned under protest from the mine-owners. A further attempt is promised, but in the meantime the Commission is helpless to do more than survey the ground before it and essay such limited tasks as can be achieved by persuasion. Nevertheless a study of the Coal Mines Reorganization Commission (which will henceforth be called, for brevity and euphony, the C.M.R.C.) deserves to be included in this work, not only because the State has intervened through this body in the affairs of industry but because of the hopes widely entertained that its operations, together with the statutory marketing machinery, may herald the formation of a body similar to those elsewhere discussed in this volume, and possessing a real control over the supply and distribution of coal.

The C.M.R.C. owes its statutory existence to Part II of the Coal Mines Act, 1930, but the Act has a long history behind

[1] In the Act of Parliament setting up the Commission and in other official documents this word is spelt "Reorganisation," but the solecism will not be repeated here; perhaps Mr. A. P. Herbert, M.P., will oblige with the necessary amendment to the Act.

it, and the true origin of the Commission must be sought at least as far back as the Great War. During those years of national stress, when the allied victory was slowly built on a foundation of British coal, many people began to doubt whether the mining industry was being carried on as efficiently as possible. The Minister of Reconstruction appointed a Coal Conservation Committee to study such matters, and a Mining Sub-Committee reported a number of points, especially in regard to royalties, where improved working was possible.

SIR R. REDMAYNE'S VIEWS

The problem came to the forefront in 1919 when the Coal Industry Commission was appointed with Mr. Justice (now Lord) Sankey as chairman. On March 11 Sir Richard Redmayne, who was then Chief Inspector of Mines and had an unrivalled experience of the industry from many angles, was examined[1] and startled the country by a frank declaration, "In my opinion the present system of individual ownership of collieries is extravagant and wasteful." He proceeded to state, as the advantages which would result from "collective production,"

(*a*) Enhanced production;
(*b*) Diminished cost of production; and
(*c*) Prevention of waste, by the following means:
    (1) Prevention of competition, leading to a better selling price for exported coal;
    (2) Better control of freights;
    (3) Economy of administration;
    (4) Provision of capital, allowing a quicker and more extensive development of the backward mines;
    (5) The more advantageous purchase of material;
    (6) Reduction of colliery consumption of coal;
    (7) More harmonious relations between the workmen and the employers;

---

[1] Vide Coal Industry Commission, *Reports and Minutes of Evidence on the First Stage of the Inquiry* (1919, Cmd. 359), QQ. 5208–9, pp. 210–11.

(8) Obliteration to a great extent of vested interests and middlemen;
(9) Unification of the best knowledge and skill, leading to greater interchange of ideas and comparison of methods.

Other witnesses were not lacking to support the view that an industry made up of 1,500 competing concerns, owning 3,000 pits,[1] was not organized as it should be. Subject in general to the saving clause that the size of the producing unit must not be made indefinitely large, the following experts approved a policy of larger undertakings:

Mr. (later Sir) Arthur Pease (QQ. 7852–3), Mr. C. E. Rhodes (QQ. 16766–7), Mr. Edmund Hann (Q. 18723), Lord Gainford (with further qualification, QQ. 19795 and 20096), Mr. Bramwell (Q. 21337), Mr. Thorneycroft (Q. 21355), Sir Hugh Bell (Q. 26293), Professor George Knox (Q. 26402–11), and Sir Lionel Phillips (Q. 26577).

Only one expert voice was raised against a policy of larger undertakings, that of Mr. F. Parker Rhodes, a mine-owner.

SAMUEL REPORT

In 1925 the question was exhaustively considered by the Royal Commission on the Coal Industry under the chairmanship of Sir Herbert Samuel.[2] The members had before them the evidence given to the Coal Industry Commission, and they themselves heard further testimony to the same effect from Sir Richard Redmayne and Mr. Charles Markham, head of one of the most important combinations in the industry.[3] They had evidence in a contrary sense on behalf of the organization of mine-owners, the mining engineers, and the mine managers, but, as they pertinently implied, these bodies could not fail to be influenced by the stand which they had already taken against nationalization,

---

[1] That was the state of the industry at the time.
[2] *Report* (1926, Cmd. 2600), pp. 44–62.
[3] Doncaster Collieries Association.

and against anything which might appear as a step towards nationalization.

The Commissioners set out six arguments in favour of larger units. They may be abbreviated as follows:

(1) All the economies of large-scale production become possible, particularly in the provision of electric power, in the purchase of supplies, in maintaining the stock of stores, and in the economical running of repair workshops. In some cases the organization of the pumping of the mines on a well-considered general plan may be facilitated. In others the question of the barriers and coal reserves, left between separate mines, may be dealt with in a more efficient manner than when each is in separate ownership.

(2) The sales organization is in a stronger position to secure favourable prices.

(3) Transport is facilitated, and the daily supply of railway wagons can be more easily adjusted to the production at the moment of each pit.

(4) A large enterprise is in a position to offer high salaries and to secure the best brains.

(5) The process of closing obsolete pits and opening new ones can be undertaken scientifically.

(6) The large colliery, able to draw on adequate supplies of capital, is more likely to succeed in adapting itself to the needs of the time.

The Samuel Commission noted a contention that in many cases these considerations did not apply; that the economies were in any event comparatively small; that management, so far from being improved, might be worsened through the unit becoming too large for efficient personal attention; that managers with the needed high qualifications would not be forthcoming; and that relations with the workers would be worsened through a weakening of contact. To resolve such doubts, the Commission instituted an inquiry into the actual results of the working of 613 colliery undertakings grouped according to the size of their output. These undertakings raised about 95 per cent of the total British production in the six months reviewed. The results of the inquiry were summarized in the following tables:

WORKING RESULTS OF COLLIERY UNDERTAKINGS OF VARIOUS SIZES

GREAT BRITAIN—JANUARY TO JUNE 1925

Yearly Output of Undertaking, 1,000 Tons	Number of Under-takings	Tonnage Raised		Output per Man-Shift	Proceeds	Costs	Profit (+) or Loss (−)
		Total 1,000 Tons	Percentage of Total				
(1)	(2)	(3)	(4)	(5)	(6)	(7)	(8)
				Cwt.	Shillings per Ton	Shillings per Ton	Shillings per Ton
Less than 5	10	32	—	12·78	23·51	32·01	− 8·50
5 and under 200	307	27,360	12·7	16·22	19·02	20·23	− 1·21
200 and under 400	126	36,394	16·9	17·05	18·43	19·21	− 0·78
400 and under 600	72	35,118	16·3	18·34	17·90	18·04	− 0·14
600 and under 800	28	19,132	8·9	18·86	17·58	17·82	− 0·24
800 and under 1,000	20	17,992	8·4	18·68	17·52	17·65	− 0·13
1,000 and under 2,000	42	56,280	26·2	19·66	17·77	17·49	+ 0·28
2,000 and over	8	22,744	10·6	19·76	17·39	17·11	+ 0·28
Total	613	215,052	100·0	18·32	17·98	18·23	− 0·25

LOSSES AND PROFITS BY SIZE OF UNDERTAKINGS

Great Britain—January to June 1925

Yearly Output of Coal Disposable Commercially, 1,000 Tons	Total Number of Undertakings	Number of Undertakings making a Loss per Ton of					Number of Undertakings making a Profit per Ton of				
		7s. and over	5s. and under 7s.	3s. and under 5s.	1s. and under 3s.	Under 1s.	Under 1s.	1s. and under 3s.	3s. and under 5s.	5s. and under 7s.	7s. and over
Under 5	10	5	—	2	—	1	1	—	1	—	—
5 and under 200	307	28	16	39	73	50	33	48	9	5	6
200 and under 400	126	2	5	13	39	28	10	14	14	1	—
400 and under 600	72	—	—	2	25	15	14	12	4	—	—
600 and under 800	28	—	—	—	9	8	5	4	2	—	—
800 and under 1,000	20	—	—	2	6	8	2	2	2	—	—
1,000 and under 2,000	42	—	—	—	10	6	8	15	—	1	—
2,000 and over	8	—	—	—	1	3	1	3	—	—	—
Total	613	35	21	58	163	119	74	98	32	7	6

The former of these tables showed that output per man-shift (column 5) rose with almost complete regularity from the smallest class of undertakings to the largest, while costs of production per ton (column 7) fell with complete regularity. Although the smaller undertakings were able to get at the pithead a higher price—due either to special qualities of their seams or proximity to good markets—the larger undertakings were substantially the more profitable (or less unprofitable). This is confirmed by the latter table, from which it is seen that nearly all the heavy losses were confined to the smaller undertakings.

No such thorough inquiry has since been made, but there is no reason to suspect that the forces which in 1925 made for the efficiency of the larger undertaking have ceased to operate. If a similar inquiry were made today, it could not fail to show a similar result. The conclusion reached in the Samuel Report has never been satisfactorily challenged. It has been argued that the tables did not show the capital involved,[1] with the implication that, owing to differences in capitalization, a pit with high costs of production may give a greater return to the investor than another pit with lower costs of production. But this has no relevance to the absolute efficiency of mines and was rightly disregarded in the Samuel Report. The argument reveals, as was known already, that those in control of the industry look at it primarily from the point of view of the shareholders, but is no guide to the reorganization of the industry on the most efficient lines. Capital in many colliery concerns has been "watered" so profusely that the rate of return is worthless as a guide to efficiency.

SURPLUS PRODUCTIVE CAPACITY

The Samuel Commission may therefore be regarded as having established that larger productive units than those

[1] *Report on the British Coal Industry* (Political and Economic Planning), p. 66.

in existence were desirable. This conclusion has been given
added importance by a feature of the industry which has
come into prominence during recent years, the surplus
capacity of the industry over the greatest demand likely to
be made in the next few decades, so far as can be foreseen.

It is not possible to state with any pretence to accuracy
the present productive capacity of the coal industry. Such
estimates must necessarily be little more than guesses, but
they are guesses which can to some extent be checked. A
few years ago it was commonly accepted that the British
coal industry could produce, if need be, 330,000,000 tons
a year. In the interval, many mines and seams have been
closed. On the other hand, the increase in machine mining
has tended to increase productive capacity, for it has
"changed the limiting factor from the amount of coal-face
available to the coal-winding capacity of the shafts."[1]
Though certainty is impossible, it is generally believed
among those with any claim to speak that the productive
capacity of the industry is not less than 300,000,000 tons a
year. A casual remark to that effect in a leading article in
The Times of May 29, 1936, produced an interesting correspondence. The figure was challenged by Mr. W. A. Lee,
Secretary of the Mining Association of Great Britain, on
June 2, 1936. Basing his argument on the number of days
lost through want of trade, and on the seasonal nature of
a great part of the demand for coal, Mr. Lee estimated
productive capacity at 250,000,000 to 260,000,000 tons. It
is easy to see that this method gives a lower limit to the
productive capacity, but also that it gives no more than a
lower limit. According to the returns of the Mines Department[2] the average weekly number of coal-winding days lost
through want of trade in 1935 was 0·75, or about one-eighth
of the total possible coal-winding time, amounting on the

[1] Mr. Osbert Peake, M.P., and Lord Castlereagh, M.P., in *The Times* of
June 13, 1936. These mine-owners assert that for this reason the "excess
capacity is much greater today than it was in 1930."
[2] *Fifteenth Annual Report*, Table 16, p. 134.

average to $5\frac{4}{5}$ days a week. Clearly, if this time had not been lost, the industry could have raised about 250,000,000 tons instead of 222,000,000 tons. But the Mines Department return has a significant footnote which Mr. Lee did not take into account: "It is not necessarily implied that all the persons employed worked every day coal was wound." Nor does this method take into account the concentration of production inside mines, i.e. the closing of seams which could be worked, as the best method of complying with quota requirements. Accordingly this method can give no more than a lower estimate of productive capacity.

There is a still simpler method of showing that productive capacity cannot be less than 260,000,000 tons a year. In the week ended December 14, 1935, the industry raised 5,159,500 tons, so that in a year of 52 weeks, even allowing for Bank holidays, it would certainly produce 260,000,000 tons. Anyone who regards this as the actual productive capacity would be compelled to say that in the week ended December 14, 1935, the industry could not have raised any more coal, which, as Euclid would have declared, is absurd.

We are still a long way from knowing how much greater than the 260,000,000 tons is the actual productive capacity. In the same correspondence in *The Times* to which reference has been made a useful piece of evidence was given on June 23, 1936, by Mr. J. Frater Taylor, chairman of Pease & Partners Limited. Analysing the figures for twelve collieries with which he is associated, he found that without further abnormal expenditure their output could be increased by 13·30 per cent; with a moderate expenditure their output could be increased by 34·02 per cent.

If these figures are typical, then the 1934 output of 222,000,000 tons could be increased, without abnormal expenditure, to 252,000,000 tons and with moderate expenditure to 298,000,000 tons. Admittedly twelve collieries producing 3,025,000 tons a year do not form a sufficient basis for generalization, but there is no reason to suspect that these collieries are abnormal. The Wearmouth Coal Company, for example, is announced[1] to have an annual capacity of 1,250,000 tons a year, though at present its output is restricted to 800,000 tons. The chairman of the Yorkshire Amalgamated Collieries has stated that his company is working only to two-thirds of its capacity. Powell Duffryn Associated Collieries is estimated to have a total productive capacity of over 20,000,000 tons a year, but the total output of the whole South Wales coalfield in 1935 was only 35,000,000 tons. In fact, wherever figures can be given they confirm the belief that the industry has at present a productive capacity of 300,000,000 tons a year, or at any rate could be given that capacity with moderate expenditure.

In no year since the war has the demand exceeded 276,000,000 tons, and the average annual production since 1927 has been only 230,000,000 tons.

PRODUCTION OF COAL IN GREAT BRITAIN*

(In Million Tons)

1913	1919	1920	1921†	1922	1923	1924	1925	1926†
287	230	230	163	250	276	267	243	126

1927	1928	1929	1930	1931	1932	1933	1934	1935
251	237	258	244	219	209	207	221	222

* Including particulars for Ireland up to 1921.
† Production affected by national strikes.

Unfortunately there is no reason to expect any big increase in demand. Production generally has recovered almost to the level of 1929, but coal production still lags far short. The forces which have led to the decline are still at work— development of coalfields and alternative fuels abroad, the use of oil in place of coal at sea and at home, and increasing economy in use.[2] Even a spectacular increase in the produc-

---

[1] *The Times*, June 3, 1936.
[2] Ultimately the last cause may lead to an increase in the demand, but immediately it produces a decline.

tion of oil from coal would not wholly close the gap between the potential demand for coal and the industry's productive capacity. We cannot reasonably expect a demand of more than 240,000,000 tons in any of the years immediately ahead, and productive capacity is 300,000,000 tons a year. True, that does not mean there is a surplus capacity of 60,000,000 tons a year, for demand varies seasonably, and to meet a demand of 240,000,000 tons a year the industry would have to be producing in its peak period at the rate of about 260,000,000 tons a year. But, on the most moderate estimate, the industry has a surplus capacity of 40,000,000 tons a year, and we must reluctantly acknowledge that the surplus is more nearly of the order of 50,000,000 tons a year.

This raises anew the question of amalgamating mines. It is a serious matter to close a mine before it has been exhausted, but it is also a serious matter to keep it working below its capacity. Failure to work at optimum capacity necessarily increases the costs per ton of production. Overhead charges are the same whatever fraction of productive capacity is used; and failure to work at capacity means that these fixed charges have to be divided over a smaller production, and so *ceteris paribus* costs per ton of production are inevitably increased. The coal industry is no exception to this general rule of business; and the advance of mechanization, which increases the overhead charges of a mine at the same time as it diminishes labour costs, has made the question more acute. The cost of working below optimum capacity has been estimated in the case of particular mines at as much as 2s. a ton, or even 3s. 6d. a ton in the case of a fully mechanized pit. Over the industry as a whole the increase in costs owing to working below capacity is estimated at 1s. a ton out of total costs in 1935 of 12s. 11¾d.

There is here a clear case for concentrating production on the most efficient pits, so as to enable them to work at full capacity, and closing down redundant mines. This gives added point to the Samuel Commission's inquiry into the most efficient units and greatly strengthens the case for concentrating production in large concerns.

THE ACT OF 1926

It is now time to see how far the need for larger units of production has received legislative recognition, culminating in the appointment of the c.m.r.c. Posing to itself four questions, the Samuel Commission gave the following answers:

(1) We have arrived at the definite conclusion on the first of the four questions which we have formulated, that the size of undertakings usual in the coal industry in Great Britain is not economically the best; and that there are great advantages in large-scale production which are not now being realized.

(2) At the same time we consider that it has been established that any general measure of compulsory grouping on uniform or arbitrary lines is open to grave objection. . . . The answer, then, to the second question is that a number of amalgamations have in fact been effected in the older coalfields and with advantage; that they are therefore clearly not impracticable; but that not in every case is amalgamation desirable, and that to compel parties, who object to it, to work together in a combined undertaking would be a mistaken policy.

(3) Our conclusion on the third point is—that while in some cases fusions or absorptions which are desirable have taken place, and in other cases fusions and absorptions would be attended with a balance of disadvantage and should not take place, we cannot doubt that between these two classes there are a large number in which such amalgamations are desirable, have not yet been effected, and are not likely to be effected, if the matter is left entirely to the action of the parties directly concerned.

(4) Amalgamations, where they are made at all, should in most cases be complete, but might sometimes be rather of the nature of the combined action of separate businesses for power supply, co-operative selling, or other purposes. The necessary elasticity, and harmonious working, could best be obtained if the initiative came from within the industry itself. Where one or more undertakings in an area desired to effect an amalgamation, but others, whose co-operation was necessary, refused,

or demanded unreasonable terms, there must be power in the public interest to override such opposition.

Legislation giving effect to these recommendations was introduced by the Conservative Government of the day in Part 1 of the Mining Industry Act, 1926. The most important provisions were:

1. (1) Where with a view to the more economical and efficient working, treating, or disposal of coal the owners of two or more undertakings consisting of or comprising coalmines agree to amalgamate their undertakings either wholly or partially, they may prepare and submit to the Board of Trade a scheme (hereinafter referred to as an amalgamation scheme) framed in accordance with the provisions of this Part of this Act.

(2) Where the owner of any such undertaking, or where the owners of two or more such undertakings who have agreed to amalgamate, consider that in the interests of the more economical and efficient working, treating, or disposing of coal it is expedient that one or more other such undertakings, the owners of which are unwilling to agree to amalgamate or to agree to the proposed terms of amalgamation, should be absorbed wholly or partially by the first mentioned undertaking, or by the amalgamated undertaking, as the case may be, the owner or owners may prepare and submit to the Board of Trade a scheme (hereinafter referred to as an absorption scheme) framed in accordance with the provisions of this Part of this Act.

The Act proceeded to define the contents of total and partial schemes of amalgamation and absorption, exempted any such scheme from stamp duty, and continued:

6. The Board of Trade shall consider any scheme submitted to them, and shall, if satisfied after communication with such parties interested as they may think fit that a prima facie case is made out that the proposed scheme would promote the more economical and efficient working, treating, or disposing of coal, refer the matter to the Railway and Canal Commission.

7. (1) Where a scheme has been referred to the Railway and Canal Commission, the Commission, if satisfied that the scheme conforms to the requirements of this Part of this Act, shall take into consideration all objections to the scheme which may be lodged by any person or by any class or body of persons within

such time and in such manner as may be directed by the Commission, and where any objections have been so lodged shall hear any objectors whom they consider entitled to appear.

(2) The Commission, after hearing such objectors as aforesaid, may confirm the scheme either without modifications or subject to such modifications as the Commission think fit, or may refuse to confirm the scheme:

Provided that the Commission—

    (a) Shall confirm a scheme if satisfied that it would be in the national interest to do so, and that the terms of the scheme are fair and equitable to all persons affected thereby.

Within two years of the passing of the 1926 Act, 17 separate schemes of amalgamation (subsequently reduced to 14 by further amalgamation) had been given effect.[1] They covered 172 pits normally employing about 126,000 workpeople. Of these 17 schemes only three were brought before the Railway and Canal Commission. The remaining 14 were effected without recourse to the special provisions of the Act, though the existence of compulsory provisions in the Act may have helped to bring about voluntary amalgamations. By December 1929 further schemes affecting 61 pits normally employing 43,760 workers had been confirmed by the Railway and Canal Commission or agreed to without recourse to the Court.[2]

LABOUR GOVERNMENT'S BILL

This was the position when the Labour Government, which had assumed office in the summer of 1929, began to tackle the problem of the coal-mining industry in accordance with its election pledges. The Government's original Bill did not include proposals for reorganizing the structure of the industry. Some such proposals might have been included

[1] *Report by the Board of Trade under Section 12 on the Working of Part 1 of the Act* (1928, Cmd. 3214).

[2] *Second Report of the Board of Trade under Section 12 on the Working of Part 1 of the Act* (1929, Cmd. 3454).

in a later measure which it was intended should deal with nationalization of coal royalties, but during the second reading in the Commons on December 17, 1929, Sir Herbert Samuel specified compulsory amalgamation as one of the conditions of Liberal support. The Government accepted this proposal, and on February 13, 1930, the President of the Board of Trade (Mr. W. Graham) moved amendments to the Bill providing for the formation of a Coal Mines Reorganization Commission to bring about amalgamations. He contemplated three commissioners appointed by the Board of Trade, with some doubt whether the number ought not to be five, and said it was his intention to get a leading lawyer familiar with industrial and commercial practice, someone familiar with administration in colliery districts, and someone who could command confidence on the industrial side and who had already experience of amalgamation in other industries. The cost of the Commission he put at £250,000 a year. When a private member (Mr. E. C. Davies, Lib.) moved that the number of commissioners should be raised to five, Mr. Graham accepted it on the ground that the Government would probably have to depend on part-time service, and in that case five was the proper number.

In due course the measure went to the Lords, who, on Lord Gainford's motion in committee on May 14, 1930, promptly struck out the clauses constituting the Commission and defining its duties. Their lordships, with memories of the 1926 Act passed by the Conservatives and with some sensitivity to public opinion as expressed at the election, were not prepared to delete *in toto* the proposals for compulsory amalgamation, so on the Duke of Northumberland's proposition they agreed to substitute the Board of Trade for the Commission in these proposals. It would be a not unfair summary of the debate to say that they chose the "bureaucracy" of Whitehall as a lesser evil than a "peripatetic" Commission. Further to limit the power of compelling amalgamations, their lordships accepted an amendment by Lord Melchett, whose wide experience of amalgamation in the chemical industry invested his words with peculiar authority. The precise terms will be noted later in a summary of the Act, but they were roughly to the effect that any scheme of amalgamation (*a*) must be in the national interest, (*b*) must result in lowering the cost of production, and (*c*) must not be financially injurious to any of the undertakings proposed to be amalgamated. These seemingly innocent safeguards have completely obstructed the work of the Commission, as will be seen in due course, but at the time few people, save possibly the mine-owners, perceived the full power of obstruction latent in them.

The Commons were not deterred by the truculence of the Lords and rejected their amendments on June 4, 1930. Thereupon Lord Salisbury on June 24, 1930, moved that the Upper House should not insist on the amendments killing the c.m.r.c. and substituting the Board of Trade for it, but should insist on the conditions for amalgamation introduced by Lord Melchett. This was agreed to, and on July 9, 1930, the Commons accepted these conditions without a further division. By then both sides were wearying of the struggle, and it was with immense relief that many members heard the royal assent given to the most fiercely contested measure of recent years. The Coal Mines Act, 1930, was at last law.

BALANCE OF THE 1930 ACT

The Act as it finally emerged from Parliament had a delicately balanced structure, the second part being complementary to the first and third. Part 1 provided for regulation of the output of coal and the fixation of minimum prices through the machinery of a Central Council and district executive boards. The Central Council was to assign to each district an "allocation," or maximum output, which was not to be exceeded except under penalty. The district schemes were to provide for the determination of a "standard tonnage" for each mine, for the periodical determination of the proportion ("quota") of the standard tonnage which each mine might produce, and for the determination of minimum prices for each class of coal, with penalties for infringement.

There is no doubt that such provisions were essential in the depressed condition of the industry, and they kept the price of coal stable when the prices of other commodities were falling calamitously. But they have the defect that they tend to perpetuate the existing state of affairs and to prevent, or at least delay, that reorganization which might have come about of itself under pressure of economic forces. Under pressure of falling demand and falling prices the least efficient pits would have been forced out of production, and probably into the bankruptcy court. This is the classic method by which hitherto efficiency has been introduced into industry. A severe depression acts like a riddle, shaking out the weaker members. It is a ruthless process, causing widespread suffering both to capital and to labour, but it attains its object in the end. The object of "rationalization," "reorganization," and so on, is to attain this object without the attendant misery. That is the ideal method, but the "bankruptcy road," if it may so be called, is preferable to continuing indefinitely a state of inefficiency. That is what Part 1 of the Coal Mines Act, 1930, tended to do. Subject to a qualification which will shortly be noticed, each pit was to be given a fixed share of the market and a guaranteed price for its products. To say that a premium was put on inefficiency would be going too far, but at least this part of the Act tended to smooth out the difference between efficient and inefficient producers. It tended, therefore, to defeat that movement towards concentrated production which we have abundantly seen to have been necessary. Pits which might have gone out of existence

H

under the free play of economic forces were kept working, and acquired an artificial market value. True, even in Part I of the Act there were counterbalancing forces. By sub-section 2 of section 3 of the Act provision was made for the transfer of quotas. A district scheme, it was laid down, might provide "for enabling arrangements to be made by the owners of coalmines in the district, whereby the output of coal or any class of coal from any such mine may exceed the quota fixed for that mine, as respects coal or that class of coal, so long as the output of coal or that class of coal from some other mine in the district is lower than the quota fixed for that other mine, as respects coal or that class of coal, by an amount not less than the excess." Out of this provision has grown a regular trade in quotas. Owners of efficient mines, anxious to work at their optimum capacity, are prepared to buy quotas from other mines up to, say, 3s. a ton, and the other mines are prepared to sacrifice their right to produce coal for this easy return conferred on them by Parliament. This trade in quotas has led to some concentration of production. Moreover, the same sub-section laid down "that a district scheme may make provision for the determination of the standard tonnage of, and quota for, any two or more coalmines in the district which are worked for the same colliery undertaking as if they were one coalmine." As a result colliery companies owning a number of pits have been able to concentrate production on the most efficient without losing quota rights. In virtue of these provisions Part I has to some extent encouraged concentration of production, but its general tendency, by the regulation of output and fixation of minimum prices, has been very much in the other direction. To this general tendency Part II offered a corrective.

Furthermore, Part III provided for a decrease of half an hour in the maximum daily hours of work, and this would in itself have had the effect of increasing costs of production, though by what fraction is highly problematical.

Reorganization would afford some set-off to increased costs, and so Part II is complementary also to Part III.

DUTIES OF THE COMMISSION

Part II of the Coal Mines Act, 1930, required the Board of Trade to appoint five Commissioners, one of them as chairman, for such period as the Board might determine. There was no restriction on the persons who might be appointed save that members of the House of Commons were excluded, and Commissioners were required to dispose of any interests they might hold in a coal business in Great Britain.

The duties of the Commission were defined in these terms:

12. (1) It shall be the duty of the Coal Mines Reorganization Commission to further the reorganization of the coal-mining industry with a view to facilitating the production, supply, and sale of coal by owners of coalmines, and for that purpose to promote and assist, by the preparation of schemes and otherwise, the amalgamation of undertakings consisting of or comprising coalmines where such amalgamations appear to be in the national interest.

13. (1) If it appears to the Coal Mines Reorganization Commission that it is expedient for the purpose of promoting the more economical and efficient working, treating, or disposing of coal that an amalgamation scheme or an absorption scheme under Part I of the Mining Industry Act, 1926, should be prepared and submitted with respect to any two or more undertakings consisting of or comprising coalmines, the Commissioners shall require the owners of those undertakings to prepare and submit to the Board of Trade an amalgamation scheme or absorption scheme with respect to those undertakings framed in accordance with the provisions of Part I of the Act of 1926, and if the owners fail to submit such a scheme within such a time as may have been specified by the Commissioners, the Commissioners shall themselves prepare and submit such a scheme to the Board of Trade, and for the purposes of that Part of the Act any scheme so prepared and submitted by the Commission shall be deemed to have been prepared and submitted in manner provided by sub-section (1) or (2), as the case

may be, of section one of that Act, and that Act shall apply accordingly. . . .[1]

(2) In the consideration by the Railway and Canal Commission of a scheme submitted by the Board of Trade under this section, the following paragraph shall be substituted for paragraph (a) of the proviso to sub-section (2) of section seven of the Act of 1926 (which relates to consideration of schemes by the Commission):

"(a) Shall not confirm a scheme unless satisfied—
    (i) That it would be in the national interest to do so, and
    (ii) in the case of an amalgamation scheme that the scheme
        (a) will result in lowering the cost of production or disposal of coal, and
        (b) will not be financially injurious to any of the undertakings proposed to be amalgamated, unless the scheme contains provisions for the purchase, at a price to be fixed in default of agreement by arbitration, of any such undertaking; and
    (iii) that the terms of the scheme are fair and equitable to all persons affected thereby."

The differences introduced by the Act of 1930 may be summarized, without essential distortion, in a few words.

(a) Under the 1926 Act the initiative for preparing schemes, whether of amalgamation or absorption, had to come from the industry; under the 1930 Act a Commission was constituted which might take the initiative.

(b) The 1926 Act provided for schemes of voluntary amalgamation and compulsory absorption; the 1930 Act envisaged in addition schemes of compulsory amalgamation. To give an example, under the 1926 Act A, B, C, and D could amalgamate by a voluntary agreement; or if B, C, and D were unwilling, A could draw up a scheme for their compulsory absorption which might be confirmed by the

---

[1] A proviso here follows to the effect that coalmines in "vertically integrated" undertakings, e.g. coalmines ancillary to iron and steel works, shall be exempt from compulsory amalgamation.

Railway and Canal Commission and be made effective. Under the 1930 Act the c.m.r.c. could require A, B, C, and D to amalgamate although all four were unwilling.

(c) Under the 1926 Act the Railway and Canal Commission was required to confirm a scheme if satisfied that it would be in the national interest and was fair and equitable to all persons affected thereby. Under the 1930 Act the emphasis was somewhat different. The Court was not to confirm a scheme unless satisfied on these two points. Far more important, however, than the question of emphasis were the two additional points on which, under the 1930 Act, the Court had to be satisfied before confirming a scheme of amalgamation, to wit, that the scheme would result in lowering the cost of production or disposal of coal and would not be financially injurious to any of the undertakings to be amalgamated (unless provision was made for the purchase of any such undertaking).

MEMBERSHIP OF COMMISSION

The Coal Mines Reorganization Commission was constituted in December 1930 as follows:

> Sir Ernest Arthur Gowers, k.c.b., k.b.e. (Chairman).
> Mr. Lawrence Dunning Holt, j.p.
> Mr. Joseph Jones, j.p.
> Sir Felix John Clewett Pole.
> Sir William Edward Whyte, o.b.e., j.p.

Sir Ernest Gowers was Permanent Under-Secretary for Mines from 1920 to 1927, and thereafter was Chairman of the Board of Inland Revenue, which post he vacated to take up the chairmanship of the Commission. Mr. Lawrence Holt is the well-known ship owner who was Lord Mayor of Liverpool in 1929. Mr. Joseph Jones was then General Secretary of the Yorkshire Mine Workers' Association and subsequently became President of the Mine Workers' Federation of Great Britain. Sir Felix Pole was General

Manager of the Great Western Railway from 1921 to 1929, when he became Chairman of Associated Electrical Industries Limited. Sir William Whyte was a retired local government official of Scotland and chairman of the Scottish Executive Board of the National Gas Council. There has been no change in the membership of the Commission since it was constituted.

The Commission was formed with great care. At its head was a distinguished civil servant possessing a close acquaintance with the industry; it included a trade union official with all labour questions at his finger-tips; and the other three members had between them a thorough personal acquaintance with four great coal-consuming industries— shipping, railways, electricity, and gas. In a Commission of five it is not possible to get every aspect of coal production and consumption represented; nor indeed do the members serve as representatives. But it is desirable that the members should have as wide an acquaintance as possible with the production and disposal of coal, in addition to being impartial judges on the questions before them, and from this point of view a better balanced Commission could hardly have been found. The exclusion of anyone with a financial interest in coal made it impossible to have a coal-owner or mine-owner on the Commission; and there was at the time some criticism that, in view of this limitation, a miners' official should have been included. But the exclusion was clearly desirable, and there is no evidence that any Commissioner has at any time approached his work in anything but a spirit of strict impartiality.

THE COMMISSIONERS' REMUNERATION

Highly qualified as the Commissioners were, neither they nor any other persons available should have been paid the fantastic remuneration offered for their services. It must ever remain one of the great paradoxes of British politics that a Labour Government should have offered such remuneration for work in the public service, even though that Government had only a minority following in the House of Commons and in the matter of the c.m.r.c. acted throughout "under instructions" from the Liberal group. Although the Commissioners had been appointed in December 1930, it was not until February 26, 1931, on a supplementary vote of £14,100 for the salaries and expenses of the Mines Department, that Mr. Shinwell announced that Sir Ernest Gowers, as full-time chairman, was to receive a salary of £7,000 per annum. Three of the Commissioners were to be paid for their part-time services at the rate of seven guineas a day, with a guaranteed minimum of a hundred days a year. One Commissioner, Mr. Shinwell stated, would not accept remuneration. His name has not been publicly disclosed, and it would be invidious to do so here.

The House was staggered by these figures, and not least those members who sat behind the Government. Sir Ernest Gowers, they recollected, was leaving a high post in the Civil Service bearing only £3,000 a year, and no one doubted that when the work of the c.m.r.c. came to an end he would be able to return to the Civil Service. Sir Ernest's superiors in his new post would be the Secretary for Mines, with a salary of only £1,500 a year, and the President of the Board of Trade, who received £5,000 a year, and their tenure of office was far more uncertain than the chairmanship of the c.m.r.c. Sir Ernest Gowers was certainly an outstanding figure in the Civil Service. Energetic, firm, easily approached, hard-working and conscientious, with a wide knowledge of the industry and a clear brain, he has abundantly justified his choice. But nothing can justify a salary of £7,000 a year for such a post, nor the remuneration offered to the part-time Commissioners; and in the debate Mr. Shinwell made it obvious that, while accepting responsibility for the proposals inasmuch as they came under his department's vote, they were thoroughly unpalatable to him.

Nevertheless the full force of criticism was not felt when the proposals were first announced. They were so surprising as to numb criticism, and it was then believed that Sir Ernest Gowers was surrendering pension rights for which he deserved compensation. Accordingly a Conservative amendment to reject the vote was lost by 156 votes to 96. The supplementary vote came up again on report on March 13, 1931. It was then made clear that Sir Ernest Gowers was not surrendering pension rights, and the Government's best defence was that the salaries, large as they were, amounted to a small fraction of the £250,000 a year which the Commission was expected to cost.[1] The House was in rebellious mood, and the supplementary estimate was carried by only five votes—173 to 168; the minority included a number of Labour members.

The staff of the c.m.r.c. includes the following officers at the salaries stated:

Secretary	£1,360 to £1,650 (with an allowance of £303)
Accountant and Establishment Officer	£900 to £1,000
Assistant Secretary	£634 to £738
Mining Engineer	£634 to £738

Mr. C. S. Hurst was seconded from the Mines Department for the key post of secretary. In his youth he had captained

---

[1] An explanation of this figure was given by the President of the Board of Trade (Mr. Graham) in moving the financial resolution for the Coal Mines Bill on January 28, 1930. He then expressed his belief that £250,000 would cover the remuneration of the Commissioners, subsistence and other allowances, and technical and other assistance, including valuers and other expert help. As the Mining Industry Act, 1920, placed a limit of £250,000 on the annual expenditure which the Mines Department might incur, it was necessary to make provision for the additional expenditure under the Bill. In practice, owing to the frustration of its work, the cost of the c.m.r.c. cannot have been anything like £250,000 a year; and this is borne out by the figures for the total expenditure of the Mines Department.

the Uppingham and Oxford cricket XI's, and had also played hockey for his University; to a smaller circle he was known as the very able secretary of the Samuel Commission. He and his staff took up their offices at 55 Broadway in the building made notorious by Mr. Epstein's sculptures, and the C.M.R.C. began to survey the ground.

EIGHTEEN MONTHS OF PERSUASION

The Commissioners on beginning their labours found "certain signposts" indicating the direction in which they should go.

One was that the Act implied a decision by Parliament that the coal-mining industry was to be reorganized by means of amalgamations. The second was that, as between the alternatives presented to us, common sense required us to "assist" amalgamations by stimulating the industry to make its own before we fell back on "promoting" them by trying to force upon it schemes devised by us. The third was that, so far as attempts to stimulate voluntary action might fail, we must not shrink from invoking the powers of compulsion that the Act provides.[1]

Accordingly the Commissioners spent eighteen months in studying the facts and in trying to evoke voluntary action. Sir Ernest Gowers got into touch with the chairmen of district colliery owners' associations, who arranged meetings with him in nineteen places. He dwelt on the need of the industry to deal with its over-production by a policy of elimination and concentration; urged the owners to frame their own schemes of amalgamation; offered to help in any way that he could; and pointed out that if there were no response the Commissioners would have no alternative but to use their compulsory powers.

In August 1931 the Commissioners issued a memorandum stating as their ultimate goal the division of the country

[1] Coal Mines Reorganization Commission, *Report to the Secretary for Mines* (1933, Cmd. 4468), p. 5.

*

into six great geographical units, in each of which there should be only one undertaking. It was perhaps a tactical mistake, even though they qualified it by saying that this goal could not everywhere be reached in one stride; that certain undertakings now in existence might be not worth bringing into an amalgamated concern; and that it might sometimes prove wiser to begin with amalgamation into smaller units. But it soon became clear that, whatever tactics the Commission employed, the mine-owners were not to be won over.

The Commissioners were disappointed with the results of this first move, and especially to find that areas where amalgamation had already been mooted were foci of particularly strong opposition. They found also a disposition "to regard the Commission merely as a temporary inconvenience which need not be taken too seriously."[1] As a second step the Commission visited each coalfield in a body during the autumn and winter of 1931-2 and invited the chairmen of all substantial colliery concerns to appear separately before them, with any of their colleagues and staff whom they pleased. They summarized the result in the following words:

> We talked across the table to over 800 people, representing about 450 undertakings responsible for nearly 95 per cent of the output of the country. Their courtesy and frankness towards us were unexceptionable, but on the whole they remained disappointing in their attitude towards our mission.[2]

At the same time a new difficulty presented itself. Many colliery-owners had presumed that a change of Government would mean the repeal of Part II of the 1930 Act, and when that change came in 1931 the Mining Association formally asked the Government to put an end to the Commission. The Commissioners' work was for long hindered by this uncertainty, but it was removed on May 31, 1932, when

---

[1] Loc. cit., p. 6.   [2] Loc. cit., p. 7.

the Attorney-General, speaking in the House of Commons, bade the Commission "take up the task that was committed to it by Parliament with energy, and a certainty that the Government not only hope, but intend that it should proceed with its task." Fortified with this assurance, the Commission sent out another communication to the industry in an attempt to dispel misunderstanding, and in particular repudiated "all idea of amalgamations that might result in the prosperous partners being saddled with the debts of those that had been less fortunate."

A "TWO-STOREY" STRUCTURE

In a speech before the Cardiff Business Club in February 1933, Sir Ernest Gowers gave a further exposition of the Commission's aims. He reaffirmed its view that an inferior scheme of reform carried out voluntarily was preferable to a superior scheme imposed compulsorily. The only reservation he made was that the Commission could not be content with a scheme that aimed at maintaining prices and no more. There also he adumbrated his celebrated conception of a "two-storey" building as the structure to be aimed at in the industry. The desirable structure, he indicated, was not so much the creation of great financial mergers as the formation of operating units of moderate size linked together in associations falling short of complete financial merger. The "ground floor" was thus to be built by "total" amalgamation, the "upper" floor by "partial" amalgamation. Operating units, brought where necessary to a desirable size by financial mergers, were to be associated for such purposes as control over development, co-ordinated selling, and concentration of production.

In March 1933 delegates from the Central Committee of the Mining Association sought an interview with the Commissioners, and argued that it would be impossible ever to establish before the Court a case for compulsory amalgamation. The proof of that thesis makes a second chapter in the history of the Commission.

COMPULSORY SCHEMES

While still "fanning an uncertain spark of voluntary effort,"[1] the Commissioners felt at length that they could no longer refrain from exercising the compulsory powers with which they were endowed, and which they were expected to use, by Parliament. They contemplated schemes of total amalgamation for Cannock Chase, Warwickshire, Fife, the Lothians, the Forest of Dean, Leicestershire, the south-west part of Lancashire, and the south-west part of Nottinghamshire and Derbyshire. In Durham, South Yorkshire, West Yorkshire, and Nottinghamshire and Derbyshire the Commission aimed in the first place at partial amalgamation of all the principal concerns, though it was not doubted that some measures of total amalgamation would sooner or later be necessary in these districts. In the case of South Wales the Commission was satisfied with the progress of voluntary amalgamation.

The Commission completed schemes of total amalgamation for the Lothians, South-West Lancashire, and the Forest of Dean. In no case was the scheme acceptable to the owners, but in the Lothians and South-West Lancashire voluntary co-operative schemes of central selling were prepared, and the Commissioners agreed to hold their own schemes in abeyance for the time being. The Forest of Dean, a small coalfield, was not regarded as suitable for a test case. Schemes of total amalgamation were also completed for Cannock Chase, Fife, and Warwickshire. The Commission began to prepare schemes for the south-west part of Nottinghamshire and Derbyshire, but decided not to proceed with total amalgamation in Leicestershire.

[1] Loc. cit., p. 3.

THE WEST YORKSHIRE SCHEME

Of the districts in which the Commissioners meant to begin with partial amalgamation. they found the greatest measure of support in West Yorkshire. A scheme had been drawn up by influential colliery-owners as an alternative to suggestions made by the Commission, and the Commissioners, in conformity with their general principles, substantially accepted this as their own. The scheme proposed machinery for co-operative action in selling, in the closing of redundant pits, in the purchase of stores, and in certain other matters. It was to comprise about sixty concerns, of which only four, accounting for about 12 per cent of the total production, opposed it. The Commission proposed to enforce the scheme compulsorily, and it was brought before the Railway and Canal Commission in May 1935. The Court rejected the scheme, both on its merits and in law, in a decision of the utmost importance for the future of the Commission.

The Court held that before confirming the scheme it had to be satisfied on five points. It had to be satisfied, in the first place, that the scheme was a partial amalgamation scheme within the meaning of Part 1 of the 1926 Act. It had to be satisfied, in the second place, on each of the four points specifically mentioned in section 13, sub-section 2 of the 1930 Act, which amended section 8, sub-section 2, of the 1926 Act, namely, that the scheme would be in the national interest, would result in lowering the cost of production or disposal of coal, would not be financially injurious to any of the undertakings, and would be fair and equitable to all persons affected thereby.

On all five points the Court found against the Commission. The paramount consideration was that the scheme did not constitute a scheme of amalgamation, even partial amalgamation, within the meaning of the 1926 Act. Mr. Justice MacKinnon, in giving judgment, said that amalgamation was not a term with a definite legal meaning. Basing himself on a judgment given in 1904 by Mr. Justice Buckley, he observed that in each case it had to be decided whether the transaction was such that, in the meaning of commercial men, it was comprehended in the term amalgamation. Still basing himself on the language of Mr. Justice Buckley, the learned judge decided that in amalgamation: "You must have the rolling together somehow or other of several concerns into one; you must weld those several concerns together and arrive at an amalgam, a blending together, of the constituent elements." He continued:

Now under this scheme, or so-called scheme, that has been put before us, there is no fusion or rolling together of any of these entities in any shape or form. Each entity is to remain entirely separate and distinct. Nor is there any creation of a new corporation which shall in any way own the shares or the undertakings of the separate entities. All that is proposed by the scheme is that an authority should be created which shall have powers to control the independent action of the various separate entities; that authority is ultimately the voting power of each of the separate entities by what is called the tonnage vote, but subject in every case, and as regards the decision of every single piece of proposed business, to the decision of an arbitrator. It is true that section 4 of the 1926 Act says that a scheme may provide for the constitution of a joint committee for the joint exercise of the powers or conduct of the business or operations with certain results; but I think the whole of that section is to be read together. That contemplates that part of the machinery of a partial amalgamation scheme may be the constitution of a joint committee. I cannot agree, however, that directly you provide for a joint committee as controlling the affairs of various separate entities, you thereby create a partial amalgamation scheme. The Act only provides that if there is a partial amalgamation scheme its terms may provide for the constitution of a joint committee. Such a scheme must, within the meaning of the Act, be a partial amalgamation scheme before the propriety of its machinery falls to be considered at all.[1]

[1] Coal Mines Reorganization Commission, *Report to the Secretary for Mines,* January 13, 1936 (Cmd. 5069), pp. 8–9.

The procedure contemplated in the scheme for committees whose decisions might always go to arbitration made it impossible for the Court to satisfy itself that, in fact, the scheme would be in the national interest, or comply with the other requirements of the 1930 Act. As these points are subordinate to the main issue, we need quote only a single sentence from the judgment given by Sir Francis Taylor. He observed: "It is in the national interest that inefficient or uneconomic coalmines, or even undertakings, should be closed down,"[1] and he noticed that he could find no provision (or no express provision) of that kind in the proposed scheme. Clearly the contention of the Mining Association, which would have a good deal of support among the workers, that it is in the national interest to spread unemployment geographically, could not be maintained at law.

The Court's decision placed the Coal Commissioners in a dilemma. They took the result to mean that no scheme could be imposed compulsorily which did not provide for some financial merger of the constituent concerns; for otherwise it would not be regarded by the Court as a scheme of amalgamation at all. On the other hand, the Commissioners did not see how a scheme which provided for a financial merger could be made to satisfy the Court. How, in particular, could they satisfy the Court that it would "not be financially injurious to any of the undertakings proposed to be amalgamated"?

The Court's decision suggests that the distinction between "total" and "partial" amalgamation cannot be made; that, in fact, "partial" amalgamation is a contradiction in terms. It meant that the Commissioners had to change their plans in the important districts of Durham, South and West Yorkshire, and Nottinghamshire and Derbyshire. They revoked the notices given in those districts and were beginning to make inquiries with a view to compulsory schemes of total amalgamation, when the Secretary for Mines

[1] Loc. cit., p. 11.

(Captain Crookshank) asked them, on July 28, 1935, to refrain from initiating any fresh inquiries pending consideration by the Government of the whole position and powers of the Commission.

A NEW BILL

In February 1936, legislation to give the Commission the powers which Parliament intended it should possess was promised. The text of the proposed legislation was published on May 6 as the Coal Mines Bill, 1936. Under this Bill the first three sub-sections of section 13 of the 1930 Act[1] were to be repealed, so that henceforth it would not be required to be proved that an amalgamation scheme would result in lowering the cost of production or disposal and would not be financially injurious to any of the undertakings to be amalgamated. The Bill laid down the following procedure for the Commission in preparing schemes of amalgamation:

(*a*) Firstly, a scheme for submission to the Board of Trade (hereinafter referred to as a "reorganization scheme") providing for the formation of a company (hereinafter referred to as the "transferee company"), and for the transfer to that company of such property of the owner of every undertaking or part of an undertaking to be amalgamated (hereinafter referred to as a "transferor company") as may be provided by the scheme; and

(*b*) Secondly, as soon as may be after an order approving any reorganization scheme has been made by the Board of Trade under this Act, a scheme in connexion therewith (hereinafter referred to as a "participation scheme") making provision for securing that the amalgamation effected by the reorganization scheme will be carried out upon terms and conditions that are fair and equitable to all persons affected thereby and will enable the undertaking of the transferee company to be efficiently carried on with due regard to the interests of all such persons.

Under the Bill the C.M.R.C. was obliged to inquire into any non-frivolous objection to a reorganization scheme,

[1] The first two sections are quoted *supra*, pp. 227-8.

and empowered to make modifications after such inquiry. The scheme, with any modifications, was then to be submitted to the Board of Trade, along with all objections not withdrawn. The Board of Trade might themselves modify the scheme, and then lay before Parliament the scheme and a draft order approving it. Unless within twenty-one parliamentary days either House resolved that the scheme ought not to be approved, the Board was authorized to make the order of approval. The C.M.R.C. was then required to frame details of the necessary "participation scheme." The division of schemes was a convenient way of ensuring that the C.M.R.C. did not draw up elaborate financial plans until the principle of the amalgamation had been approved.

It will be seen that under this Bill the Railway and Canal Commission disappeared from the procedure. Colliery undertakings to be amalgamated could protest to the Board of Trade, but the mine-owners felt that the C.M.R.C. was itself a branch of the Board of Trade. There was the possibility of obstruction in Parliament, but its success would depend on the attitude adopted by the Government of the day and their Whips. No provision was made for appeal to the Courts[1] against a reorganization scheme save on the ground that it was *ultra vires*; legal appeal was to be allowed against a participation scheme on the ground of being unfair or inequitable.

GOVERNMENT YIELD TO MINE-OWNERS

Although the Courts might be greatly perplexed to know what is fair and equitable, it does appear that this Bill would have given to the C.M.R.C. those powers which Parliament in 1930 intended it to possess. So apparently the coal-owners thought, for at once they raised a violent agitation against the Bill. Two-column advertisements were published in the newspapers, a deputation waited on the

---

[1] The High Court in England, the Court of Session in Scotland.

Secretary for Mines (and came away satisfied), fierce lobbying was undertaken, and when the President of the Board of Trade (Mr. Runciman) moved the second reading on May 19 he announced that the Government would propose three amendments in committee:

(1) The new compulsory powers were not to take effect until July 1, 1938.
(2) Coalmines ancillary to undertakings not primarily engaged in the production or treatment of coal[1] were not to be included in any compulsory amalgamation schemes.
(3) Instead of inquiry by the Commission, or by someone appointed by the Commission, "an independent, impartial authority" was to be set up to hear objections.

At once the Opposition protested that these proposed amendments altered the character of the Bill, and that to give it a second reading would be a farce. Government supporters joined in the protest, and eventually the Government dropped the second reading, with a promise to issue a White Paper explaining the changes and to reintroduce the Bill in the autumn. This capitulation by a Government commanding an enormous majority in the Commons, and assured of the support of the Lords, to a section of employers is one of the sorriest chapters in the annals of Parliament. And though the autumn has made way for winter (December 1936) there is as yet no sign of a revival of the Bill, even in its emasculated form.

So the situation remains for the time being, and it does not yet appear how the Government intends to give the Commission real powers. The mistake which has been made in dealing with the Commission is to treat it and the coalowners as two opposed bodies between whom arbitration (in the form of appeal) is desirable. The plain fact is that the necessity for amalgamation of coalmines was proved

---

[1] E.g. iron and steel works. By the Coal Mines Act, 1930, such coalmines could not be included in schemes of compulsory amalgamation. The Coal Mines Bill, 1936, as unamended, would have permitted this because the provision of the 1930 Act was repealed.

years ago, at least as far back as the Samuel Commission; and the C.M.R.C. is the body appointed to give effect to the community's will for amalgamation. It is in effect a branch of the Civil Service[1] appointed to carry out the declared will of Parliament, and it should be under no necessity to prove its case before the Courts (except to rebut a contention that it is acting *ultra vires*).

In fact, the C.M.R.C. has been successfully obstructed at every turn by the mine-owners. It may be asked why the mine-owners are in general so bitterly opposed to amalgamation. If amalgamation is economically desirable, why do not the mine-owners recognize it, for surely they would stand to gain?

RESISTANCE A POINT OF PRINCIPLE

A prime reason is that resistance to amalgamation, and especially to amalgamation under the compulsory powers of the C.M.R.C., has become a matter of principle. The mine-owners have long been noted as the most individualistic of employers, and they are reluctant to believe that methods which were good enough to build the British coal trade are not good enough to preserve it. They are in general a body of hard, unyielding men, whose inherent individualism has solidified into a rock-like tenacity under pressure from the C.M.R.C. and public opinion. Resistance to the C.M.R.C. has become a watchword and a shibboleth.

Psychology will account for much, and economics for the rest. The efficient concerns do not think amalgamation desirable. They have a haunting fear of having to carry the burdens of the weak undertakings, a fear which the C.M.R.C. has tried in vain to dispel. Colliery-owners have long obeyed, without complaint, the law of the economic jungle, and what the strong concerns would like to see is the liquidation

---

[1] The Commissioners are not, of course, civil servants in the strict sense of the term, though commonly so called in controversy.

of the weak undertakings, whose markets they would then absorb. But it has already been shown how Part 1 of the 1930 Act tends to keep these inefficient undertakings in existence, and here indeed is one of the main reasons for the creation of the c.m.r.c.

THE CONDITIONS FOR AMALGAMATION

A big stumbling-block to the Commission's work has been the obligation to prove that schemes of amalgamation are

(i) in the national interest;
(ii) will result in lowering the cost of production or disposal of coal;
(iii) will not be financially injurious to any of the undertakings to be amalgamated.

On the surface, these may appear to be not unreasonable conditions. The first is, indeed, so vague that it need not in itself cause much difficulty. The second may be difficult to *prove* in a particular case, though it is easy to demonstrate as a general rule that the amalgamation of mines, concentration of production, and closing of redundant pits will lead to a lowering of the cost of production, provided only that excessive compensation is not paid for the pits to be closed. The third condition is perhaps the most serious. For amalgamation may very well injure one or more of the amalgamated undertakings, either because they are weak and are now enjoying a bounty under the 1930 Act, or because they are strong and may have to help in carrying the weaker brethren. To require amalgamation to fulfil all these conditions is impossible; it is to ask to eat one's cake and yet have it.

These conditions cannot, in fact, be fulfilled, and are not in general fulfilled in voluntary schemes of amalgamation, whether of coalmines or of any other industrial undertakings. It is easy to show, and it is shown in this essay, that as a general rule such schemes of amalgamation will fulfil the conditions, but to *prove* this in a particular case is quite another matter. When the owners of two or more coalmines agree to amalgamate them, they would be rash to assert categorically that the fusion will result in lowering the cost of production of coal and will not be injurious to any of the undertakings amalgamated; they may hope that such will be the case, and on the evidence before them they may believe that it will indeed be so, but any scheme of amalgamation must to some extent be a gamble or, if the metaphor be preferred, an act of faith. The conditions for amalgamation inserted in the Coal Mines Act, 1930, have therefore had the effect of completely frustrating the will of Parliament that amalgamations be effected, if necessary by compulsion. Though the Government of the day resented these conditions as limiting the discretion of the Court, there is no evidence that it realized the full power of obstruction contained in them. If the mine-owning peers did recognize this, they must be congratulated on their prescience, for no subtler weapon could have been devised with which to ward off the Commission from its task.

UNIFICATION OF ROYALTIES

When the Government returns to the question of the c.m.r.c., the problem of royalties will also have to be taken into account. The Government's election manifesto stated: "We have further decided to effect the unification of coal-mining royalties, a step which will enable greater progress to be made with the organization of production and thus improve the efficiency of the industry." To quote the Samuel Report,[1] in advocating such a step, "it will be necessary to establish an authority which will act on behalf of the State in acquiring and administering the valuable property which will come into national ownership." The

[1] P. 83.

report proposed the appointment of a body, to be entitled the Coal Commissioners, in whom would be vested the ownership and administration of the property. Those Commissioners now exist in the c.m.r.c., and this body should have the administration of the nationalized royalties. It will perform for the State the necessary task of collecting royalty payments as they fall due, and its special task of bringing about amalgamations will be greatly facilitated through its powers as universal lessor of the coal. For instance, it could refuse to renew leases as they fall due unless its requirements in the matter of amalgamation were met.

Armed with this weapon, the c.m.r.c. could make rapid progress in its task of facilitating amalgamations, and within a reasonable time each district might be brought under unified control. It would then be fairly easy, through the existing machinery of a Central Council and District Executive Boards, strengthened and improved, to bring the whole industry into public ownership and to run it in the public interest.

8

THE AGRICULTURAL
MARKETING BOARDS

by

W. H. JONES

A BRIEF review of the position of British agriculture in the post-war period will indicate the circumstances in which the marketing boards came into existence. The repeal of the Agriculture Act in 1921 marked the beginning of a period in which the policy of limited interference in agriculture was adopted. Farmers were at the time disappointed and to some extent disheartened; they had been promised guaranteed prices for certain products and an assurance that returns would be related to costs of production. They had also been promised additional security of tenure. To add to the difficulties a rather severe fall in the prices of agricultural commodities began about this time. Between 1921 and 1924 there was much real distress in the industry: the value of farm produce was rapidly declining, whereas costs of production remained comparatively high. Further, a large number of farmers had purchased their holdings either during the war or in the years that followed, and had paid rather high prices for them; at that time interest rates were high and many of the new owner-occupiers were burdened with high if not exorbitant charges on heavy mortgages. It was also contended that the margins between wholesale and retail prices of agricultural products were in some cases unduly inflated. Middlemen were accused of retaining too high a proportion of the price paid by consumers for their food. Farmers in the main were obliged to meet the situation as best they could; there was a tendency to move away from the most risky undertakings, especially those in which capital was turned over somewhat slowly.

A decline in the number of persons engaged in agriculture in England and Wales occurred each year between 1921 and 1931 with one exception, i.e. 1924. It is calculated that there were 869,000 employees engaged in the industry in 1921, together with 840,000 persons interested as occupiers of farms or close relatives of occupiers, which gave a total of 1,709,000 individuals. By 1932 the number of employees had fallen to 697,000 and the number of others to 780,000; the total therefore only stood at 1,477,000—a reduction of 232,000 in the course of eleven years, or an average decline of over 21,000 persons a year. The re-establishment of the agricultural wages boards, however, in 1924, probably served to maintain wages during the years that followed at a higher level than would otherwise have been the case. It was realized, of course, that in pre-war years general rates of wages, and between 1922 and 1924 those in some counties, had been extremely low, and it was desirable to prevent a further relapse even if the policy resulted in a slight acceleration of migration.

The general decline of prices between 1921 and 1931 can be seen from column 1 of the Table opposite, and it is not difficult to realize that during this decade the industry was severely handicapped by this movement. Other columns of the Table show the movements in prices of some commodities for which Marketing Schemes were established at a later date.

In 1923 a Committee was set up, under the chairmanship of Lord Linlithgow, to inquire into the methods and costs of selling and distributing agricultural, horticultural, and dairy produce in Great Britain, and to consider whether, and if so by what means, the disparity between the price received by the producer and that paid by the consumer could be diminished. The Committee was led to the conclusion that the spread between producers' and consumers' prices was unjustifiably wide and that distribution costs were a far heavier burden than society would permanently consent to bear. The view was recorded that individual traders and groups of traders were in some cases making higher profits than was warranted by the services they performed. It was also pointed out that there were too many profit-making agencies engaged in the process of distribution. Public interest, it was stated, demanded a far more determined effort on the part of all concerned

INDEX NUMBERS OF PRICES. 1911–13 = 100

Year	All Agricultural Commodities (1)	Wheat (2)	Milk (3)	Bacon Pigs (4)	Potatoes (5)	Hops (6)
1921	219	219	263	220	232	211
1922	169	146	179	180	189	123
1923	157	130	174	157	113	152
1924	161	152	170	133	257	102
1925	159	160	170	163	204	114
1926	151	164	170	180	151	126
1927	144	152	160	144	174	137
1928	147	132	161	135	171	126
1929	144	130	169	160	117	51
1930	134	105	162	154	106	47
1931	120	76	147	107	188	105
1932	112	78	144	91	197	99
1933	107	70	150	102	104	173
1934	114	64	163	112	119	101
1935	117	68	176	103	133	105

to bring about reform and to increase the efficiency of the marketing and distributive machinery. Further, the Committee declared that it was necessary for producers to give greater attention to the conditions governing the marketing, transport, and sale of their produce, as it was clear that most farmers had little knowledge of the working of the distributive system.

In the final report of the Agricultural Tribunal of Investigation[1] the majority state that "Nothing stands out more markedly in a comparsion of British and foreign agriculture

[1] Cmd. No. 2145.

than the backwardness of co-operation in this country. Rapid strides have been made and are being made in the British oversea dominions, but in England, Scotland, and Wales headway has been relatively slow."

The State had rendered assistance to the agricultural co-operative movement for several years, but particularly from 1917 onwards, and considerable efforts were made in this country to encourage farmers to market their produce on co-operative lines, but only a limited degree of success was achieved. The total contribution made by co-operative movements towards the solution of the problem of marketing farm products in the decade that followed the close of the war cannot be regarded as very important as it did not affect the situation to any appreciable extent. In Ireland, however, the co-operative movement had attained a reasonable degree of success. From the close of last century up to the present time great strides have been made; the success achieved in that country of course was to a large extent due to the work of Sir Horace Plunkett. The problem of selling agricultural produce and of buying farmers' requirements have been tackled and recent reports indicate that the movement is showing continued growth. In both Scotland and Wales results of a somewhat similar character have been obtained. Farmers have realized the advantages of joint effort and definite progress has been made in recent years. Each of the four countries[1] now has its own Agricultural Organization Society, and in each case a large proportion of the financial support is obtained from affiliated societies.

DEVELOPMENT OVERSEAS

From 1921 onwards there were important developments in oversea countries with regard to the production and marketing of food, and these had some very serious effects

[1] Saorstaat Eirean, Northern Ireland, Scotland, and Wales.

upon the prices of foodstuffs at home. In most of the countries from which we obtained our food supplies, active attempts were being made to improve the quality of the product placed on the British market. In fact, the advance made in this direction put oversea products in a highly competitive position. Detailed studies were being made of the requirements of the British market, prices were frequently more favourable than those of the home-produced article, and it was clear that the British public was in most cases supplied with a good article from abroad, and in some instances a taste for it was gradually being acquired. The rise of the Grain Pools in America is of importance in this connection; in 1920 the first wheat pool was organized in the United States of America; this was followed by others. This development of wheat pools on a voluntary basis after 1920 enabled the American grain crops to be marketed comparatively quickly, and it was stated at the time that, in consequence, prices for a period became unduly depressed. Nevertheless, remarkable progress was made towards what appeared to be a solution of the wheat marketing problem, and it was realized that a high degree of control of the industry was essential before success could be attained. A form of contract with farmers was later evolved providing, *inter alia*, for the grower to deliver to the organization all the wheat grown by him, except that kept for seed. All grain of similar grade was then pooled and producers received the same basic price for an article of similar quality. A system of this kind was in direct contrast with that commonly found in this country. In Britain each farmer sold his own wheat as best he could to the agent or corn merchant. It was difficult for the home producer, unorganized as he was, to stand in competition with the oversea supplier. The latter also possessed many advantages not only in marketing but also in the production of grain, and as a result, it is not surprising to find that there was a definite movement away from wheat production in this country. Farmers turned to other systems of farming, but in many cases home products came into keen competition with oversea supplies.

The slump in prices of meat after 1920 was a very serious matter to the New Zealand exporters; at the time large quantities of meat were lying in store and buyers in this country were reluctant to enter into contracts. The Meat (Export) Control Act was passed by the New Zealand Government in 1922 and the Meat Export Control Board came into being. The Board were given the fullest powers to regulate exports, including the right to take over the whole organization for marketing New Zealand meat in any importing country. Expenses were provided from the proceeds of a levy on meat exported. The Board have used their powers in several ways—including the control of grading and methods of shipment, negotiations of freight rates, advertisement, and in other directions they have attempted to safeguard the interests of producers. Such activities, particularly those regarding the regulation of shipments, had an appreciable effect upon the trade in this country, and again the unorganized home farmers suffered.

In Australia the Meat Council was established in 1922; its tasks included a review of the huge livestock industry of the Continent and a study of producers' interests; it aimed at improving the quality of the products sold by supervising the breeding and grading of stock; it also did much work in seeking better markets for Australian meat in other countries.

In South America, meat companies of great influence and strength have recently acquired a high degree of control. There has been amalgamation into large-scale units, and this has undoubtedly been conducive to efficiency in processing and distribution. Representatives of these large companies meet periodically to discuss matters connected with the trade, and the power exercised by these voluntary organizations has placed the chilled beef trade in a very strong if not in an unassailable position.

In the dairy produce trade also farmers in this country have been confronted with powerful organizations abroad, and in the case of butter and cheese the prices of the home product have been very largely determined by those of the imported articles. In Denmark the co-operative movement has become highly efficient; in the post-war years that country has, in fact, supplied us with about one-third of our butter requirements. Under Danish law strict State control of the methods of producing, processing, and selling butter is maintained, and care is taken to supply the British market in an orderly manner. New Zealand butter also became a serious competitor in the British market in the post-war years, especially after the Dairy Produce Control Board was set up; this body possesses important powers, including the control and direction of the export industry.

DEVELOPMENT OF UNION ORGANIZATION

Between 1919 and 1929, therefore, certain developments occurred which had far-reaching consequences upon British agriculture. The trade in foodstuffs obtained from other countries was closely studied and carefully guarded by powerful groups of producers and traders, and these were often aided by the Governments of the countries concerned. Supplies were arriving in this country in increasing quantities, the quality was improving, prices were often relatively favourable, and competition with our own products was often intense. The home industry, on the other hand, was largely unorganized, most farmers were pursuing their own methods irrespective of the interests of others, marketing was in the hands of a multitude of dealers and wholesalers, and only in a few cases was any voluntary attempt made to control the work of marketing.

The interests of farmers in this country have been guarded to some extent in recent years by the National Farmers' Union. The Union is essentially a trade union, and definite business activity, such as buying or selling, is outside its scope. As the Union, however, only includes a minority of the farmers, its effects are only indirectly felt.

Some new form of organization in this country was obviously necessary to meet the changed conditions of competition in the markets for foodstuffs, and the Agricultural Marketing Acts have now enabled British producers to combine in order to improve their methods of marketing. By the establishment of Marketing Boards it was expected that farmers would be in a better position to stand in competition with other organized groups in the field. One of the conspicuous weaknesses of the voluntary marketing organizations, commenced in the post-war years, was the intractable minority. A small proportion of those interested in a movement would often stand aside and leave to others all the responsibilities, and, when some important rules could be disregarded with impunity, unity of action was impossible.

The Agricultural Marketing Act, 1931, is an enabling measure. It enables the producers of any agricultural product[1] to organize themselves for group action, and when a board is set up to administer a marketing scheme it becomes incumbent on all the producers of the article in the area concerned to comply with the regulations in force in so far as they have not been exempted therefrom.

A Marketing Board set up under the 1931 Act exercises jurisdiction only over commodities produced within the area of the scheme, which might be a small area or the whole of Great Britain. Later it was realized that in the case of several foodstuffs, especially those which suffered

[1] Agricultural products include any product of agriculture or horticulture and any article of food or drink wholly or partly manufactured or derived from any such product.

from overseas competition, reorganization at home would be difficult if not ineffective unless imports were also controlled to some extent. In 1933, therefore, the second Marketing Act was passed. Powers are provided in this Act to enable the Board of Trade, after consultation with the Minister of Agriculture and with the Secretaries of State concerned with agriculture in Scotland and Northern Ireland respectively, to regulate the importation into the United Kingdom of any agricultural product if it appears that there have been or are being taken practicable and necessary steps for the efficient reorganization by means of agricultural marketing schemes of that branch of the agricultural industry in whose interest the regulation is made. The 1933 Act also makes provision for the compulsory regulation of sales of a home-produced commodity. If the importation of the commodity is controlled, and it appears to the Minister of Agriculture and the Secretaries of State concerned that regulation will conduce to the efficient reorganization of a particular branch of agriculture or is necessary to secure its economic stability, such regulation may be secured by Order. The compulsory regulation of sales of a home-produced commodity is therefore dependent upon restriction of imports.

Schemes in force when any change of government occurs will remain and their operation must continue. Tariffs and quota systems may be modified or removed very quickly, much more quickly in practice than the schemes themselves. The tariffs or quotas may be made dependent on schemes, and in theory schemes may be made dependent on the existence of tariffs or quotas, although it is important to notice that the former is the present position. But whatever the theory may be, in practice the existence and operation of some schemes cannot be made entirely dependent on the existence of tariffs or quotas. Wherever the operation of a scheme supersedes the organization which existed for the conduct of a particular trade and the scheme is operated long enough to make effective removal of that organization, it is almost impossible to contemplate the possibility of ceasing to operate an organized scheme. Cessation of operations would lead to chaos, and would make necessary the building up of another form of organization for that particular branch of marketing.

Moreover, in so far as regulation of imports is obtained by the quota method, it is of great importance to realize that the organization of imported produce will be very greatly strengthened under this plan. With the existence of a strengthened organization for exporting or for importing, the imported produce would be a source of special danger in the event of disorganization of the home supply through any existing marketing scheme ceasing to operate. Close organization of imports will be almost sufficient of itself to require equal organization of the home supply.

Some of the objects visualized in these movements included the regulation of marketing so that the home-produced supply could flow in a more orderly manner towards consumers, the control of quality, and the stimulation of improvement in quality. The exercise of some control over conditions of sale so that producers could command a larger proportion of the money paid by consumers for their food was also contemplated. Home producers, by effective combinations, would be placed in a better position to stand the competition of other organized groups. The weakness of the existing system was particularly obvious, and the prevailing conditions had proved disastrous to producers, and might ultimately have proved injurious even to consumers.

The method of control is fully representative of producers, since before a scheme can come into force there must be a poll in which all the producers who are affected by it are entitled to vote. Moreover, the majority of the members of the Board, which is the body entrusted with the administration of the scheme, is composed of elected representatives of the producers. Yet to confine the membership almost entirely to producers seems unjust, as the Boards exercise jurisdiction over a wide field and must take cognizance of both distributors' and consumers' interest.

THE BOARDS AND THEIR POWERS

Schemes are now in operation for the marketing of milk, bacon, pigs, potatoes, and hops. These have now been in operation for about three years. There is a good deal of variation in the powers exercised by the several Boards. As they all operate on a commodity basis, it is for the committee preparing the scheme to select those powers which are required to meet the needs of a particular case. The 1931 Act being an enabling measure, as it was drafted with a view to meeting the needs of marketing a variety of agricultural products, made provision for a broad array of powers.

Except where a farmer is concerned only, or mainly, with one commodity, no single scheme will embrace all his interests in the sale of produce. But amongst the dairy farmers of the country there is a considerable proportion whose sole or main interests lie in the production and sale of milk. The degree, however, to which any scheme absorbs all the producer's interests in the sale of produce will vary from one scheme to another, but many farmers may find themselves included in several schemes, and some may, therefore, find all their selling interests covered.

It has appeared, in fact, that some English farmers may soon be in much the same position as the Danish producer, who is a member of several co-operative societies, including a dairy, a bacon factory, an egg depot, and a requirement store. Some British farmers may now find themselves "registered producers" under the milk, pigs, and potato schemes if they are producers of these commodities, and also members of a requirements co-operative society. In such cases all their major economic interests except those

I

arising from renting land and employing labour would be covered.

The main powers which a board may acquire are wide and far reaching, and can be conveniently stated as follows:

(1) A board may buy all the product over which it has jurisdiction, and may sell, grade, pack, store, adapt for sale, insure, advertise, and transport the commodity.
(2) A board may require the producers to sell any kind, variety, grade, or quantity of the product only to or through the agency of the Board.
(3) A board may be empowered to buy and to sell or let for hire to producers anything required for the production, adaptation for sale, or sale of the product.
(4) A board may determine the price at, below or above which the terms on which, and the persons to, or through the agency of whom, the product may be sold.

A board may be equipped with all or only some of these powers; in fact, three rather different types of organizations can be set up under the Acts. In the first place, a trading body may be established, i.e. a body acting as the sole agent for the sale of the product handled. The second kind of organization possible is a regulatory body (in other words, a trade union with powers of compulsion); this body would undertake no trading itself and would limit its functions to the issue of instructions regarding the methods and operations connected with the marketing of the article. The latter type of organization has been common in the dominions, and under certain circumstances it may be effectively introduced in this country. The third type of marketing authority envisaged is a body exercising both trading and regulatory functions to a varying extent.

SAFEGUARDS

The granting of such important powers to producers' organizations is a serious matter, and the provision of safeguards against their possible misuse is obviously necessary.

Once a scheme comes into operation the rules made by the Board are binding on all non-exempt producers; safeguards are provided, therefore, first in the interests of producers. Every scheme must include provision to enable an aggrieved producer to refer a matter in dispute to arbitration. The Minister of Agriculture may also refer to a Committee of Investigation any complaint made to him regarding the operation of a scheme, and the Minister and Parliament have the statutory power to secure the rectification of the matter in complaint on the recommendation of the Committee of Investigation.

Special arrangements are also made to guard the interests of consumers. The Minister of Agriculture was required to appoint a Consumers' Committee immediately the first scheme came into operation. The duty of this committee is to consider and report to the Minister the effects that any schemes in force have upon consumers and on any complaints which may be made to the committee regarding either the schemes themselves or consumers' interests as affected by the schemes. This committee, therefore, watches, in a general way, the operations of the various schemes from the consumers' standpoint. Reports of the Consumers' Committee are submitted to the Minister, who in case of serious complaint must refer them to the Committee of Investigation. On receipt of a report from the Investigation Committee the Minister of Agriculture is obliged to act in one of certain ways. If the committee report that any act or omission of a board is contrary to the interests of consumers of the regulated product or of any other persons affected by the scheme and is not in the public interest, the Minister may require the Board administering the scheme to rectify the matter, or, after consulting the Board of Trade, he may lay before each House of Parliament a draft of an Order which includes such amendments in the scheme as he considers necessary for the purpose of rectifying the matter, or he may in the same way proceed to revoke the scheme.

Provision is also made in the first Act to meet the situation where a number of producers feel that a scheme is contrary to their interests. It is possible for them to take joint action and to move for its amendment or revocation. This involves a poll of producers, and if the result shows that the majority favour the discontinuance of a scheme, it ceases to function. But, of course, a board administering a scheme is not deemed to be dissolved by reason only that the scheme has been revoked, and so much of the scheme as relates to its winding up continues. In the case of revocation of a scheme, however, a chaotic state of affairs might result, as part of the machinery available for the distribution of certain commodities would disappear. Provision is therefore made in the 1933 Act to enable the Minister of Agriculture and the Secretaries of State concerned with agriculture in Scotland and Northern Ireland to impose by Order certain regulatory measures upon the producers of any agricultural commodity in cases where the importation of the commodity is regulated.

THE MILK MARKETING BOARD

Powers to function as a trading organization have been acquired by the Milk Marketing Board; but chiefly this body constitutes itself as a party to all contracts relating to the sale of milk, and distributors of milk cannot legally obtain supplies except through the Board. In this way the Board have secured complete control over supplies, as they are in a position to determine the description of milk, the prices (after the first year of operation), and the terms on which milk may be sold. In addition, they may acquire premises for the manufacture of dairy products. In fact, the Milk Marketing Board is now the only medium between producers and distributors, and in consequence it occupies a highly responsible position.[1]

[1] For a full description of the work of the Milk Marketing Board see the Report of the Milk Reorganization Committee for Great Britain, Ministry of Agriculture, Economic Series No. 44, 1936.

Under the Milk Marketing Scheme, England and Wales is divided into eleven regions, and in each region producers of milk receive a "pool" price which is arrived at by distributing among them the total proceeds of the sale of milk (after certain small adjustments) in proportion to the quantity of milk sold by each. Since the inception of the scheme several methods have been adopted to fix the price of milk; between October 1933, when the scheme came into force, and September 1934 the prices paid to the Board by wholesalers and retailers were fixed by a group of independent persons appointed for the purpose by the Minister of Agriculture.

During the first six months of the operation of the scheme, i.e. the first contract period, a clause was inserted in the contracts to the effect that the price at which milk could be retailed should not be below the prevailing retail price in the district. The "prevailing retail prices" were not specified and districts were not defined; actual prices were, therefore, left to be settled by retailers in each district. There was, however, a great deal of variation in retail prices, apparently without sufficient reason, and in general the system proved unsatisfactory. At the end of the first six months of operation the Consumers' Committee reported to the Minister that they did not accept the principle of fixing retail prices as a corollary of fixing wholesale prices. They appreciated, however, the difficulties involved in working a scheme which did not contain some provision for controlling retail prices. They suggested, therefore, that instead of fixing prices at the consumers' end, the minimum permissible margin over the wholesale price should be determined. At the same time distributors were to be allowed a reasonable return in cases where the work was done economically and efficiently. In the second six months of the Board's activity provision was made for establishing minimum "appropriate retail" prices; these were defined as prices exceeding the wholesale price by not less than a definite margin, which varied from 8d. a gallon in rural areas to 10d. a gallon in cities.

During subsequent years minimum retail prices have been fixed by the Board for different districts according to the size of their populations. Higher prices have been prescribed for the larger cities than for the smaller towns. Subsequent to April 1934 an important clause has been included in the contracts to the effect that the Board could reduce the minimum permissible prices in any district if retailers in the area recommended a reduction. The Board have already sanctioned price reductions in many districts. The Consumers' Committee have been watching the situation carefully, but in the absence of adequate data relating to the costs and profits of milk distribution some difficulty has been experienced in judging the adequacy or otherwise of the margins permitted to distributors.

Some of the main objects of reorganizing the milk industry included the strengthening of the producers' position in order to enable them to negotiate with distributors as a solid body and to ensure that the agreements made were universally observed. Before the advent of the scheme many producers were obliged to accept prices below the costs of production. Now a large proportion of producers, particularly those situated at some distance from consuming centres, are receiving far more remunerative prices than was formerly the case. In fact, the returns from sale of milk appear more favourable than those obtainable from several other branches of farming; in consequence, large numbers of farmers have turned to it. The organization has resulted in a considerable increase in the quantity of milk offered for sale in this country.

Milk used for manufacturing into dairy products commands only a comparatively low price, and the larger the proportion of the whole that is used for this purpose the smaller will be the return to producers. The movement for increasing the sale of milk to school children has, however, proved reasonably successful, but large numbers of children are still without supplies. The Board are also making strenuous efforts to improve the quality of milk in the country. As from May 1935 producers whose methods of production and quality of milk reach certain standards receive higher prices.

It is seen that the Board have been active in certain respects; they have of course endeavoured to improve the position of producers by enabling them to obtain prices that are at least better than those which prevailed before; they have also introduced measures to improve the quality of the supply. They have also endeavoured to arrange prices so that distributors can command profits in proportion to the efficiency of their businesses and to the nature of the services which they render. Very little, however, has been achieved in stimulating the demand for milk, and large numbers of people are still unable to obtain adequate supplies, although the quantity produced has shown an appreciable increase.

Official complaints, however, regarding the operation of the scheme have not been numerous. Apart from the reports of the Consumers' Committee mentioned above, the Committee of Investigation reported in 1934 on two complaints submitted to them. The first came from the National Association of Creamery Proprietors and the second from the Amalgamated Master Dairymen Ltd. Both complaints, however, dealt with the relations between the Board and members of the manufacturing and distributive trades.

In September 1935 the Board made fuller use of the powers they possessed; the prices at which milk was available to the distributive trade for the year 1935-6 were prescribed by the Board on their own responsibility. The Board were determined to obtain better returns for producers, and at the same time it was recognized that retail prices could not be advanced; to achieve this end, therefore, distributors' margins had to be curtailed. The Central Milk

Distributive Committee immediately lodged a complaint against the operation of the Milk Marketing Scheme, and this was referred to the Committee of Investigation. After an exhaustive inquiry into all the relevant aspects of the problem, including the costs of milk production and of distribution, a report was issued in April 1936. The Committee found *inter alia* that the wholesale price of milk as prescribed by the Board was too high, and was contrary to the interests of purchasers of milk by wholesale, and also not in the public interest. They also recommended that no increase should be made in the scale of minimum retail prices.

THE HOPS MARKETING BOARD

The other trading body now in existence is the Hops Marketing Board; this body came into operation in September 1932. Certain important amendments were incorporated in the scheme in 1934, with the result that the Hops Marketing Board have acquired powers which give them very wide jurisdiction over both the production and marketing of hops, and very close control is now exercised over the industry. Each producer is allotted a certain basic quota, which is related to the annual average quantity of hops picked on the farm during the five years 1928 to 1932. The Board also estimate the total effective demand for English hops during each season, and the quantity so determined is taken to be the "market requirement." The quantity to be sold by the producers under the quota is then related to the "market demand."

In proportion as any hop-grower's production quota stands to all production quotas, so shall his selling quota be to the total "market demand" for English hops. If in any season the "market demand" falls short of the total basic quota and any producer offers the Board hops in excess of his selling quota, the Board will select the hops of highest value for payment under the quota plan. These quota provisions of the scheme remain in operation until 1939.

The two parties now primarily interested in the business of marketing hops are the Hops Marketing Board and the Brewers' Society. In 1934 it was realized that close collaboration between these two bodies was very desirable. A Permanent Joint Committee was therefore set up to determine the long-period policy; many important matters concerning the industry came under their jurisdiction, including production, the estimation of total demand in each season, and the negotiation of prices. It should not be forgotten, however, that it is the Board who ultimately possess the authority for determining the prices paid to producers, and they have undertaken the complete management of the trade in English-grown hops and are equipped with powers to fix both prices and quantities sold. In 1932, the first year of operation, the average price realized for hops was £8 17s. 2d. per cwt., but in the following year it had risen to £15 1s. 8d. per cwt. The 1933 crop, however, came on to the market under very favourable conditions. The demand from the United States of America was increasing as that country had "gone wet," and prices on the Continent were greatly in excess of those fixed for English hops. The reduction in the beer duty may also have stimulated demand to some extent. The 1934 crop was fairly heavy and rather indifferent in quality. Producers' selling quotas were 3 per cent below their production quotas, and the price obtainable only slightly above the 1932 figure.

An official complaint was lodged by the Brewers' Society regarding the high prices charged for the 1933 crop, but the Committee of Investigation reported to the effect that there was no justification for the complaint. Much criticism could be brought to bear on the Board regarding the general policy adopted. Hops, however, are different from most other commodities with which the Boards deal, as the demand for them is indirect, largely depending upon the

*

demand for beer, and the cost of this raw material is only a small proportion of the total cost of the final product. When in any year the supply is in excess of demand the price fall might be very injurious to producers and to future production. Regulation of production appears permissible to a certain extent because demand has been relatively inelastic, while supplies have been variable, and prices have shown wild fluctuations. With control of supply firm control of prices may be exercised. Yet the authority which the Board have to destroy hops in excess of a pre-ascertained demand may appear difficult to justify.

THE PIGS AND BACON MARKETING BOARDS

Examples of the regulatory type of organization are to be found in the Bacon and Pigs Marketing Boards. These schemes may be regarded as component parts of the same structure. Both came into operation in September 1933, and were designed, amongst other matters, to secure a larger share of the market for the home industry. The proportion of home-produced pig meat to the total supply had been gradually falling for some years; between 1926 and 1930 only 6,000,000 cwt. of our yearly requirements were home produced, whereas nearly 13,000,000 cwt. were imported.

Reorganization of marketing methods was definitely needed, otherwise home producers would find it increasingly difficult to withstand competition from overseas. Pig production was really a gamble, as prices fluctuated enormously, and, as a result, there was a very wide yearly variation in the number of pigs offered for sale. In addition, there was an enormous superfluity of breeds and types, and this fact, coupled with some inefficiency in the technique of feeding and management, resulted in somewhat unsatisfactory products being placed on the market. Bacon factories were very unevenly distributed, and many of them were unable to obtain an economic throughput, and these, too, showed some inefficiencies.

The schemes deal only with bacon pigs and bacon, the pork trade is not included. The quantity of bacon normally consumed in this country was thought to be known within narrow limits, and with this knowledge it appeared to be possible to plan the industry to the advantage of both pig and bacon producers. The methods adopted for the improvement of the trade involve the introduction of the contract system. A standard contract is arranged between the Pigs and the Bacon Marketing Boards, and individual producers of bacon pigs who so desire can arrange forward contracts with individual curers through the Pigs Marketing Board. The Pigs Marketing Board itself also disposes of some pigs sold on contract. The Bacon Marketing Board, in consequence, are in a position to supply information regarding future supplies of pigs available for the factories, and the home output of bacon can therefore be calculated over a period with a high degree of accuracy. From this information it is possible to estimate our requirements of bacon from overseas, and the import quota system can be more effectively applied.

The idea of making contracts to supply animals not yet born was, however, rather new to pig producers, and some encouragement was needed before farmers would accept it. As the prices of pigs in previous years had been closely related to those of feeding stuffs, and as the profits in the enterprise were dependent upon this relationship, a system of linking the two sets of prices was introduced. Under the new system curers were obliged to pay for pigs according to the price of feed; this really meant a return to producers more or less in proportion to the cost of production. As from May 1, 1934, however, a new method was introduced which aimed at relating pig prices not only to the cost of feed but also the price realized for bacon and offals. This improvement has relieved curers from the risks of loss in the event of feed and bacon prices moving in opposite directions. In 1934 an important provision was incorporated in the Bacon Marketing Scheme to enable the Board to determine the quantity of bacon which may be sold during any year by any curer that comes under its jurisdiction.[1]

Official complaints relating to the schemes have dealt with comparatively minor points. A good deal of criticism has, however, been levelled at the Boards in view of the increase in the price of bacon since the advent of the schemes. Early in 1930 there was a very substantial decline in bacon prices, and they remained low during the two years that followed. Since November 1932, however, when restriction of imports was initiated, the prices of both the home and imported product have stood at much higher levels. Quotations for imported bacon in 1934 were higher on the average than in any year since 1930, and have shown a slightly greater advance than those of the home-produced article.

In 1935 a new body came into existence, viz. the Bacon Development Board. This body consists of members drawn from the Pigs and Bacon Boards, together with some others. The work of the new Board will cover the development of the industry generally. All large bacon factories will be licensed by the body, and it is expected that this plan will lead to greater efficiency in the production of bacon. The Board will be in a position to rationalize the output of bacon on a national basis to meet the volume of demand. The jurisdiction which they may exercise over pig producers is also far reaching, as they may regulate the sale of pigs by determining the kinds and grades of pigs, and the prices at which they may be sold. The Board will also act as a sort of court of appeal; this means that should the Pigs and Bacon Boards fail to agree upon certain matters, both Boards may decide, by resolution, to hand the matter over to the Development Board.

The quantity of bacon and hams imported has been

[1] Certain small curers are exempt from the scheme.

regulated since the advent of these schemes. Foreign supplies in 1934 fell to 64·4 per cent of our total requirements compared with 83·5 per cent in 1932. Both home and empire supplies, on the other hand, rose, the former from 12·6 per cent to 21·7 per cent, and the latter from 3·9 per cent to 13·7 per cent during the same period.

THE POTATO MARKETING BOARD

The only other regulatory board as yet in existence is the Potato Marketing Board, which has acquired only very limited trading powers. Great Britain is almost self-sufficient in main-crop potatoes, but in view of the comparative stability of demand and the rather wide variation in supply, prices in many years have shown enormous fluctuations.

The Board have powers to regulate the marketing of potatoes by determining the description of potatoes that may be sold; these powers are generally implemented by prohibiting sales of potatoes for human consumption that pass through a riddle of a prescribed gauge. Partial control of production has also been attempted by determining the acreage of potatoes which each producer can normally grow. Producers who desire to grow more than the allotted acreage are required to pay £5 per acre on the excess.

The Board depend very largely upon the help of the wholesale merchants for the working of the scheme, and they have introduced a system of "authorized" potato buyers. These authorized merchants have agreed, amongst other matters, not to buy from producers other than on the terms prescribed by the Board. Sales of potatoes on commission have been prohibited, as such transactions were not considered conducive to the efficient working of the scheme or in the general interest of producers.

Much valuable information regarding market conditions has been collected by the Board, and as a result they are in a position to give much reliable information to the trade.

As the powers of the Board are almost entirely of a regulatory nature, a supply of accurate information is indispensable to the efficient working of the scheme. The Board have only been in effective operation a little more than two years, and it is as yet difficult to measure the influence they have had upon the trade. The time necessary to enable regulatory boards to accomplish any perceptible results may, in general, be appreciably longer than in the case of trading boards.

SOME GENERAL RESULTS

It is probably true that only by results can the Marketing Boards be fairly judged. In view of the fact that they have only been in existence for a comparatively short period, the full effect that they have had upon the positions of producers, distributors, or consumers may not as yet be apparent. During the first two years of operation a large number of factors, more particularly the developments in food-exporting countries, were exercising their influence upon British agriculture. The imposition of tariffs in this country and the conclusion of certain international agreements regarding the importation of food also played their part. It is, therefore, rather difficult to evaluate the influence of the Marketing Boards upon the problems of food production and distribution. It is true, however, that the prices of most of the commodities covered by the schemes have risen, and that the rise has on the whole been more conspicuous in the case of these commodities than in others, and this rise may at least in part be ascribed to the activities of the boards. In the case of fresh milk and potatoes, however, the schemes deal with products little subject to the influences of imported supplies, in which rather more than average recovery of prices from depression level might be expected, and in the case of hops some special considerations apply.

The level of prices of agricultural commodities was

extremely low in 1932, and a continuation of such conditions for any appreciable length of time would no doubt
have caused considerable damage to the agricultural industry. The community could not expect a continuation of
conditions that only enabled a proportion of producers to
command returns that covered costs of production. The
raising of prices to producers from the low level to which
they had fallen was undoubtedly essential. Farmers who
conducted their businesses in a reasonably efficient way
were fully justified in seeking to improve the conditions
that prevailed at the time. While it is essential that prices
shall be maintained sufficiently high to cover the cost
of producing the bulk of any particular product, in no
circumstances is there any justification for raising prices to
a level that enables inefficient producers to continue in
business.

During recent years there had been a tendency for the
spread between the wholesale prices of farm products and
the retail prices of food to widen; in consequence producers
had been obliged to take less, and consumers had not always
benefited. The depression in agriculture had been partly
ascribed to the persistent fall in the wholesale price level of
agricultural commodities, and in cases where retail prices
had not declined to the same extent the expansion of
consumption was hindered. Rapid developments have been
made in the technique of food production both in this
and in other countries, and considerably greater supplies
have become available. As some difficulty was experienced
in disposing of the comparatively heavy supplies in certain
cases wholesale prices showed a definite tendency to fall,
and demand was often curtailed by the high level of retail
prices relative to wholesale prices and to the purchasing
powers of large masses of consumers. A disequilibrium
therefore arose between supplies and effective demand, and
this was harmful both to producers and consumers.

It is true, however, that both the quantity and quality of

distributive services are gradually changing; consumers now require more regular delivery and better service than was the case in pre-war days. Greater expenditure is incurred in handling and packing commodities, and in general they are sold in smaller lots. Distributive charges have been higher in consequence of these changes, but such factors need not adversely affect producers' prices. The additional cost of handling should normally be passed on to the consumer. There is a great deal of evidence to show, however, that middlemen's margins have been unduly inflated; and even when allowance is made for higher distributive costs, retail prices in many cases have remained unduly high.

The disequilibrium between the available supply of food and the effective demand for it, or what is much the same thing, the spread between wholesale and retail prices, may be in part ascribed to several causes, including:

(a) Rapid progress in the technique of production.
(b) The existence of strong combinations of the interests operating between the producer and consumer which could exploit the situation to advantage.
(c) Lack of organization in the processes of marketing leading to waste and inefficiency in distribution.

It is the duty of the Boards to study these problems and to ascertain the reasons for their existence, and, further, to administer schemes that will lead to the removal of the difficulties. While over-production in this country has certainly not been the primary cause of trouble, it should be borne in mind that Great Britain imports a large proportion of some foodstuffs and that these have been available at relatively low prices during certain years.

PRODUCERS' AND CONSUMERS' INTERESTS

Although many criticisms have been heard, farmers in general are certainly not dissatisfied with the schemes. There have been many complaints, but this was anticipated, as it was difficult for the old type of farmer, who had been accustomed to considerable liberty, to adapt himself even to a small amount of control. Many administrators despaired of the success of the new plan, as they believed that persons who were notorious for their individualism would prove intractable, and that such friction would follow the application of compulsory powers as would render the working of the schemes extremely difficult. In general, however, the schemes have appealed to producers, as they offered them something tangible in return for a certain degree of discipline. Although there is no available body of facts upon which an estimate can be made of the total effects that the schemes have had upon farmers' incomes, what evidence there is shows clearly that the great majority of producers who come under the jurisdiction of marketing boards now enjoy higher incomes than was the case three years ago.

Comparisons of the retail prices of commodities in 1932 with those that prevailed in later years indicate that in the case of certain commodities there has been a marked advance. The expansion of demand with the improvement of trade was discouraged, and this occurred when home production was increasing. Surely the movement of commodities into consumption with as little friction as possible must at all times be one of the main objects of the boards, and this can only be secured by keeping prices to consumers as low as possible.

Minimum retail prices of milk have recently been fixed by the Milk Marketing Board, although actual prices are fixed by distributors, and in many cases these are higher than formerly. Prices have advanced by about 20 points since the advent of the scheme, which is considerably more than the rise in the index number of all food or the cost of living index. It is generally claimed that the demand for milk does not change appreciably with alterations in its price. There is, however, a good deal of evidence to show that the price of milk has a very important effect upon demand amongst the poor classes. It is known that an appreciable proportion of poor families rely upon the inferior varieties of tinned milks and do not purchase any fresh milk, and it has been proved that there is a close relationship between the daily quantity of milk taken per household and the family income.

Considerably greater quantities of milk would undoubtedly be taken by many classes of people in this country if it were available at a lower price. Much criticism can be brought to bear upon the Board for their policy in this aspect of their work; retail prices have advanced at a time when producers' sales are rapidly rising and when the quantity of "surplus" milk is expanding.

Very little has been done to improve the efficiency of distribution. In the smaller towns large numbers of small producer-retailers are still to be found. Milk rounds generally overlap, and the amount of time taken to deliver the milk requirements of the population is far in excess of the necessary minimum. In the larger cities the work is generally in the hands of powerful combines, which are now guaranteed a margin for distribution higher than that they formerly commanded. They have, therefore, been able to show extremely good profits. A margin of about 11d. to 1s. a gallon is an unnecessarily high allowance for the work of distribution, as it is known that it can be done for considerably less when efficiently conducted.

The whole organization of the milk industry and the work of the Milk Marketing Board has been critically surveyed by the Reorganization Commission appointed for the purpose in their recent Report (published by H.M. Stationery Office, Economic Series No. 44, 1936, 1s. net). The Commission makes a number of far-reaching proposals for reform, and their Report is a most important document.

All the schemes have undoubtedly fallen far short of the expectation of the supporters of the original plan, as the boards have done scarcely anything to reorganize the ultimate distribution of commodities, although the Marketing Acts were drafted with a view to improving the methods of handling commodities from farm to consumers. To omit dealing with the retailing aspect of the problem amounts to a neglect of its biggest and most difficult part. In fact, the Milk Marketing Board have to some extent hindered the important developments of the last few years. Co-operative societies, which were formerly engaged in handling members' milk on the profit-sharing principle, are now obliged to maintain prices with other wholesalers and retailers.

The Milk Marketing Board have clearly recognized the monopoly which they hold over the liquid milk market, and the wide differences in the value of milk in different uses. In view of the increase in producers' offers and the low prices obtained in the manufacturing market, an attempt has been made to maintain profitable conditions of production by keeping liquid milk prices at a comparatively high level. Extraction from the liquid market of some support for the other market was definitely essential, otherwise there would be a danger of short supplies at some periods of the year, but the action of the Board has gone beyond the maintenance of the necessary reserve. The Board are, of course, composed of representatives of producers, and it is their duty to guard the interests of those for whom they speak. They have succeeded so far in making milk production far more profitable in many parts of the country than was formerly the case. They have done this partly at the expense of suppliers near towns, but a fair proportion of the support has come from the exploitation of the liquid market. In addition, the industry has been supported by State "advances." The Government in 1934 guaranteed, for a period of two years, a minimum manufacturing price of 5d. a gallon in summer and 6d. a gallon in winter. The cost of this subsidy was estimated to be from £1,500,000 to £1,750,000 a year. The money is repayable between 1936 and 1938 if prices have risen sufficiently high to make it possible. In addition, a sum up to £2,000,000, which is not repayable, has been allocated towards increasing the consumption of milk, as by aiding the milk-in-schools scheme and for the purpose of enabling higher prices to be paid to producers who improve the quality of their supplies. It is very doubtful whether it was the intention of the originators of the new marketing plan that the public should be called upon to provide support for milk prices in the form of a direct subsidy from the Treasury and then suffer exploitation in the liquid market.

It is almost inevitable that the State, as the guardian of national interests, should exercise control with a view to remedying the present situation. Hitherto the State has been concerned with the protection of public welfare against existent or possible dangers, largely with negative control. Henceforward it must be more concerned with its promotion, but at present it is hardly leading the way. There is a rising public consciousness of the possibilities of increased production and consumption and of the existence of certain obstacles to the realization of these possibilities. If the increase of milk production and of consumption are both objects of national policy, there is conflict between the methods adopted. Milk consumption is restricted by the maintenance of high prices for liquid milk in order to subsidize manufacturing supplies. There is little doubt that the increase in direct consumption of milk should be the first object of national policy, and in this case it is almost inconceivable that unrestricted exploitation of the monopoly in liquid milk will be allowed to continue.

From November 1933 the importation of bacon and hams has been regulated by order under the 1933 Marketing Act, and in subsequent years there have been considerable reductions in the quantities imported compared with those of 1932. Overseas supplies in 1933 were 18 per cent lower, in 1934 there was a further decline of 13 per cent, whilst for 1935 the total quantity arriving in this country was 37 per cent below the 1932 figure. In spite of an increase in home production there was an appreciable rise in retail prices during these years. Restriction is based on a yearly bacon and ham consumption of 10·6 million cwt., which was the average of annual retained imports plus estimated home production for the years 1925–30. Some severe criticism has been forthcoming as to the advisability of fixing so low a figure, as no allowance was made for a possible increase in consumption. The demand for bacon and hams in this country might show an increase with an improvement in industrial conditions; with consumption at about ½ lb. per person weekly it is difficult to believe that there is no room for expansion. However, only the regulated supply was limited to this amount, and there is an unknown but apparently increasing quantity outside the regulated supply.

NEW MARKETING AUTHORITIES

As at present constituted, the boards represent producers' interests almost entirely, but provision is made for co-opting on to each board two "independent" persons. Before the latter can be co-opted, however, the Market Supply Committee must be consulted. This Committee was set up under the 1933 Marketing Act to review the circumstances affecting the supply of agricultural products in this country and to make representations as to any steps which they consider essential for regulating the supply. The Committee also gives advice and assistance in regard to any measures taken to control the description and quantities of any home-produced commodity which may be sold, and also any steps taken regarding the regulation of imports.

No other provision is made in the Marketing Acts to ensure that persons other than those who directly represent the interests of producers are elected to the boards, neither is any provision made to ensure that the persons co-opted to the boards represent the interests of either distributors or consumers. It is doubtful, therefore, whether the boards, as at present constituted, will function directly to the advantage of the community as a whole. The work of providing food for the people cannot effectively be divided into several independent and semi-antagonistic sections. Conventionally the field is considered as falling into four different sections, viz. production, assembly and transport, wholesale marketing, and distribution. This field, however, covers the whole business of food provision, and it is clear that before the work can be done to the satisfaction of the community it must be tackled in all its phases. No partial reform or readjustment can be permanently advantageous to everybody concerned without consequent reforms at other stages.

The present forms of organization, as evolved under the Marketing Acts, have resulted in producers' representatives gaining initial control over almost the whole field. The boards are, *inter alia*, in a position to secure a measure of control over the quantity of a foodstuff produced, or to take steps to secure such powers of control. In this way they are able to curtail production if necessary. As they are entitled to prescribe the descriptions of commodities which may be sold, they are also in a position to limit the amount of regulated foodstuffs which is placed on the market. The boards also enjoy very considerable powers over the distribution of commodities, as apparently they can determine not only the wholesale prices but also retail prices.

The only fair method of controlling the whole series of processes would be to entrust the work of controlling the production and marketing of food products to bodies composed of representatives of all interested groups. It is the consumers who must ultimately decide what kind of commodities are needed, if opportunities of choosing are available. In very undesirable circumstances certain products may be forced upon them, but a system in which consumers were not allowed a fair degree of liberty to choose would be an extremely unfavourable one. Under present arrange-

ments the producers' interests receive primary consideration, with the result that the general community is liable
to suffer.

Marketing bodies should have undisputed jurisdiction over
the whole field of producing and distributing commodities,
but they should be composed of representatives of all
interested parties. At present marketing boards are obliged
to guard the financial position of producers, as the great
majority of members are elected by producers and must
answer to them. Yet the boards have powers which extend
over distributors' businesses, and they are in a position to
influence very considerably the income made by persons in
the distributive trade and to some extent to influence changes
in the processes of supply.

For the purposes of administration the work of food provision can be conveniently divided into two sections, viz.
(*a*) production and (*b*) distribution.

Production problems are really confined to the farm,
whereas those relating to marketing and distribution cover
the handling of the commodities from the time they leave
the farm until they reach the final consumer. This work
would in many cases include a certain amount of processing
and manufacture. In view of the fact that the work of
supplying food is of primary importance to the people in
general, it is clear that any statutory body which is given
wide powers relating to food supplies should be composed
of representatives of producers, distributors, and consumers,
and provision must eventually be made for statutory bodies
based on this principle before any degree of fairness can be
introduced into the system.

For each major food commodity produced in the country
three authorities need to be established, viz. :

(*a*) A producers' board.
(*b*) A distributors' board.
(*c*) A commodity council consisting of members elected by
     the two boards together with consumers' representatives.

PRODUCERS' BOARDS

Problems relating to the production of a commodity should be relegated to the producers' board. Such a body, with regional committees, should be built up on a national basis, i.e. there should be only one for each commodity produced in Great Britain. The powers delegated to these boards should relate mainly to problems of production, but they should also be equipped with certain marketing powers in order to enable effective control to be applied over the total output.

A producers' board should be given the powers to buy and sell the regulated product, and provision should also be made to compel producers to sell the commodity if necessary only to the board, as this body would then be in a position to exercise control over the total output. The work of dealing with certain financial matters would also devolve upon the producers' boards, as all payments for commodities (except perhaps those accruing to small producers or for small lots) would first pass into their hands, and it would be for them to distribute the proceeds amongst producers.

These boards, in addition, should be provided with powers to enable them to buy, sell, or let for hire to producers anything required for the production or adaptation for sale of the product, and they should be in a position to co-operate with other organizations, such as those trading in farmers' requirements.

DISTRIBUTORS' BOARDS

These bodies should be composed of representatives of distributors and processors and should be equal in numerical strength to the producers' board. It would be desirable to have equal numbers on the two boards, as they might sometimes meet for business purposes. It would probably be sufficient to legislate in general terms for the establishment of this new type of board and to leave the details regarding the method of arranging and allocating seats to the drafters of each separate scheme. In view of the complex nature of the trade in farm products and the enormous variation in its character from one commodity to another, it would be rather difficult to draft a plan of electing distributors' boards that could be applied in every case. Persons engaged in the trade should to a certain extent be left to devise methods of electing their own boards.

The distributors' boards should have powers somewhat analogous to those possessed by producers' boards. These would include the right to buy from the producers' board or in the absence of contrary regulation direct from producers. The distributive boards could be made responsible for collecting sums due from distributors for the commodities they had received, and these moneys would be handed over to the producers' boards. They could also deal with the credit problem which arises amongst their members and other matters of a detailed character relating to the trade.

COMMODITY COUNCILS

These bodies would be composed of representatives of the different classes of people directly interested in each commodity, i.e. producers, distributors, and consumers. They should have a statutory basis and be equipped with wide powers. Each council should be made up as follows:

One-third elected by the producers' board.
One-third elected by the distributors' board.
One-third nominated by the Minister of Agriculture after consultation with the President of the Board of Trade to represent consumers' interests.
An independent chairman nominated by the Minister of Agriculture after consultation with the Home Secretary.

Each council would deal in a comprehensive way with the

whole business of marketing one particular food commodity; they would watch the interests of all concerned,
and be able to make representations to any body that was
constituted to advise the Government on the regulation of
imports. The councils would have facilities for studying in
broad outline all measures relating to the particular industry
in which they were interested; detailed questions relating
to problems of production or distribution would be relegated
to the respective boards.[1]

Very important powers should be conferred on the commodity councils; each should be enabled to fix both the
wholesale and retail prices of the product handled. It is
obvious that to ensure success in such ventures the confidence
of producers, distributors, and the public must be commanded, and this would be far more easily obtained when
it was known that each party was equally represented on
the council. This body would also constitute an effective
organ of co-operation, as it would establish a fair balance
between the interested parties.

Each council should be empowered by statute to demand
information relating to the costs and profits of producers and
distributors, and should be at liberty to inspect the accounts
of those who carry on business in the field, but such information should of course be treated in confidence in so far as
any individual or firm is concerned.

It is known that considerable harm is done to producers
in general by certain persons who place commodities of
comparatively low quality on the market. In fact, British
agriculture has suffered considerably from the attempts
made by certain producers to market inferior articles. As a
result, consumers have frequently lost confidence in the
home-produced commodity and have turned to the imported

[1] Since this chapter was written, the Report has been published of the
Reorganization Commission for the Milk Industry (H.M. Stationery Office,
price 1s.). This contains, *inter alia*, proposals for establishing a permanent
Milk Commission with large and important functions. The Report should be
carefully studied in connection with Mr. Jones's suggestions.—EDITOR.

product, the quality of which is sometimes more reliable. The time has undoubtedly arrived when producers and distributors should not be at liberty to deceive consumers, as under such conditions the whole home industry is likely to suffer. Power should therefore be given to the commodity councils to license producers and distributors, and to subject them to such conditions with regard to methods of producing and handling the commodity as in their opinion are necessary in the interests of the community. They should also be enabled to revoke licences of persons who contravene a condition on which the licence was granted. Each commodity council should also be able to purchase by agreement any premises used for producing or distributing the product and to dispose of such premises. This authority would be necessary, as in certain cases the council may deem it advisable to remove inefficient persons from the business.

In order to ensure that the council is in a position to acquire the fullest information about the industry and to secure compliance with the scheme they should be able to empower certain persons to enter and inspect any premises used for producing or marketing the commodity. The imposition and the recovery of penalties from persons who contravene the provisions of the scheme would also be part of the councils' work. In addition, provision should be made to enable the councils to conduct education and research in connection with the production and marketing of the commodity over which they exercised jurisdiction.

IMPORT CONTROL

The successful operation of some marketing schemes is obviously dependent upon an adequate regulation of imports. One of the primary objects of introducing a centralized method of marketing control is to steady the prices of certain food commodities and to maintain them at a reasonable

level above costs of production. This could hardly be
achieved if imports were left unrestricted, since oversea
supplies might upset any marketing plan in operation. At
present the rigid control of the quantity of any product
imported does not precede an attempt at reorganizing the
home industry in regard to that product.[1] In fact, an assurance that the home industry is efficiently conducted is
required before the control of imports by the quota method
can be put into force. This form of regulation presents
some very severe difficulties. The production of agricultural
commodities is of necessity somewhat risky owing to climatic
and similar factors, which give rise to variations in the
quantities produced from year to year. On the other hand,
to maintain a reasonably steady price level it should be
possible to adjust the supply of a commodity easily and
quickly to the demand for it. It is probable that only certain
limited classes of food commodities can be effectively subjected to this method of control. The demand for such
products must be reasonably stable and must not fluctuate
unduly over comparatively short periods, otherwise frequent
adjustments will be necessary, and such interference would
undoubtedly be very damaging to trade.

Under the quota system of import control it is necessary
to forecast the market demand for a commodity over an
appreciable length of time, as arrangements must be made
with oversea suppliers. Danger would be run by placing
a fixed limit on the quantity of a commodity to be
imported when either the demand was likely to fluctuate
appreciably or the quantity produced at home was liable
to show wide variations. Quotas for farm products must be
fixed for fairly long periods, as sufficient time must be
allowed for farmers to arrange their plans. In the case of
most agricultural commodities the quantity produced cannot
be altered easily and quickly to meet changes in demand,

[1] There is "voluntary" or "agreed" control of imports prior to organization
of the house supply—as in the case of eggs.

and in general a surplus must be carried, otherwise consumers may run the risk of a shortage. Under the policy of
laissez-faire an abundant supply of a food commodity was
moved into consumption as a result of a decline in its price;
this brought in additional buyers, whilst those who had
taken only comparatively small quantities at a certain price
level generally bought more when the price was lowered.
Such a system was extremely flexible, and usually resulted
in the equation of demand and supply, although, of course,
price variation was common.

In planning supplies of food commodities, however, cognizance would have to be taken of total or potential demand
as well as the amount bought at any given price. Under
present conditions total demand for certain products is
seldom met, as the great bulk of the poor people of this
country are unable to pay the price charged. In arranging
the quota system for any particular commodity, therefore,
the demand for foodstuffs would of course have to be pre-
ascertained. Ideally, provision should be made so that each
person gets sufficient. It is intolerable that limits should be
placed on supplies when certain classes of people are unable
to get enough.

The quantity of any foodstuff demanded in this country
during any period in the past is no adequate guide to the
real requirements of the community. Large sections of the
community are inadequately fed, and the potential demand
for many of the most essential foodstuffs far exceeds the
quantities actually passing into consumption. Yet under the
quota system, as at present applied, no provision is made
for meeting the requirements of the whole community.
Under any quota system, however, the quantity of any
foodstuff allowed to enter this country must be decided
beforehand; the line must be drawn at a certain point, and
great responsibility falls on those who have to decide where
it shall be drawn. Any measure which serves to exclude
commodities, and, as a result, deprives certain persons of

the necessaries of life, constitutes interference of the worst kind.

It is realized that the cost of producing many farm products is much lower in many oversea countries than in Great Britain. In consequence, certain imported foods can be sold in this country at comparatively low prices, with the result that some home producers, in the present state of our agricultural industry, cannot effectively withstand free competition. It seems hardly justifiable from the consumers' viewpoint, however, to adopt a policy of limiting supplies of food in order to maintain prices in this country at an artificially high level. The country will not indefinitely tolerate a plan which ensures a satisfactory return to home producers without regard to organization of the industry.

It is apparent that under the quota system as now administered in this country first consideration is given to producers, since the general policy involves limiting supplies in order to maintain profitable conditions of production. Some reorganization of our methods of farming would no doubt result in a considerable reduction of costs of production, as in many districts primitive and obsolete methods are still in vogue. No advantage to the country as a whole can be derived from a system which aims at maintaining prices at a sufficiently high level to ensure that certain systems of farming prove remunerative, when no measures are taken to see that production is conducted in the most efficient way.

In the case of some commodities, particularly those which can be produced relatively cheaply in oversea countries, it may be necessary, in the interests of British farmers, to differentiate between the price of the home-produced and the imported article. Under certain conditions, as, for example, those which have prevailed during the last few years, it may be essential to enable the home product to command a higher price than the imported supply. It is possible that consumers may be asked to support such a plan and to give it their assistance. But the work should be done without inflicting any unnecessary hardships and without penalizing the poorer sections of the community.

In order to maintain differential prices, however, it is not necessary to restrict the supply so that a partial scarcity is created, with the inevitable forcing up of the price of all supplies. Methods of administration may take many forms, but it is desirable to avoid duplication of authorities. Under the plan outlined here it would be unnecessary to create any statutory bodies in addition to those which had come into existence to deal with home supplies. As the commodity councils would be composed of all groups interested in the marketing of food products, they would be competent to deal with the problem of imports. Final powers over the control of imports, however, should not be granted to commodity councils concerned with the marketing of particular commodities. They should in this matter work in conjunction with some authority, such as the Import Duties Advisory Committee, set up for the purpose of dealing with the regulation of all classes of products imported into this country.

9

THE POST OFFICE

by

JOHN DUGDALE

THE Post Office is by far the oldest of all the public concerns described in this volume. It is in fact the only State enterprise that has continued to function uninterruptedly throughout the last three hundred years of British history. It was established in the reign of Charles I as a mail-carrying organization. Already in those days it was felt that there were certain important functions that private enterprise could not be trusted to perform either efficiently or with enough disinterestedness. The maintenance of law and order was one of these functions, and the provision of a means of communication between every subject within the realm was another. It was with this idea in view that the Post Office was created.

For over two hundred years it acted purely as a mail-carrying organization. Until 1840 it charged its customers roughly in accordance with the service that it gave to each one of them. In that year, however, Rowland Hill introduced an entirely new principle, which was to charge a uniform and very low rate for all letters below a certain weight whatever the distance they had to be carried. The introduction of the penny post revolutionized the Post Office, and from then on its business increased at a phenomenal rate, until to-day over seven thousand million letters are dealt with each year.

It was not, however, until the latter half of the last century that the Post Office began its remarkable series of advances into new and entirely unexpected fields. To-day, while the mail-carrying business is still the basis of its work, the Post Office is responsible for the organization of some half a dozen separate services, each one of which employs many thousands of people. So rapid has been the growth of these new services that, together with the mail-carrying business, they form the largest single commercial unit in the country, with a staff of 241,500 employees.

The organization of a service of this magnitude is not an easy matter at any time. It has, however, been further complicated by reason of its origin. As we have already seen, the main reason for the foundation of the Post Office was that the work of mail carrying was considered too important to be left in private hands. So important was it considered, indeed, that there was a feeling that it should be under the direct day-to-day control of the Government. The manner in which this control is exercised is well enough known to most people, but it may be as well to give a brief résumé of it before proceeding to a consideration of the internal organization of the Post Office.

The head of the Post Office is appointed by the King on the advice of the Prime Minister. He is a Minister of the Crown, but he is not usually a member of the Cabinet. In most cases he is either a young and promising politician who is being tried out with a view to promotion to one of the higher offices of State, or else a person of importance but not very great ability for whom a Government position has to be found for some reason or other. He has under him an Assistant Postmaster-General and a Parliamentary Private Secretary.

Since he is a member of the Government, his appointment terminates automatically when the Government falls. This means that his maximum period of office is five years and his minimum can be anything down to five days. When the National Government was first formed after the resignation of the Labour Government and before the General

Election of 1931, a new Postmaster-General was appointed. He remained in office till after the election—a period of exactly eight weeks. But, while legally he may keep his position for as long as the Government of which he is a member remains in office, the average life of a Postmaster-General is considerably less than this. If he is at all successful he is likely to be transferred to a higher position.

Even while he is actually Postmaster-General he cannot devote all his time to the running of his office in the way that the head of an ordinary business can do. The mornings may be spent there, but every afternoon while the House is sitting he must attend and record his vote in the division lobby like any ordinary Member of Parliament. He must also be ready to answer questions about his department. Any Member may ask any question he likes on the running of the Post Office. Notice must, of course, be given, and the answers are usually prepared by the permanent staff, though the Postmaster-General must be ready to deal with supplementary questions arising out of the original one. Finally, he is responsible for introducing and defending the Post Office annual estimates, and for carrying through any particular piece of legislation sponsored by the Post Office.[1] He can, of course, hand over any portion of this work to the Assistant Postmaster-General. In practice the latter answers all minor questions and winds up the debate on the Post Office estimates. The Parliamentary Private Secretary is not a Minister of the Crown, and is unable therefore to answer any questions in the House with reference to his department. His position is that of semi-official assistant to the Postmaster-General.

Such, in brief outline, is the position of the Postmaster-General. The disadvantages of this particular system of governmental control are obvious enough. It makes for extreme rigidity. The fact that a Member of Parliament

---

[1] In addition he is responsible in certain ways for the B.B.C., which is the subject of another chapter in this book.

may ask for information not only on points of general policy, but on every conceivable aspect of the work of the Post Office, from the flotation of a ten-million-pound loan to the establishment of a call box in a small Highland village, puts all Post Office officials on the defensive. They are inclined to feel that the best course is to leave things alone, and that it is dangerous to make any new innovation for fear that a question will be raised about it in the House. Naturally this is only a tendency, and innovations are in fact constantly being made throughout the Post Office service, but it is apt to be a very dangerous tendency in a service that is already prone to over-centralization and the lack of initiative consequent thereon. The advantages of the system are equally obvious. No public body in the country is subjected to severer criticism, much of it of very great value.

Victimization of members of the staff is difficult, if not impossible, with the power of the Post Office Unions to get a question put in Parliament asking for an explanation of the alleged victimization. The Post Office cannot afford to leave out certain classes of the public from the services it provides, for every class or district can get a question asked in the House as to why it is deprived of these services. To sum up, parliamentary control makes it unlikely that there will be any grave abuses in the Post Office service, but at the same time it produces a tendency to discourage any outstanding innovations.

The fact that the Postmaster-General is a Minister of the Crown, with parliamentary and other interests outside the Post Office, and with no security of tenure, makes the position of the permanent officials extremely important. That position has been radically altered during the last few years as a result of the Report of the Bridgeman Committee, which was set up in 1932 to inquire into the manner in which the Post Office was run. Before describing the alterations that have taken place, it may be as well to give an

outline of the headquarters organization as it existed at the
time when the Bridgeman Committee reported.

The chief official was the permanent secretary, who in
theory occupied the same position as the permanent secretary
of any other Government department. In practice, however,
he had come to be the sole means of communication between
the Postmaster-General and the entire Post Office staff,
except in cases where disputes were actually brought by the
Post Office Unions, when the Postmaster-General or his
assistant was himself present to hear the men's claims. How
long this state of affairs had existed it is difficult to estimate,
but it had presumably grown up gradually with the growth
of the Post Office. It meant, of course, that the Postmaster-
General had very little real contact with the service and
was apt to derive all his views of it from the permanent
secretary. It may be of interest to add that when the
Bridgeman Committee reported the Post Office had had
the same permanent secretary for a period of no less than
twenty years.

Under the permanent secretary and under the deputy
secretary were the heads of the two main sections into which
the Post Office was divided, the Director of Postal Services
and the Director of Telegraphs and Telephones, who controlled respectively the work connected with the mails on
the one hand and telegrams and telephones on the other.
The work was subdivided into eight branches, each under
an assistant secretary, dealing with mails, inland telegraphs,
overseas telegraphs, telephones, buildings, establishments,
staff and chief clerk's duties, the last four branches being
under the direct charge of the assistant secretary. In addition
to these eight, the investigation branch and the publicity
section were connected with the secretariat, though they
were neither of them under the direct charge of an assistant
secretary. The publicity section until recent years was,
indeed, only a very minor branch of the headquarters
organization, but recently it has risen to a position of

considerable prominence, and its work will be discussed separately at a later stage.

Parallel with the secretariat branches, but subject to their general authority, were seven headquarters departments, namely, those of the comptroller and accountant-general (who is the accounting officer of the Post Office and comptroller of the Post Office revenue), the comptroller of stores (who is also responsible for Post Office contracts, other than those for manufacture and erection *in situ*, and for the control of the Post Office factories in London and Birmingham), the engineer-in-chief, the controller of the savings bank, the controller of the money order department, and, finally, the solicitor to the Post Office and the chief medical officer.

The secretariat was the centre of all authority, and, as is natural in an organization the size of the Post Office, it had tended during the years to withdraw more and more into itself and become somewhat divorced from the general work of the Post Office service, issuing its orders and expecting them to be obeyed. The report of the Bridgeman Committee in 1932 drew attention to this fact in the following words:

The Post Office secretariat has come to assume a position which has no parallel in the secretariat of any other Government department, and is in fact the sole source of authority under the Postmaster-General. For instance, we understand that no executive department of the Post Office can give instruction to another department, nor can it through its own officers do anything for which it has not secretariat authority, either general or specific.[1]

Two factors had increased this tendency to the separation of the secretariat from the rest of the Post Office service. The first was one to which reference has already been made, namely, the right of Members of Parliament to raise questions in the House of Commons on any and every matter

[1] Cmd. 4149, p. 32.

connected with the Post Office. The head of any department who knows that he may be questioned publicly on any aspect of his department's work is naturally careful, and perhaps over-careful, to see that he knows every detail of what is going on in that department, and may even try to prevent any action of other than the most minor importance from being taken without his consent. This is, however, a difficulty experienced by all Government departments, and as long as the Post Office is under direct parliamentary control it is inevitable.

The second factor is capable of being remedied far more easily. The administrative staff of the Post Office is recruited in quite a different manner from the rank and file, namely, through the Civil Service Administrative Class examination. On joining, they are appointed to the secretariat, and although during the first few years of their service they may be sent for a short period to the provinces to gain experience, they never have an opportunity of acquiring any thorough training in, or even experience of, the actual executive work of the Post Office. Except for this short period of provincial training they are kept for the rest of their service enclosed within the four walls of the General Post Office, controlling the execution of services of which they have very little practical knowledge.

As a result of the recommendations of the Bridgeman Committee, the Post Office secretariat has now been re-organized in the form of a functional board. The permanent secretary and his assistant are now known as the director-general and assistant director-general, and the alteration in title is significant as indicating an alteration in status. The director-general is no longer in a position of isolated splendour, but is now considered as *primus inter pares*. Periodical meetings between him and the heads of the various departments who constitute the other members of the board, with the Postmaster-General in the chair, have been substituted for the old system, with a marked improvement in the spirit of the organization. At these meetings each man present is expected to give his opinion, though the final responsibility on matters of policy still rests with the Postmaster-General.

We come now to the all-important question: How does the Post Office secretariat see that its instructions are carried out by the thousands of different offices throughout the British Isles? The best description that has so far been given of the metropolitan and provincial organization of the Post Office as it existed up till 1933 is again contained in the report of the Bridgeman Committee. The details of Post Office organization are, indeed, so clearly set out in this report that one cannot do better than to quote a few paragraphs from it.

Outside headquarters there are two systems of organization, the metropolitan and the provincial. In London the three communications services are organized separately by services, under a controller of the London postal service and a controller of the central telegraph office respectively. In the provinces, geographical areas and not services constitute the basis of administration.

Outside Inner London, the country, excluding Edinburgh, is divided into twenty-two districts for Post Office purposes; of these, thirteen are under the charge of surveyors and nine, comprising nine of the largest towns and the immediately surrounding area, are under the charge of postmaster surveyors.

In Scotland the Post Office organization is under the general charge of the secretary in Edinburgh, who in turn is responsible to the secretary of the Post Office. There is a controller in charge of the postal and telegraph services in Edinburgh and a small surrounding area.

The surveyor or the postmaster-surveyor is the Postmaster-General's chief provincial representative and is responsible for all the Post Office services within his district—postal, telegraph, and telephone—although he has no authority over the superintending engineer. He has certain powers delegated to him within which he can act upon his own authority. For instance, the number of letter deliveries and collections are prescribed by headquarters for large cities, medium-sized towns, and rural areas, but the times and other arrangements for these services are prescribed by the surveyors and postmasters according to local requirements.

A surveyor has a certain amount of disciplinary power, but cannot dismiss or degrade established staff who have passed their probation. He has power to make promotions from the manipulative to the first supervising grade. He can engage temporary staff, subject in the latter case to statistical justification to the accountant-general.

Any matter which requires authority beyond the powers delegated is referred to the secretariat of the Post Office.

Each surveyor has under his control some thirty to forty head Post Office districts. To assist in the supervision and inspection of this area, he has a staff of assistant surveyors, first and second class, an assistant traffic superintendent for telegraph work, and an office staffed by the usual Civil Service clerical grades.[1]

The Bridgeman Report then proceeds to a consideration of the telephone organization, after which it continues with its analysis of postal and telegraph work, as follows:

The head office areas into which a surveyor's district is divided are each under the control of a head postmaster situated generally in the largest town in the area. The head postmaster is responsible for all Post Office activities in his area except the direction of the telephone traffic, and is in direct charge of all staff and buildings. Under the head postmaster the postal centres are organized into (1) branch offices, (2) salaried sub-offices, (3) scale payment sub-offices. Generally speaking, these types of office may be described as follows:

1. Branch offices are outposts of the head office in the busier parts of large towns, and their functions are practically confined to counter work. They are staffed by Post Office civil servants.

2. Salaried sub-offices may be either similar to branch offices but conducting a smaller volume of business, or they may be the principal office in a smaller town within the head office district but outside the head office town area, in which case they act as postal, dispatching, and delivery centres in addition to providing counter facilities. In both cases, like branch offices, they are staffed by established Post Office staff.

3. Scale payment sub-offices are in effect agencies which generally combine Post Office duties with private business. The Post Office work is provided for under contract by the sub-

[1] Cmd. 4149, p. 30.

*

postmaster, who, in return for an inclusive scale payment based on the volume of work, provides accommodation, fittings, and indoor staff.[1]

There are approximately twenty thousand scale payment sub-offices, and by far the greater amount of counter work is performed by them. To the majority of those living in the country districts they represent the whole vast organization vaguely known as the Post Office, and great numbers of people living in the towns never use any but a scale payment sub-office. Yet, while in many cases they employ a staff of postmen paid directly by the Post Office for delivery purposes, they remain first and foremost shops, owned by shopkeepers who are ready to earn a little extra money by doing Post Office work in their spare time.

The postal and telegraph organization of this country is undergoing very considerable alteration as a result of the Bridgeman Committee's report. A departmental committee was set up, and this committee recommended certain alterations in postal organization, which are being carried out in two trial areas. The aim of these is to create "regions," each the size of two or three surveyors' districts, in charge of a regional director. The survey district is to become merged in these new regions, but postmaster-surveyors are to continue to exercise their powers in so far as their head office and its subordinate sub-offices are concerned. The two "trial regions" are Scotland and the north-east of England, and it is anticipated that when the whole scheme is in operation there will be six regions in all. The regional director is to be in complete control of all the functional headquarters officials, except for the technical control of the engineer-in-chief and the financial control of the comptroller and accountant-general over the engineering and financial branches respectively. He will have under him five principal officers, in control of mails, telephones (service and sales), finance, engineering, and personnel and buildings,

[1] Cmd. 4149, p. 31.

the last to deal with the staff and buildings of all branches of the Post Office service in its region. These officers, together with the regional director, will form a board which will meet frequently to discuss all important matters connected with the region. Lastly, the clerical staff, drawn from the former surveyors', superintending engineers', and district managers' officers, is to be interchangeable between the various functional branches. It is hoped that the creation of these regions will facilitate the devolution of many of the powers at present concentrated in the hands of the secretariat.

The problem of Post Office organization within the London area is, of course, somewhat different, and the departmental committee issued two separate reports for the London area. The first of these, which was published early in 1936, stated that the density of the population of London and its position as a centre for international as well as national communications made it advisable to concentrate in one authority the extensive control of the whole of the Post Office business of London. It was recommended that London should be divided into two "regions," one for telegraphs and telephones, and the other for postal services, and a sketch was made of the organization of the former. In its second report the committee proposed a scheme for the organization of a London postal region.

It is suggested that the inner and outer areas of the London postal region, with a radius of roughly ten and twenty-five miles respectively from the centre should be combined to form the London postal region. This region would cover much the same ground as the London tele-communications region, and, like it, would be controlled by a regional director, assisted by a deputy and a number of heads of functional branches.

One of these branches would be responsible for the efficient operation of the public services, including the collection, dispatch, and delivery of correspondence and the work done at the public counters. Another would concern itself with questions of buildings and staff; while a third would be responsible for the regional budget, which amounts at present to £8,000,000 per annum. The remaining branch would deal with transport, including not only the very extensive mail-van services, but also the Post Office tube railway and the travelling post offices. It is probable that this form of organization will before long be adopted by the Post Office for its London area.

When we come to the telephone service, we find that until recently the position was not altogether satisfactory. The telephone service is an integral part of the Post Office. It shares the same buildings, and in thousands of cases the same staff, as the postal and telegraph departments. There was at one time a vigorous campaign by a number of vociferous people for the separation of the telephone service from the rest of the Post Office, but even the most cursory examination of the position shows the impossibility of this. The local scale payment sub-office, for example, is the only convenient or available place for people to telephone from in many thousands of villages, and the sub-postmaster naturally keeps the Post Office telephone accounts. Even in the larger offices separation would be exceedingly difficult and costly, since the whole network of telephone lines for the district leads generally to the Post Office. A separate telephone system might have been evolved originally, but it is certainly quite impractical to-day.

Assuming, then, that the telephone service has to be part of the Post Office, sharing the same buildings and staff in many cases, the question then arises as to whether the method of organization by which it is linked with the rest of the Post Office is the best possible one. We will describe first the old method which existed from the time when the telephone service was taken over.

The unit of operations for the telephone service was the district manager's area. Normally, this area was coterminous with that of the Post Office surveyor, but in some cases a surveyor's district contained two district managers. The surveyor had general authority over the district manager, but in practice left him to manage all telephone matters. These were divided into three sections, traffic, contract, and clerical, or, in ordinary language, service, salesmanship, and accounting. While these three sections ought to have continual contact with one another in order to ensure the smooth working of the service, they were not in fact brought together anywhere in each district manager's area except within the central office of that area. As each district manager's territory extended over a wide field, this meant in practice that commercial telephone matters were dealt with in the first instance by three entirely separate bodies, which resulted both in delay in the provision of service and much confusion on the part of the public.

So far we have considered only the commercial aspect of the telephone service. The engineering side, which is responsible for the equipment and maintenance of the telephone and telegraph services, was entirely separate both from the surveyor and the district manager. It was divided into areas of its own, each under a superintendent engineer, and again further divided into sections, each in charge of an engineer, with a subordinate staff of assistant engineers, inspectors, and skilled workmen. Neither the surveyor nor the district manager was in a position to issue instructions to the engineering department, which received its orders direct from headquarters.

It is easy enough to see the disadvantages of a system such as this. To make a concrete case, let us suppose that Mr. Smith wanted a telephone. He would write to the local post office, and in due course his letter would find its way to the sales department. A salesman, or contract officer, would then visit Mr. Smith, and meantime the traffic or service section would have been informed of his desire to have a telephone. This section in turn would investigate the position, and would report to head office, who would instruct the engineering section to deal with the matter from their point of view. All this passing backwards and forwards of correspondence had the effect of slowing up the job in question, namely, the provision of a telephone for Mr. Smith, who after a time became irritated and complained about Post Office slackness. A thousand Mr. Smiths all complaining soon gave the Post Office telephone service a bad name, and there were many interests who were only too ready to take advantage of the situation and add fuel to the fire.

As a result of adverse comments on this form of organization contained in the Bridgeman Report, the departmental committee (already referred to) was set up to inquire into both metropolitan and provincial organization. It concentrated largely on the telephone service, and recommended the adoption of the following plan. Local telephone units were to be set up in which a sectional engineer, an accounting section, and a representative of the sales and service organizations would be brought together. The unit chosen was the sectional engineer's area. Each one of these units would be in charge of a telephone manager, having local responsibility for, and control of, all engineering, accounting, service, and sales matters within his area. Persons in any branch of the Post Office service were to be eligible, and selected officers were to undergo a special course of training. These units were to be under the general superintendence of the regional director. When it has been completed this new organization should run smoothly from the secretariat right down to the scale payment sub-office.

THE FINANCE OF THE POST OFFICE [1]

Four years ago the Post Office underwent a financial revolution. From the date of its foundation until 1933 it

[1] The accounts on which the following analysis of Post Office finance are based are the Post Office commercial accounts, published annually by order of the House of Commons. They are drawn up by the Comptroller and Accountant-General of the Post Office and audited by the Comptroller and

had been considered financially as a department of the Treasury. Revenue and expenditure were kept entirely separate, the former being paid over intact to the Exchequer and the latter being voted by Parliament on the annual estimates, with the exception of capital expenditure on telephone and telegraph construction and on Post Office sites and buildings. Capital expenditure was financed by loans, representing the estimated expenditure over a period of years, raised by the Treasury through the National Debt Commissioners and repaid through annuities which were charged upon the Post Office vote.

The result of this system was, as can easily be imagined, to discourage all initiative among Post Office servants towards improving the financial position of their department. No matter whether the surplus was one or ten million pounds, the Post Office did not receive an extra penny. It was in the condition of a woman whose bills are all paid for by a faithful but none the less grudging husband, and who has to hand over anything she herself may earn to him. Now this position may possibly be suitable for ordinary Government departments, though this is questionable, but it is certainly most unsuitable for a revenue-producing business such as the Post Office. The system was initiated long before there was any idea of the State being responsible for the running of certain important industries. There was thus no precedent for the financial arrangements of a Government business, and the Post Office was treated not as a business but as an ordinary non-revenue-producing

Auditor-General of His Majesty's Government, in accordance with the Exchequer and Audit Departments Act of 1921. "The Post Office net receipts," as shown in the weekly revenue returns and in the Budget statement, is a different figure. It takes account only of the revenue collected by the Post Office and the expenditure out of the Post Office Vote, excluding on one hand sums due by customers and the value of the work done for other departments without actual cash repayment, and on the other Post Office liabilities and expenditure by other departments on Post Office account. By bringing in these items the Post Office commercial accounts render an accurate record of Post Office finance comparable to the profit and loss accounts of private firms.

department such as the Foreign Office. Of late years, however, the formation of such public concerns as are referred to in this book made many people ask whether it was not possible for the Post Office to be run on a similar commercial basis.

The Bridgeman Committee paid special attention to this matter, and their principal recommendation was that the Post Office should contribute a fixed sum annually to the Treasury, and that any surplus which remained over and above this amount should be placed to its credit in a Post Office fund. This recommendation was agreed to by the Chancellor of the Exchequer and adopted by the Postmaster-General, and was given effect to in the Finance Act, 1933.

The accounts for 1934–5 were the second to be presented to Parliament since this innovation in the financial practice of the Post Office was made. In that year the Post Office, after paying over to the Treasury the full amount of its net surplus of £11,944,567, received back the sum of £1,126,817. The position is thus a compromise between the original situation and the grant of financial autonomy to the Post Office. It means in practice that, while it is still subject to Treasury control and is bound to pay the greater part of its present surplus over to the Treasury, the Post Office is now able by its own efforts to make a considerable surplus each year for itself.

The capital invested in the Post Office amounted to a total of £161,434,329 in the year 1934–5. By the word "capital," however, was understood only engineering plant and stores for telegraph, telephone, and electric lighting, together with land, buildings, and the Post Office (London) railway. All other fixtures owned by the Post Office, including motor vehicles and cycles, are not treated as capital, their cost being charged against the revenue of the year. The Post Office finds its money by means of loans, representing the estimated expenditure for a period of years, raised by the Treasury from the National Debt Commissioners and repaid through annuities which are charged upon the Post Office vote. The loans outstanding on March 31, 1935, amounted to just over £100,000,000. The Post Office is therefore in a very sound financial position, the value placed on its capital investments being nearly two-thirds as much as the total of its outstanding loans. The money has been borrowed at varying rates, the highest amount being 6 per cent in 1921 and 1922 and the lowest 3½ per cent in 1934. In the year 1934-5 a sum of just over £10,000,000 was provided for capital repayments and interest, the latter averaging out at around 5 per cent.

Before passing on to a detailed financial consideration of the various units which comprise the Post Office, it may be as well to mention three points which concern each one of them. The Post Office carries its own risks and does not insure against any contingencies. All services given to or received from other Government departments are accounted for at cost. The annual cost of accommodation is distributed through the general rent account on the basis of user.

How far may the Post Office be said to be a financial success judged by ordinary commercial standards? Let us take first the Postal Service. In 1934-5 this showed a net surplus, after charging interest on capital, of £10,910,819 out of the total net surplus of £11,944,567 earned by all the departments of the Post Office together. It will be seen, therefore, that the postal service is responsible for the overwhelming part of the Post Office net surplus. This service, however, cannot be considered as an ordinary commercial concern. The Treasury depends on the Post Office for a regular contribution to the national funds each year, and this sum may be considered either as rent paid for the monopoly conferred on it or as taxation paid by users of the Post Office. The greater part of it comes from the payment made by the public for the carriage of letters. Possessing, as it does, a monopoly of this absolutely necessary service, the State can charge within fairly wide limits what it wants. For example, during the war letter rates were raised from a penny to twopence. In 1922 they were reduced to 1½d., a reduction of 25 per cent. The result was an increase of only 5 per cent in business and a loss in revenue of £5,000,000 a year. It has been reliably estimated that the net annual loss to the Exchequer through the introduction of penny post would be in the neighbourhood of £5,500,000. The fact that it charges 1½d. for letters means that it considers that the senders of letters should contribute the sum of £10,910,819 (less that portion handed over to the Post Office Fund) towards the total national revenue.

When we come to the other branches of the Post Office, however, the position is entirely different. Let us take first the telegraph service. The business of sending telegrams was originally undertaken by a private concern. The Post Office bought out this concern in 1869 for a sum of £8,000,000. Capital stock was created between the years 1869 and 1877 for the purchase and development of the telegraph service, and interest on this stock, at the rate of 2½ per cent in perpetuity, is being paid to-day on all but a small amount which was redeemed some years ago. The total amount of annual interest is £271,691.

For many years now the telegraph service has continued to show a loss. In 1912–13 this was £1,175,347; during the war years, when there was a tremendous increase in the number of telegrams sent, it dropped to around £500,000; but in 1920–1 it was up again, this time to the highest figure it has ever reached, namely, £3,728,779. Since then, however, it has gradually decreased, and for the year 1934–5 it was only £651,235. Does this loss go to show that the service is unintelligently managed, and that it would be better for the public if the whole telegraph business were turned over to a private company, as many people have advocated? Comparisons have often been made with the Western Union Telegraph Company of America

and other private concerns. The Western Union manages
to-day to make a comfortable profit on its business, and it
has been argued that this is because it is run as a private
concern and not under Government auspices.

The fact is that the Western Union is in a very different
position to the Post Office telegraph system. The United
States covers a vast area and offers infinite scope to a
telegraph service. As the Bridgeman Committee said in
their report (p. 11): "The telegraph service as such . . .
is in the unfortunate position of lying between the upper
and nether millstones of an expanding telephone service
and of a postal organization which, with relatively minor
exceptions, ensures delivery of a letter anywhere within the
boundaries of the British Isles within twenty-four hours of
posting. No close comparison with the American telegraph
system is therefore possible. In the United States a large part
of the profit is derived from night letter telegrams, the
equivalent of which can in this country be sent by post at
a cost of a penny halfpenny." Since this report was issued
night letter telegrams have as a matter of fact been instituted
in the British telegraph system, but in spite of a wide
advertising campaign they have brought in only a comparatively trifling revenue to the Post Office.

It is fair to say that until a few years ago some at any
rate of the telegraph service's loss was due to the use of
out-of-date methods in the sending of telegrams. As a result
of the report of the Committee presided over by Sir Hardman
Lever in 1927, however, a departmental commission conducted a thorough examination into the telegraph service
in the United States. In consequence of its investigation a
considerable measure of reorganization has been carried
out, and the service may now be said in general to be run
on somewhat sounder lines.[1] The day of the inland telegraph

[1] Two aspects of the telegraph service which would repay investigation
are the special facilities offered to the Press and the policy of the Postmaster-
General in regard to the employment of telegraphists.

service is, however, past, and all that can be done now is to cut the loss on it and gradually merge it in with the telephone service.

When we come to telephones the position is a very different one. Here is a business which in fact is eminently suitable for comparison with similar businesses in private hands. Does an examination of its financial position show that it is a success or a failure?

For the year 1934–5 the telephone service had a surplus, after charging £5,544,306 for interest on capital, of £1,684,983. The net income of £7,229,289 represents a yield of nearly 6 per cent on the mean of the capital invested in telephone plant and stores.

Since the Post Office took over the telephone service from a private company in 1911 for the sum of £12,470,264, it has had only two bad years, 1919–20 and 1920–1. During these two years it lost nearly £6,500,000 before paying interest on its capital. In every other year it has been able to pay the full amount of interest due on the whole of its capital and to provide a fund for its redemption. Besides this it has made a profit varying from £107,391 in 1917–18 to £1,596,917 in 1923–4. Taking the whole period, including the years 1919–21, it has continually paid 5 per cent average interest on capital and made over £2,000,000 profit besides.

The purchase of the telephone system by the Post Office has in fact been a definite commercial success. It might conceivably have been a greater success, and a private firm might possibly have made a greater profit from it. But there are not many large private concerns that have as good a financial record during the last twenty-four years. To raise the whole of the capital required by the issue of fixed-interest-bearing securities and to earn enough to pay full interest on all of them is a remarkable achievement these days. An undertaking that can do this and, in addition, make a million pounds has every reason to be considered a success. The ability to make a profit cannot, however, be considered the sole or even the most important criterion of success in the case of a publicly operated service. It must be remembered, too, that the telephone, unlike the letter, is a luxury. Even the poorest can, and do, send letters, but as yet only a limited number of people in England have telephones. The Post Office, while not in competition with a rival telephone service, is in fierce competition with other firms providing luxuries. "Shall we have a telephone or a wireless? Shall we economize in telephone calls and spend more on going to the movies? Will a call to America cost more than the business it will bring in?" All these questions, and many others besides, are asked every day by thousands throughout the British Isles, and it depends on the cost and efficiency of the telephone service how they will be answered.

SERVICES OTHER THAN COMMUNICATIONS

We have considered up to now only the communications departments of the Post Office. But there are, of course, a number of other departments that come directly under the Post Office, although they are in no way connected with any form of communication.

The principal one of these is the Post Office savings bank. While the postal service cannot be said to have any competition worth speaking of, and the telephone service only in so far as its "goods" compete with other luxuries of a different nature which people might possibly buy in preference to telephones, the Post Office savings bank is in a definitely competitive position. It competes in the first place with other savings banks, such, for instance, as the Yorkshire Penny Bank, the various trustee savings banks, and the Birmingham municipal bank. But it may also be said to compete, at least in some degree, with the joint stock banks. In general the latter deal only with the larger accounts and the Post Office savings bank with the smaller ones. But there is a large area where the two kinds of banking overlap, and to this extent there is actual competition.

The Post Office savings bank was started in 1861. So careful were its founders to see that it did not compete in any way with the private banks that they placed a limit of £30 on deposits in a single year and £150 in all. To-day the yearly limit has been increased to £500, and there is no limit to the total deposits that may be made. Two pounds may be withdrawn on demand at any office, and approximately half the total withdrawals are of this amount.

Starting as a very small concern, the Post Office savings bank to-day has a total of £390,000,000 deposited with it. During 1935–6 25,000,000 deposits were made at Post Offices, and for the second time in the history of the bank the amount of these deposits exceeded £100,000,000. Withdrawals reached the high figure of 13,628 with a total of £5,000,000 in amount. The number of post offices transacting savings bank business was increased during 1935 by 430, making a total of 16,300. The Post Office savings bank is, in fact, a very flourishing concern.

The Post Office performs a number of miscellaneous services for the Government, mainly connected with the collection of revenue and the payment of pensions. Licences for dogs, guns, motor vehicles, and wireless sets may be obtained from it, and their sale occupies a considerable amount of Post Office time. The cost of this work is, with the exception of the sale of wireless licences, borne by the Post Office, together with the cost of dealing with the payment of pensions and separation allowances and the sale of national health insurance stamps. It amounts to rather over £1,000,000 annually, and, while the Government does not pay for it, the Post Office credits itself with this sum in the commercial accounts. The Post Office is, however, actually paid in cash for its services in collecting wireless receiving licences. It receives 10 per cent of the amount collected for expenses of management, and in 1934 this was £348,000. The cost of the work was estimated at £312,000, so that the Post Office surplus on this particular business was £36,000. Some idea of the volume of work falling on the Post Office in connection with these miscellaneous services for the Government may be obtained by a glance at the number of "customers" served. Six million wireless licences are issued each year, while two million people draw their old age pensions through the Post Office. Finally, some £70,000,000 worth of insurance stamps—mainly health insurance—are sold each year in post offices.

RELATIONS WITH EMPLOYEES

The Post Office is the largest single employer of labour in the country. The types of labour that it employs differ widely, including as they do officers who have passed the Civil Service administrative class examination and been through a university, sub-postmasters who are in reality shopkeepers trying to earn an extra penny by doing Post Office work in their shops, highly skilled engineers, and the postman who delivers the letters every morning.

It is obvious that such a varied collection of workers tends to be organized at least to some extent along craft lines. There are, in fact, a number of separate unions in the Post Office, each catering for a particular class of employees. Three of these, however, contain between them the overwhelming majority. These are the Union of Post Office Workers with 108,000 employees, the Post Office Engineering Union with 23,000, and the National Federation of Sub-postmasters with 12,000. Rather more than half the employees of the Post Office are thus comprised in three unions.

The first Post Office unions were recognized in 1906 by Sydney Buxton, then Postmaster-General, who allowed duly constituted associations of Post Office servants to employ officials outside the service and to make representations to

him for improvements in the conditions of Post Office
employment. To-day there are departmental councils meeting at regular intervals whereat the Postmaster-General or
the Assistant Postmaster-General presides, and the unions
state their claims at these meetings. Besides these there are
joint committees appointed *ad hoc* from time to time, while
each head office has its Whitley Committee. In this way it
is possible for most questions to be settled by agreement
between the Post Office and the unions. All cases that
cannot be settled by negotiation are referred to the Industrial Court, which is the final arbitrator between the State
and its employees, and in this respect the Post Office is in
the same position as any other Government department.
Strikes are forbidden by law.

The Post Office unions have, however, a potent weapon
which is denied in great measure to every other body of
workers outside the Government's service. This is the right
to raise matters connected with the employment of their
members in the House of Commons. It is, of course, true
that in certain cases questions may be asked in the House
on the conduct of any business, private or public, within
the British Empire. But there is not the same continual fire
of questions about other industries as there is about the
Post Office. The Union of Post Office Workers has its
representatives in Parliament, and they are able to question
the Postmaster-General in public upon any and every aspect
of Post Office work. This continual ventilation of grievances
by the staff has a most wholesome effect in preventing
serious abuses. A running fire of questions, for instance, on
the hours and rate of pay of auxiliary postmen may force
the Post Office to give serious consideration to the improvement of their position. It is impossible to estimate what
Post Office workers owe to this right of parliamentary
questioning; it is certain, however, that their conditions are
infinitely better than they would be without it.

Until eight years ago the Post Office unions were affiliated to the Trades Union Congress, but the Trades Disputes and Trade Unions Act, 1927, has forced them to sever this connection. The Labour Party is pledged to the repeal of this Act, and in due course the Post Office unions may once again find themselves entitled to join with their fellow workers in other industries, though it is doubtful if they will ever be given the right to strike.

There are 241,500 people employed directly by the Post Office. Somewhere around two-thirds of these are "established" and eligible for pensions under the ordinary Civil Service rules. The majority of the other employees, while not pensionable, are nevertheless in what is in practice permanent employment. A large proportion of the Post Office staff started as messenger boys at the age of fourteen. Every boy joining the staff is now given a pledge that, subject to good conduct, he will receive permanent employment in the Post Office. On reaching the age of sixteen he is allowed to enter for a limited competition and placed in a certain category corresponding to the standard he attains in this examination. Those who secure the top places go generally on to the indoor staff or into the engineering department, while the majority become postmen.

The postmen form the largest single grade in the Post Office and number over fifty thousand. They do not necessarily remain postmen during the whole of their career, but may enter a limited examination for promotion to the class of sorters, clerks, or telegraphists. This latter class is known as the indoor staff. They, in turn, may be promoted to supervising or clerical grades through limited competition.

The clerical class is recruited in an entirely different way to the rest of the service. In the main its members are composed of those who have passed one of the open competitions conducted by the Civil Service Commissioners.

The engineering staff is recruited, in so far as the rank and file are concerned, partly by the selection of men to start as labourers and partly through the class of youth-in-training. The youths are selected partly from applicants who have had a secondary school or equivalent training, and partly from Post Office messengers who show a definite bent towards engineering. The higher ranks of the engineering staff are recruited partly by promotion from below and partly by open and limited competition for appointments as inspectors and assistant engineers. Above the grade of assistant engineer advancement is entirely by promotion.

The Post Office combines the system of examination with that of selection for the recruitment of its staff. It is no doubt true that there is, as in any large concern, a certain proportion of neglected talent. It would indeed be a miracle if there were not. But it is a significant fact, as Sir Evelyn Murray points out in his book, *The Post Office*, that at least a dozen officers earning a thousand pounds a year or more began their official careers as messenger boys, telegraph learners, or in other junior positions on the manipulative staff.[1]

The wages and hours of employment of Post Office workers are regulated in the main through Whitley Councils. While its standards are comparable with those businesses employing a similar grade of worker, the Post Office cannot be said to take a lead in improving the conditions of its employees. The matter of the forty-four hour week is a case in point, and the Post Office might well be expected to take a lead in its establishment.

RELATIONS WITH THE PUBLIC

The Post Office has by far the largest number of customers of any undertaking in the British Isles. They include, in fact, the entire population of nearly fifty millions. The relations that it has with the public are therefore of the

[1] For further discussion on the personnel aspect see E. J. Waldegrave, "The Middle and Lower Grades of the Civil Service," in *The British Civil Servant*, edited by W. A. Robson.

utmost importance to its welfare. They affect to some extent
its commercial success, but they affect still more the spirit
among its own employees. A body of workers who are being
continually criticized and whose work is never appreciated
is not likely to be as good as one that receives its due amount
of praise. An irritated public is not going to make Post
Office transactions any easier, and will be ready to pounce
on the smallest mistake and find fault because of it with
the whole Post Office management. A business the size of
the Post Office may carry through several million transactions a day, ranging from the sale of a penny stamp to
the connection of a subscriber with a telephone number in
Australia. Out of these millions it would be a miracle if
there were not a few thousand that were imperfectly carried
out. No one ever hears of the million successfully managed
transactions, but a dozen people will be told of each one
of the mistakes. The problem of successful relations with the
public resolves itself, therefore, first of all into decreasing
the number of faults in the Post Office service and, secondly,
into realizing that there must still be a vast number left,
and that the important thing to do is to tell the public
openly that the Post Office realizes that it is not perfect and
is trying to do its best. Once the public are taken into the
confidence of the Post Office the battle is largely won.

The importance of goodwill to a business is only a
comparatively recent discovery in this country, though it
has been appreciated in the United States for many years.
British firms have been famous for their "take it or leave it"
attitude in the past, and perhaps the majority of them still
do their business along these lines. The most successful ones,
however, are to-day spending large sums of money and
employing a highly paid staff simply in trying to please
their customers. The Post Office until recently has been
behindhand in this part of its business. The natural distaste
of civil servants for anything savouring of publicity made
the Post Office reluctant to launch out on a scheme of

advertising and high-power salesmanship. Members of the Post Office secretariat rather liked the feeling that they were right and the public in its ignorant criticisms was wrong. At any rate, they preferred it to the feeling that they were trying to "put themselves across" to the public. Yet the difficulty of creating a feeling of goodwill between the Post Office and its customers may be appreciated by reference to a paragraph in the report of the Bridgeman Committee:

The habit of condemning the telephone service began when it was in the hands of private enterprise, and still continues, probably with diminishing force; but in this country habit dies hard. It is difficult to adopt an unprejudiced attitude regarding an instrument which, if it is one of the blessings of civilization is not altogether an unmixed blessing.

The telephone service is only one part of the Post Office, but an attack on it reacts on the whole service, since people very naturally do not distinguish it from the rest of the organization. When the natural irritation of the public against it is exacerbated, as it was during recent years, by interested parties who wished to see someone else making profits out of the service, the Post Office was bound to suffer in public esteem.

This was the position in 1931. In that year, six months before the Labour Government went out of office, the problem of Post Office relations with the public was first tackled. A Publicity Committee, composed of some of the leading men in the advertising world, was appointed, and an exhaustive inquiry was conducted into the whole method of Post Office salesmanship. Post Office methods left much to be desired. In fact, so far as advertising went, they might be said to have been without any method at all.

As soon as these reports were in the hands of the Postmaster-General things began to move. A public relations officer was appointed, and a new department created for him. Advertising by poster and in the Press was developed; a Post Office film unit was started, and films of Post Office

work have been shown to thousands of people; while since
1931 the Post Office has held numerous highly successful
exhibitions. Meanwhile, there was a big increase in the
number of telephone salesmen, and the old staff as well as
the new were given a course of training in salesmanship.

All these activities have revolutionized the relations of the
public with the Post Office. A prominent newspaper owner
once said at a public dinner: "The advertising columns in
our newspapers are, of course, frequently reflected in the
editorials." Before 1931 the Post Office scarcely ever advertised in the Press. To-day it takes a considerable amount
of space, and the result can be seen in the way it is treated
by the Press. Instead of articles about people who have had
to wait for half an hour before they could get a simple
connection on the telephone we see articles about golden-
voiced telephone girls and bright-eyed telegraph boys. Such
are the methods by which public opinion is formed to-day.
The Post Office has at last appreciated these methods, and
to-day its relations with the Press are entirely different from
what they were for the past twenty years.

Besides cultivating good relations with the Press, the Post
Office has taken immense trouble during the last three or
four years to improve the relations between its staff and
the public. The Brighter Post Office Movement is an
obvious illustration of this, but less striking instances may be
seen any day in the method of approach of the Post Office
staff to their customers. They seem now to treat customers
as people who are welcome instead of looking upon them
as burdens that have to be borne. And the effect on the
customers is equally remarkable. Instead of a continual
undercurrent of abuse breaking out sometimes into an open
campaign against the Post Office, there is to-day a slow but
steady growth of goodwill as the public comes to understand
the variety and difficulty of the services which this great
organization is providing for it.

Lastly, the Post Office depends in its public relations to

some extent on direct consultation with bodies representing various sections of the public. There is a Post Office Advisory Council at headquarters, on which are a number of men and women prominent in various walks of life who are sufficiently interested in the Post Office to meet several times a year to discuss with the Postmaster-General methods of improving the service. Smaller councils are being set up to-day in various towns throughout the country, and it is hoped in this way to get a further insight into local Post Office needs. Such bodies as the Association of British Chambers of Commerce and the National Chamber of Trade help the Post Office by studying and crystallizing the needs of their members and affiliated bodies in respect of Post Office services.

To summarize the position, it is no exaggeration to say that five years ago the Post Office took less trouble than any other big business in its public relations. To-day it is in the forefront of those who have developed the study of public relations to a fine art.

CONCLUSIONS

The Post Office presents to-day an example of an efficient and rapidly developing Government business. There are many faults that can still be found with it, and it would indeed be surprising if there were none in an organization employing a quarter of a million people and serving the entire population. But a considered judgment of the Post Office by the Bridgeman Committee contained the following appreciation of its work:

> While in our opinion these criticisms are not devoid of some substance, we have formed the impression that in general the standard of efficiency shown by the Post Office in the performance of its duties is very satisfactory. We doubt whether the public fully appreciate how high this standard is.

The Post Office has given the world an example of a concern run every bit as efficiently as that of any private employer, and far more efficiently than the vast majority of businesses in this country. The spur of private profit and the fear of incurring the wrath of ever-watchful shareholders, which are said to be the main driving forces towards efficiency, are entirely absent from the Post Office. Their place is taken by the spur of parliamentary questions and committees of inquiry.

The British Post Office has shown what orthodox State socialism can do. During the last ten or fifteen years there has grown up a strong movement away from just this type of organization and towards the establishment of public utilities directed by small boards with only the minimum of parliamentary interference. There is much to be said for the new type of organization, which may indeed prove to be the best for most socialized industries. But even if this be so, it is of the utmost importance that there should be at least one great concern run entirely differently to act as a measuring-rod against which the efficiency of each of the new public boards may be judged. There is no body better able to perform this service than the Post Office.

10

THE ORGANIZATION OF THE CO-OPERATIVE MOVEMENT

by

GEORGE WALWORTH

THE co-operative movement differs from other national organizations considered in this volume in that the national character is the result of purely evolutionary development without statutory establishment. The origin of the movement rests on voluntary association of parties of similar interests without any legal compulsion, and even to-day the entire movement operates on the basis of local, voluntary, and autonomous associations of producer or consumer members. Any federal or national activities, whether in production or distribution, are controlled on a democratic basis by the local co-operative associations or societies, which, of their own free will, become shareholding members of the larger national bodies. Thus the various agricultural and industrial societies of the country may determine that the wholesale societies must enter into actual production of certain commodities, but this implies no obligation on the part of the constituent societies to absorb the total output of production.

The co-operative movement has the curious quality of being regulated by a large number of local autonomous units, many of which may operate an isolationist policy in their own areas. Nevertheless, this gigantic voluntary organization, known as the co-operative movement, probably works more uniformly and nationally than most of the national organizations fixed or authorized by statute.

The underlying principle of co-operation is probably traceable more to the fundamental gregarious instinct in man for self-defence than to any principle developed in civilization. The industrial revolution is usually credited with inspiring the Industrial Co-operative Movement, but actually the poverty of this period only led to the establishment of a few scattered societies of working-class consumers, societies of quite different types and probably unknown to each other in the early days.

The ultimate ascendency of one type of industrial society was undoubtedly due to the discovery of the "dividend principle," whereas the development of agricultural and productive societies was in the main due to social aspirations for self-supporting communities. The overseas development of co-operation was mainly of later date, and traceable to educational or religious propaganda in Europe, followed by a world-wide development among agricultural exporting countries.

ORIGIN OF THE MOVEMENT

The idea of self-supporting communities occurs in More's *Utopia*, in various attempts of philanthropists to set up colonies, and later in socialist attempts to replace currency by labour tokens.

Robert Owen, a pioneer of British co-operation, in publications of the period 1813–16 admitted his indebtedness to John Bellers, a Quaker, who published a tract on self-supporting communities in 1696, and to the settlement founded by the Shakers in the United States of America. Although Owen became associated with the Industrial Co-operative Movement, his views coincided far more with the social ideals of self-supporting communities than with the simple trading efforts of the Rochdale weavers, who are now regarded as the parents of the industrial movement.

The movement did not develop as the result of a policy. One of the early co-operative attempts in 1767 was the establishment of a corn mill in Wolverhampton. This mill was built by public subscription for the use of the poor. Similar charitable ventures followed in various parts of the country round about 1795. In the same period, shops were opened by charitably disposed people round London to supply the poor with food and household necessities near to cost price.

In 1793 Friendly Societies first obtained Government recognition under the first Friendly Societies Act. These societies frequently entered into trade, but mainly to break high prices in such commodities as bread or coal. It is interesting to note that until 1852 any co-operative societies which were formed were registered under the Friendly Societies Act.

Robert Owen undertook a large-scale social experiment in New Lanark, and included on the estate a model factory. This was purely a social venture.

In 1824 the London Co-operative Society was established as a definite co-operative trading body endeavouring to sell commodities at minimum prices. In 1825 a further attempt was made in community organization at Orbiston, where about one hundred colonists were settled on the land on communal lines. On the death of the founder the estate was sold and the colonists dispossessed. At Ralahine, in County Clare, Ireland, a co-operative estate was established in 1831, and wages were mainly paid in the form of labour notes. This experiment was a great success, but unfortunately the estate was rented under the owner, who finally lost his property to creditors. The co-operative society was not a body corporate in law, and so was not recognized as tenant, thereby losing all its improvements and rights on the transfer of the estate. A larger experiment at Queenwood collapsed after seven years for lack of capital. Alongside these experiments, but totally independent of them, local co-operative societies were set up in many parts of the country purely as traders. It is estimated that by 1830 there were probably about three hundred such local societies in existence in the country, and some of them undertook some degree of production; for example, the Brighton Society possessed 28 acres cultivated as a nursery and market garden. Some Northern societies were occupied in weaving, and a few in agriculture. Most of these early societies, however, eventually collapsed without having become part of any large-scale co-operative organization.

In 1832 a so-called National Equitable Labour Exchange was established in London, where goods were paid for by labour notes.

In the same year the co-operative societies commenced their annual congresses, the first of which was held in Manchester, but at these early congresses there was very little cohesion between societies and considerable difficulty in obtaining representative assemblies. From 1835 the annual congresses were discontinued for several years, and co-operation very seriously declined. It is at this stage that the industrial revolution really did provide an impetus for a different type of co-operative movement. Trade unions were being recognized, the Chartists were issuing propaganda, and added attention was being paid to public health and education.

In 1844 the Rochdale Pioneers opened their small store. The poverty of Rochdale was indescribable, and it appears that a group of poor weavers collected the necessary funds to open a small shop for the sale of butter, sugar, flour and oatmeal, as well as candles. This society differed from previous co-operative societies in that it attempted to sell its goods at prevailing local prices, it restricted interest on capital to a fixed rate, it refused credit, and, what is more important, distributed its profits in proportion to purchases. The society adopted open membership for all customers, and members had only one vote irrespective of shareholding. A further novelty was the holding of frequent members' meetings for discussing the society's business and welfare. Balance sheets were provided for all members. The society was successful, and gradually other societies on similar lines extended in all directions. As the industrial movement extended, joint support was given for the establishment of wholesale warehouses, publishing societies, local productive societies, and, finally, for the co-ordinating machinery of the Co-operative Union. It is rather surprising that the original aims and objects of the Rochdale Pioneers are still the basis of the modern co-operative movement. The idea of self-supporting communities has been abandoned, but the idea of an ultimate co-operative commonwealth still remains. Gradually the industrial co-operative movement has attempted to secure the control of industry and commerce on an ever-widening scale, and at the present time the annual turnover of the retail societies of the country amounts to £209,000,000. The trade union influence is strong, with the result that co-operative employment represents a high standard of wages, security of tenure, and almost 100 per cent trade unionism among employees.

It should not be imagined that the Industrial Co-operative Movement was the only co-operative development in the country from 1844. The social side of co-operation developed very rapidly in various directions, and ultimately resulted in considerable development of trade unionism and in the recognition of co-operative societies by Parliament. At the same time, although the co-operative idealists involved made considerable headway in co-operative production, their activities practically faded by 1860. Up to 1848 the Christian Socialists, under the influence of Ludlow, Maurice, and Charles Kingsley, developed the principles of co-operation as a social ideal. They imported the idea of productive co-operative societies from France, and set up the "Castle Street Tailors' Association" on similar lines in 1850.

Vansittart Neale, a wealthy barrister, gave considerable help in establishing productive co-operative societies, and he was mainly responsible for obtaining the Industrial and Provident Societies Act of 1852, which legalized the position of such productive associations. This Act was the first example of statutory regulation of co-operative associations.

It gave rights for such associations to hold real property in their own names and to allow the selling of goods to the general public. The previous Friendly Societies Act gave no such protection, whilst registration under the Joint Stock Companies Act of 1844 involved stated amounts of capital and transferable shares, both of which encouraged capitalism rather than socialism. Co-operative associations function on the basis of unlimited capital, non-transferable shares with limited interest, and the return of profits in the form of dividends to purchasers. Having obtained statutory recognition for co-operative associations, Neale then prepared rules for the formation of co-operative stores. He established a central wholesale house to co-ordinate the various co-operative associations, and this wholesale society, the Central Co-operative Agency, continued until 1857. He was also responsible for the formation of a Co-operative League, established in 1852, to act as an administrative centre for co-operation and to hold annual congresses between all co-operative interests. He thus anticipated both the Co-operative Wholesale Society and the Co-operative Union, but he was in advance of his time and neither of his institutions survived. A great many productive societies were established, but eventually the Christian Socialist Movement dwindled away, after seeing the collapse of most of its productive societies. The movement did, however, secure legal status for co-operation, and played a considerable part in consolidating trade unionism and education. It is rather curious that the Christian Socialists, although establishing wholesale warehouses, would not agree to wholesale societies entering into production. In fact, the present wholesale society, which was established in 1863, had originally no powers to undertake production.

The present wholesale society was the outcome of the Rochdale type of co-operative development, and was only rendered possible by an amendment to the Industrial and Provident Societies Act in 1862. The question of the wholesale society entering into production was discussed for many years, but societies were very resistant to the principle of co-operative production by the wholesale society.

By 1870 a Central Board was established representing all co-operative societies in the country, and maintained on a contribution of one penny per member from the various societies. This Board operated in five sections, each section being independent but controlled at the central office by a committee of two representatives from each section. The central committee was termed the United Board, and became the effective governing body of the co-operative movement and responsible for the annual congress. This was the origin of the Co-operative Union, which still persists as the central administrative body for the Industrial Co-operative Movement.

In 1871 the first co-operative newspaper was established under the title of the *Co-operative News*, and this is still the central paper of the Industrial Co-operative Movement.

In 1893 the Independent Labour Party was established, mainly in conjunction with trade unions, but it was many years before any working arrangement was made between the Labour Party and the co-operative movement.

The Co-operative Wholesale Society which now exists was established in 1862, receiving the present title of the Co-operative Wholesale Society in 1872. The society did not undertake production prior to 1873, and from this date it very quickly set up collecting and purchasing centres abroad. In 1870 the wholesale society had a share capital of £19,015 and an annual turnover of £678,000. By 1900 the share capital had increased to £884,000 and the annual trade to slightly over £16,000,000.

With the powers given by the 1876 Industrial and Provident Societies Act, the wholesale society converted its deposit and loan department, established 1872, into a banking department.

Although co-operative productive societies, under the

guidance of the Christian Socialists, had failed, the idea of profit sharing and co-partnership was revived, principally by Edward Owen Greening and Thomas Blandford. By 1882 the Co-operative Productive Federation was formed to co-ordinate the activities of various co-partnership ventures. Many of the ventures failed or were rescued by the c.w.s., but the Federation is still in existence, with headquarters at Leicester, and controlling a number of highly successful factories engaged in printing, manufacturing of boots, and hosiery.

Meanwhile agricultural co-operation had proceeded on totally different lines.

Two labourers' societies farmed about 350 acres at Assington from about 1835 to 1876, when the agricultural depression led to the collapse of the societies. Mr. J. Lawson, of Blennerhassett, Cumberland, attempted various forms of profit sharing with his farm labourers from 1864. E. O. Greening established his "Agricultural and Horticultural Association" in 1868 to sell reliable seeds and fertilizers. Otherwise, agricultural co-operation was merely a theoretical policy of a now successful industrial co-operative movement. Abroad, the co-operative idea was applied to marketing and grading rather than to production, but these overseas associations led to serious competition in this country, aided by cheap transport for grain, refrigeration for meat, and Danish specialization on butter, bacon, and eggs. There were too many middlemen in England to permit of quality standards and grading, and no centralization of supplies where the market was at the door. Royal Commissions in 1879 and 1893 could suggest no remedies except State aid and rating relief.

Horace Plunkett in 1888 returned to Ireland from Canada and gained the support of the Co-operative Union to establish agricultural productive associations. He established a co-operative creamery at Drumcollogher in 1889, and by 1894 had fifty creameries, ten requirement societies, and a credit bank in Ireland. The societies worked on the Rochdale principle, with farmer members, payment on quality basis, and distribution of profits as dividends on purchases. The credit bank was based on Raiffeisen's German system, devised in 1862, with unlimited liability and registration under the Friendly Societies Acts.

In 1894 the Irish Agricultural Organization Society was established to co-ordinate agricultural co-operative activities. This body was commenced by public subscription and later received Government aid. The I.A.O.S. broke away from the Co-operative Union owing to the C.W.S. taking over Irish creameries. In 1897 the Irish Agricultural Wholesale Society was formed from the previous agency society, mainly as a wholesale selling agency. Although most of the societies were under-capitalized, the wholesale society did break trade rings dealing with manures and machinery and raised the standards for tested seeds. Considerable improvement in quality of supplies resulted from the Irish co-operative venture.

By 1900 England only had about twelve agricultural societies, with a membership of 500 and an annual turnover of £10,000. In this year Charleton, of Newark, formed an English Agricultural Organization Society, largely supported by the Co-operative Union, which had two members on the Board. In 1905 Scotland made a similar arrangement.

In England societies for the provision of agricultural requirements have always been more successful than agricultural productive societies. From 1900 to 1914 the general tendency was towards organized companies in production and distribution, and the industrial co-operative movement reflected similar development, the C.W.S., in particular, entering into production to break monopolist trade rings. State control was advocated politically, but seldom regarded as a practical possibility before the war. During the war State control became a reality in many directions. Labour

*

problems led to the formation of the Ministry of Labour in 1916, and Wages Boards operated in agriculture under the Corn Production Act of 1917. An attempt was made at food control with a Consumers' Committee (including co-operatives) in 1918, and considerable success was attained. The Ministry of Reconstruction, set up in 1918, attempted to extend national control in the interests of peace, but the collapse of world prices in 1921 destroyed the Ministry. By 1921 unemployment reached over 2,000,000, prices were low, strikes occurred in industry, and agriculture suffered relapse, especially as overseas competition became keener than pre-war. About 1920–1 the industrial co-operative movement, through the c.w.s. and local societies, enlarged its interests in farming, culminating in the purchase of about 80,000 acres of farms. Over-capitalization, falling prices, and lack of efficient control led to considerable losses in this direction and tended to widen the gap between agricultural and industrial co-operative societies. The position was not improved by the tendency for the wholesale societies to develop trading sections and depots in connection with overseas co-operative marketing associations, so that retail societies in England encouraged imported goods, often to the disadvantage of home produce. As a result of falling prices and increased competition with imports, the agricultural co-operative societies began to get into difficulties, and about 1923 appealed to the industrial movement for assistance. In some cases the c.w.s. made arrangements which kept the societies in being, but, unfortunately, there was no concerted action on the part of the industrial movement to maintain contact with the agricultural side.

The Agricultural Organization Society collapsed in 1924 under circumstances which drew the industrial and agricultural movements further apart. Finally the National Farmers' Union agreed to act as a central body for agricultural societies, but, strictly speaking, there has been no real agricultural co-operative movement from that date, although up to one hundred agricultural societies have maintained membership with the c.w.s.

In 1926 some attempt was made to bring agricultural and co-operative societies together for trading relations, but this attempt was doomed to failure, largely on political grounds. About 1932 a second attempt was made, and, whilst it resulted in no particular co-ordination between the movements, the agricultural societies did obtain some recognition from the National Farmers' Union. On an inter-trading basis, business between agricultural societies and the c.w.s. has increased, but now is having to face the added difficulty that inter-trading is becoming extremely difficult under the various national marketing schemes.

PRESENT POSITION OF THE BRITISH CO-OPERATIVE MOVEMENT

Whilst it is true that the Industrial Co-operative Movement is mainly engaged in distribution, productive activities are definitely growing. At present the movement has considerable capital in productive activities abroad, but the tendency is towards replacement by home production. Some idea of the present structure of the movement can be gained from the statistical returns for 1934. There are 1,267 societies in the industrial movement, 1,135 of which are retail distributive societies, the remainder being productive or wholesale societies. The total membership is 7,250,000 with share capital of £147,301,000. The turnover of societies of all types represents £338,000,000, and the movement employs 284,445 workers, 50 per cent of whom are employed in distribution. The English Wholesale Society has a turnover of £91,250,000, with total share and loan capital of £93,500,000. One thousand and forty co-operative societies are members of the wholesale society. The wholesale society produces goods to the value of £31,400,000. The Scottish Wholesale Society has a turnover of £17,673,844, with total share and loan capital of £10,158,731, producing goods to the value of £5,112,950. The membership is 240 societies.

The Joint English and Scottish Wholesale Society has a turnover of £7,590,000, with total share and loan capital of £4,953,299, with productions to the value of £868,003. The two wholesale societies are the only members of this joint organization.

The Productive Federation has in membership 85 societies representing 32,669 members, and its annual turnover is £5,960,000. In addition there are certain distributive federations of retail societies mainly connected with milk, bakeries, or laundries, with an annual turnover of £676,000.

The movement possesses 39,000 acres of farms owned by retail societies and 18,400 acres owned by the wholesale societies. The total productions from these farms amount to £755,000. In 1934 the net losses, after meeting interest and depreciation, were 17s. per acre on the retail societies' farms and 25s. per acre on the wholesale farms. It is interesting to note that the capital invested represents about £43 10s. per acre and the total productions about £13 per acre.

The Agricultural Co-operative Movement, as recorded by the National Farmers' Union, contains 185 societies with a membership of 70,000. One hundred and one of these societies are concerned with the purchase of agricultural requirements, thirty-three are dairy societies, twenty-three egg and poultry societies, ten deal with fruit and vegetables, three have bacon factories, and six are wool-selling societies. The total turnover is about £8,500,000, and prior to the Agricultural Marketing Schemes many of these societies were not in a flourishing condition. About one hundred of them are members of the c.w.s., but mainly for the purchase of feeding stuffs, offals, binder twine, etc. It must be admitted that, whilst the c.w.s. and retail societies purchase supplies from many agricultural societies, no serious attempt has been made to absorb the output of such societies by arrangements between the two movements as a whole. On the other hand, the societies themselves are not wholly blameless, for in many cases a considerable amount of trade is done in factoring rather than selling the productions of their members in a bulked and graded form. At the present time, largely as a result of agricultural marketing schemes and anticipated schemes, there is a much greater tendency for the c.w.s. to centralize for the handling of home agricultural produce, and there is some likelihood of closer relations ensuing with agricultural societies. One of the difficulties of the c.w.s. has been that the whole organization is of a voluntary character, so that retail societies are under no obligation to take their supplies from the c.w.s. This means that there is frequently an uncertain market for English produce and consequently no encouragement for the wholesale society to enter into definite contracts with agricultural societies. In addition, agricultural societies have the weakness of not desiring to be bound to the industrial movement as regards supplies, but in many cases preferring the open market.

The tendencies of agricultural marketing schemes have very much altered previous policies, and the policy of centralization, which has been advocated by the Co-operative Union for many years, is now being regarded by agricultural and industrial societies with much greater favour. The Co-operative Union has operated its own advisory service through its Agricultural Department since 1928, and has consolidated its position with regard to the general agricultural policy of the movement as a whole. Prior to the 1931 Agricultural Marketing Act, the Agricultural Department advocated the co-ordination of all co-operative interests on a commodity basis, and in 1929 it established a Co-operative Milk Trade Association representing the English and Scottish wholesales and all the retail or federal societies interested in the milk trade. A similar commodity association was established for meat in Scotland, and recently further Associations of Bacon Curers and Butchers have been established for Great Britain. In connection with these organized associations, the Co-operative Union is responsible for various negotiations on prices, terms, and conditions of contracts, and for legal matters connected with these industries. It is probable that this line of co-ordination will be considerably extended, and that the wholesale societies will take a very important part in future development along these lines. It is recognized that through effective commodity associations more direct arrangements can be made with agricultural producers and considerable assistance given to the establishment of agricultural marketing societies in this country.

Up to the present the official marketing boards established have not been in any sense real marketing associations. They have normally, in the interest of producers, been concerned with price fixing, and, whilst in the case of the Milk Board a comprehensive co-operative scheme for making uneconomic manufacture a charge on the profitable liquid industry has been evolved, no attempt has been made to encourage agricultural association for the collection, grading, or marketing of produce. On the other hand, the Boards have, probably unintentionally, increased the difficulty of operations between agricultural and industrial societies on an inter-trading basis.

STATUTORY REGULATION OF CO-OPERATION

It has already been mentioned that the co-operative movement was not established under any Act of Parliament. As a result of pressure by the growing movement in its early days, the Industrial and Provident Societies Acts were obtained for regulating co-operative associations, particularly with regard to registration. The main provisions of the Industrial and Provident Societies Acts are as follows:

(1) Seven individuals (who must be at least sixteen years of age) or two industrial and provident societies are required as the minimum number of members of an industrial and provident society.

(2) Societies and their rules (and any amendments thereto) are registered with the Registrar of Friendly Societies. The 1893 Act contains a schedule in respect of several matters. The word Limited must follow the name of a registered society. A registered society is recognized as a corporate body which may sue or be sued and have perpetual succession. It may carry on any industries or trades specified in its rules, whether wholesale or retail, and may include dealings of any description with land.

(3) A registered society must have a registered office.

(4) Individuals and joint stock companies may not hold more than £200 of share capital, but there is no limit to the shareholding of one registered society in another.

(5) Loan capital may be accepted if authority is given in the rules.

(6) Share capital may be either transferable or withdrawable. A society with withdrawable share capital may not undertake the business of banking, but the receipt of not more than 10s. in one deposit or £20 in all from one depositor payable on not less than two clear days' notice does not constitute the business of banking in this connection.

(7) The liability of every member as a member and not as a purchaser is limited to the number of shares he has taken up, and this liability continues for one year after cessation of membership for such debts as were contracted before he ceased to be a member and if the contributions of existing members are insufficient to meet them.

(8) Members have the right to purchase a copy of the rules, to obtain a copy of the last annual returns forwarded to the Registrar of Friendly Societies, to inspect their own accounts and the list of the members of the society, and to nominate a person or persons to whom the shareholder's property may be paid on his decease.

(9) A registered society must have its accounts audited by a public auditor once a year, and forward, not later than March 31st in each year, an annual return showing receipts and expenditure, funds and effects, of the society accompanied by the auditor's report. The society must also forward a special auditor's report at least once in three years to the Registrar showing the holdings of each person in the society, whether in

shares or loans. A copy of the last balance sheet with a report of the auditors must be hung up in a conspicuous place at the registered office of the society. Societies undertaking banking must make up a statement in specified form on the first Mondays in February and August each year, and to display this statement in the registered office or other places of business where banking is carried on.

(10) A member under twenty-one years of age may be secretary, but not a member of the committee, trustee, manager, or treasurer of the society.

(11) By special resolution a society may change its name, amalgamate with another society, transfer its engagements to another registered society willing to undertake them, convert itself into a company under the Companies Acts, or amalgamate with or transfer its engagements to such a company.

(12) Upon application from one-tenth of the whole number of members or from 100 members if the membership exceeds 1,000, the Registrar, with the consent of the Treasury, shall appoint inspectors to examine into and report on the affairs of such society or call a special meeting of the society.

These Acts constitute the only legislation dealing specifically with co-operative societies.

Any productive undertakings of societies are subject to the various Finance Acts just as are private companies. Societies were exempted from Schedules C and D of the income tax arrangements on the grounds that such societies made no profits but returned their surplus to purchasing members. The dividends returned were not regarded as profits obtained by members, but as discounts on purchases. Schedules A and B were applicable to co-operative societies in general. Under the Finance Act of 1933 the exemptions were withdrawn so that in all respects co-operative societies are treated like all other corporate bodies.

STRUCTURE OF THE CO-OPERATIVE MOVEMENT

The basis of the Industrial Movement consists of 1,135 retail societies in the United Kingdom; 883 of these are in

England and Wales, 227 in Scotland, and 25 in Ireland. The membership of these individual societies varies considerably, six of the societies having over 100,000 members, but the bulk of the retail societies have less than 2,000 members. Each retail society has its own committee of management, its own officials, and its own staff. The committees, which consist of from six to twenty-five members as a rule, are elected from the consumer members of the society. These committees are responsible for the control of the society's business and for the making of all returns required by law.

Society elections are conducted on the basis of one member one vote. The officials of a society are responsible to the committee of management in respect of purchases, sales, etc. It is very important to remember that the societies are completely autonomous. The 883 retail societies in England and Wales, together with rather over 100 agricultural societies, are shareholding members of the c.w.s.

The c.w.s. divides the country into three districts, known as the Manchester, London, and Newcastle districts. The c.w.s. is controlled by a board of twenty-eight directors, fourteen of whom are nominated by the Manchester district, eight by the London district, and six by the Newcastle district. The directors for any district, however, are elected on the basis of all the societies in England and Wales. The voting strength of societies is proportional to the trade with the c.w.s. Although the directors of the c.w.s. are elected for a period of three years, almost invariably the directors continue in office until the retiring age. The c.w.s. Board of twenty-eight directors is responsible for the conducting of the society's business, including the general business of wholesaling, banking, the control of productive factories and estates, and trading arrangements with overseas. Quarterly meetings of society members are held in the various centres, when detailed balance sheets are presented and various recommendations must be approved by the shareholders. Quarterly meetings are held simultaneously at each wholesale centre for the convenience of members, but at each centre exactly the same agenda is followed, about two directors being responsible for conducting each meeting. This is an original but convenient method of placing the facts before all shareholders on the same day. Investments of societies in the c.w.s. receive an agreed rate of interest, and surplus is used for development, reserves, and the payment of dividend on purchases. In the case of retail societies, a member's shareholding is restricted by law to £200, but no such restriction applies to the shareholding of a society in the c.w.s.

The 227 Scottish retail societies are, in the main, share-holding members in the Scottish Co-operative Wholesale Society Ltd., which is controlled by a board of twelve directors, including the secretary, who is elected. In the case of the English wholesale society the secretary is appointed as a permanent official. Similar arrangements obtain in England and Scotland regarding the wholesale societies, although the Scottish wholesale has not a banking department like the English body.

Joint committees of the English and Scottish wholesale societies undertake certain operations, including insurance, the handling of tea, coffee, cocoa, and chocolate.

Although the retail societies are members of the wholesale organizations, they are not by any means compelled to purchase requirements from the wholesale society. The relations between the bodies are purely voluntary. It usually happens that retail societies purchase an appreciable quantity of their requirements from the wholesale organizations, but it is obvious that the trade of the wholesale societies with retail societies must be largely on a competitive basis. In many respects this voluntary arrangement restricts the movement in operating any national centralizing policies of trade. If the wholesale society were prepared to establish central productive factories or to attempt to handle certain

commodities on a national scale, there would be no obligation for individual retail societies to absorb the supplies.
The result is that the wholesale societies tend to concentrate on a policy of extending trade at competitive prices
with low dividends. Retail societies, on the other hand, are
frequently less concerned with competitive prices than with
the maintenance of a high dividend. It should be noted,
however, that of recent years the tendency amongst retail
societies has been to enter into trade on a competitive basis,
with a consequent reduction of dividend. Whereas the older
retail societies, particularly in the North, paid dividend at
the rate of 2s. to 3s. in the £ or over, the tendency of the
newer societies in the South is to stabilize dividends at
between 1s. and 2s. in the £. The wholesale society, on the
other hand, normally pays a dividend of 4d. in the £ on
general sales to societies, but an additional 3d. in the £ is
paid on goods actually produced by the wholesale society.

The Co-operative Union is an administrative body of
quite a different type. Great Britain is divided into eight
sections by the Co-operative Union. Each of these sections
is sub-divided into a considerable number of districts, so
that a district is made up of a relatively small number of
retail societies, possibly averaging about twenty-five societies
per district. The societies elect representatives to their
District Committees, the representatives being usually members of society Management Committees. Societies also elect
representatives to the Sectional Boards, and the eight Sectional Boards elect representatives to the Central Board of
the Co-operative Union. This Central Board, which is the
governing body of the Co-operative Union, contains seventy-
eight members, including those elected from the Irish
Executive. The Central Board in turn elects its own Executive Committee and Educational Executive. The Executives,
together with representatives from the wholesale societies,
Co-operative Press, Productive Federation, Co-operative
Party, various educational bodies, etc., constitute the

National Authority and the Educational Council respectively.

The funds of the Co-operative Union are obtained by a payment from retail societies of 2d. per member per year and from wholesale and productive societies on an agreed lump sum basis.

The Co-operative Union includes in its administration specialist departments dealing with finance, law, labour, education, publicity, and agriculture. In connection with parliamentary and propaganda matters, joint committees with the wholesale societies are established, and recently trade associations have been set up to deal with milk, coal, pharmacy, meat, and bacon, and these are regarded as committees of the Co-operative Union.

The recent tendency is for the Co-operative Union committees to deal with matters of national and general co-operative policy, and in view of legislative tendencies Co-operative Union interest has veered towards forms of centralized trading control. Even in Co-operative Union matters, however, the association of societies is still on a voluntary basis.

A number of productive and service societies, totalling about ninety-two, are engaged in such industries as printing, the manufacture of clothing, hosiery, etc. These societies mainly operate on a co-partnership basis, under which the workers share in the management and in the surplus. These societies are linked up in an organization known as the Co-operative Productive Federation, which has headquarters at Leicester. The total trade of these societies is about £6,250,000 per year. Many retail societies are shareholding members, and the bulk of the trade, but not all, is done with retail distributive societies. In addition, there are factories formerly owned by productive societies but now under the control of a retail society, whilst groups of retail societies have established their own federal societies for bakery, laundry, or dairy business.

TRADE OF THE CO-OPERATIVE MOVEMENT

It must be admitted that the bulk of the trade of the movement is concerned with distribution, particularly of foodstuffs. The total trade in 1934 was £207,000,000, this representing the retail sales of all distributive societies. In addition, the agricultural societies have an approximate turnover of £10,000,000, an appreciable proportion of which is included in the above retail societies' sales. So far as foodstuffs are concerned, it is obvious that an appreciable proportion consists of imported material, as the following figures indicate:

Commodity	Co-operative Trade	National Trade	Percentage Co-operative
Liquid milk	137,759,350 galls.	696,655,492 galls.	19·77
Manufactured milk ..	10,163,137 ,,	246,295,792 ,,	4·1
English cheese.. ..	106,375 cwt.	857,000 cwt.	12·41
Imported cheese ..	589,613 ,,	2,868,000 ,,	20·55
English butter.. ..	Negligible	674,000 .,	—
Imported butter ..	2,284,200 cwt.	5,379,000 ,,	42·5
English meat	2,097,539 ,,	24,410,000 ,,	8·96
Imported meat ..	768,186 ,,	34,462,000 ,,	2·23
Home-produced bacon	183,780 ,,	1,800,000 ,,	10·16
Imported bacon ..	1,000,000 ,,	9,953,167 ,,	10·05
Home-produced eggs..	226,000,000	4,764,000,000	4·75
Imported eggs.. ..	281,000,000	2,244,000,000	12·5
Potatoes	3,408,980 cwt.	75,340,000 cwt.	4·5
Sugar	7,521,840 ,,	33,700,000 ,,	22·3
Home-produced wheat	2,930,000 ,,	18,440,000 ,,	15·9
Imported wheat ..	16,591,060 ,,	104,780,000 ,,	15·85

It is estimated that the annual bread output of the movement is 353,000,000 four-pound loaves, representing a trade of over £11,000,000 per year. The cash value of the coal trade of the movement is £9,637,000. All these figures are, of course, based on retail prices. In considering the extent to which the trade is met through the wholesale societies, the position of the English c.w.s. may be interesting. In this case, of course, wholesale prices form the basis. The total productions of the c.w.s. during 1934 were £32,500,000, including £8,100,000 from flour milling, £2,500,000 from the manufacture of soap, £2,100,000 from the manufacture of preserves, and £2,000,000 from the

manufacture of boots and shoes. Other productive undertakings with annual returns of approximately £2,000,000
are tobacco, margarine, and printing. The various undertakings in connection with clothing, woollen manufacture,
hosiery, and cattle foods have annual turnover in the region
of £500,000 each. The c.w.s. also purchases from agricultural productive societies to the extent of £1,500,000 per
year, and tea from the English and Scottish Co-operative
Wholesale Society to the value of nearly £5,000,000 per
year. It is obvious, however, that the bulk of the sales made
by the c.w.s. are purely wholesale sales of commodities
purchased overseas or in the open market. The distributive
trade of the various departments during 1934 is as follows:

			£
Grocery and provisions	..	..	83,000,000
Coal	..	..	3,600,000
Drapery	..	..	6,200,000
Woollens and readymades ..	..	4,000,000
Boots and shoes	..	2,500,000
Furnishing	..	..	5,200,000
A total of over	..	..	104,000,000

Since 1865 the net sales of the c.w.s. have increased from
£121,000 to £90,000,000. The Scottish c.w.s. in 1934 had
a total turnover of £17,674,000, of which their own productions represented £5,113,000.

In Great Britain the movement employs about 285,000
workers, roughly 50 per cent of whom are engaged on
productive or service work and 50 per cent in distribution.
The employees are almost entirely members of trade unions,
and in general co-operative rates of wages are in excess of
general trade union rates or rates accepted by Distributive
Trade Boards. The total wages represent about £36,500,000.
The wholesale societies, the Co-operative Union, and the
larger retail societies operate superannuation schemes.
Generally speaking, it is recognized that employees enjoy
reasonable hours, good conditions of labour, and considerable security of tenure. Officials and administrative staff

vary considerably in salary conditions, and frequently managers are paid on a basis depending on turnover in addition to a basic salary. Probably on the average it would be accepted that the salaries of the higher grades are considerably lower than those recognized in national organizations or Government offices. It would certainly be acknowledged that directors of the wholesale societies receive considerably less than directors of large private trade organizations. Usually committees of management of retail societies receive small out-of-pocket expenses for meetings attended and no definite salary. In this direction it is obvious that the voluntary nature of the co-operative movement renders comparison difficult with other large-scale organizations or public utility companies.

The national expenditure on food, clothing, and household requirements is in the region of £2,000,000,000 per year. It is very striking that the co-operative movement handles more than 10 per cent of this total national trade purely in a voluntary basis and largely controlled by committees of management not specifically paid for this service. When the fact is realized that the workers of the movement are practically 100 per cent trade union, with at least trade union conditions, it seems more remarkable that the movement has made such headway in competition with capitalist organizations not providing comparative labour conditions and presumably attracting managers and directors of outstanding ability by the substantial salaries paid to those in control. It would appear that the essential principles underlying co-operation play some considerable part in the development of the vast co-operative organization.

INTERNATIONAL ASPECTS OF CO-OPERATION

In many European countries there is very close association between agricultural and distributive co-operative interests.

In some cases both sides are actually controlled by a joint wholesale organization, so that trading between the two sides is almost completely co-operative. Typical examples of countries with considerable development of co-operative organization are: Austria, Bulgaria, Czechoslovakia, Denmark, Sweden, Germany, and Switzerland. Within recent years an International Wholesale Society has been set up for encouraging trading relationships between these various countries and the United Kingdom. The British co-operative wholesale societies are members of this organization, and have considerable influence in it, owing to the fact that they tend to be the principal purchasers of the goods handled by other European countries. For the most part continental countries are dependent on production and export, whereas the United Kingdom is mainly an importing country, with correspondingly strong development of the consumers' societies. It is probably on account of this that the Industrial Co-operative Movement of this country has developed to such enormous proportions as compared with the Agricultural Movement. The English c.w.s. has very close relations with several overseas co-operatives. The New Zealand Produce Association is a joint organization of the c.w.s. and the New Zealand Producers' Co-operative Marketing Association established in 1921 with joint shareholding. The Danish Co-operative Bacon Trading Company, established in 1902, is responsible for the sale of one-third of the Danish bacon imported into Great Britain. The organization consists of a Danish Co-operative Supply Association and buyers, including the c.w.s. in this country. Profits are equally divided between the suppliers and purchasers. The Russo-British Grain Export Company contains 50 per cent shareholding by Russian co-operative associations, 25 per cent of the shareholding is held by the c.w.s., and the remainder by a private commission and a shipping firm. In 1925 the c.w.s. Bank opened £1,365,000 credit to the Co-operative Wheat Pool of Western Australia, and several millions in the form of credits have been given since. The Overseas Farmers' Co-operative Federation, mainly interested in fruit and dairy produce, is affiliated to the c.w.s. More recently the Palestine Citrus Fruits Association has been considerably encouraged by the c.w.s., and has now become a member of the English wholesale society. In addition, the English wholesale society has direct trading relations established with various farmers' co-operative societies in the Argentine, with Westralian Farmers, Ltd., and United Farmers, Ltd., of Canada. The wholesale society also owns factories abroad, as in Denmark, and the joint wholesale societies have oreign plantations for tea, etc. In most of the leading export countries the wholesale society has its own collecting and exporting depots. Through the International Co-operative Alliance, social relationships, with European countries in particular, are closely maintained. In view of the enormous overseas trade and the more intimate relationships between co-operatives at home and abroad, it will be seen that the movement is in a position of some difficulty owing to the modern tendency for the development of legislation on the lines of economic nationalism.

SOCIAL ASPECTS OF CO-OPERATION

The principle of co-operation is based on the idea of mutual trading for mutual benefit. The international motto of the movement is "Each for All and All for Each." The idea of profit from commercial undertakings is not recognized in the fundamental principles, so that in general the various sections of the movement return their surplus to their own members (after making allowance for expenses and reserves) in proportion to purchases or sales of the members concerned. It can be stated generally that the dividend returns to consuming members of distributive societies are much higher per £1 of sales than the returns to members of producers' societies, and this is quite in line with the general experience

of profits on a turnover basis from productive and distributive private trade organizations. The movement differs
essentially from private trade organizations in that the
return to shareholders is made on the basis of the shareholders' own purchases or sales instead of on the basis of
the shareholding. Because of this principle there is one
difficulty which is frequently overlooked in comparing the
movement with private trade organizations. The private
trade organizations may be highly successful by very rapid
turnover on small margins. This would not be of assistance
to the co-operative movement, in so far as every sale by
the movement ranks on level terms from point of view of
dividend requirement. It is quite true, of course, that many
sales are made with profits too small to meet the dividend
and that in the complete working of a co-operative society
certain sales must subsidize others. As a general principle,
however, the level price must be such as to cover dividend,
which can almost be regarded as a standing charge. It is
quite true that a society is at liberty to modify its dividend
rate in accordance with its trading for the period, but the
experience of co-operative societies is that frequent changes
in dividend rate have a most unfortunate effect on the
confidence of the members. For this reason societies tend to
stabilize their rates of dividend, and two of the problems
frequently considered by the movement as a whole are the
desirability of establishing a stabilized dividend on a national
basis and whether the movement would ultimately gain by
the aceptance of a low rate of dividend and the utilization
of further surplus in reducing retail prices on a competitive
basis. The co-operative movement has very definite social
ideas. It firmly believes in maintaining a good standard of
living for its employees. It believes that on a basis of service
near cost and on regular returns of dividend on purchases,
the idea of thrift may be encouraged among the consumers
of the country. The movement regards itself as evolving
gradually but surely towards a state or commonwealth in

which the people of the country, through their own capital and under their own control, will secure the monopoly of the trade of the nation. The *principles* of co-operation are completely opposed to capitalism for private profit, and it is confidently believed by co-operators that the profits accruing from the trade of the country should be used for the welfare of the citizens of the country. In a sense, the ultimate goal of the co-operative system would be a form of national control in each country, but always for the welfare of the nation as a whole and not for the private profit of any individuals or organizations. It is rather remarkable that wide public control ideas of this character should, in many directions, cut directly across some of the ideas of socialism and of State control. In the first place, the tendency of trade unionism is to develop on protectionist lines. In advocating the welfare of the workers of a particular industry there is a natural tendency towards an upward trend of prices and towards a restriction of competing commodities from abroad. It is open to doubt whether the upward trend of prices does necessarily mean increased welfare for the workers. The essential factor is the purchasing power of the woikers, and a general upward trend of prices under the present monetary system automatically means a reduction in purchasing power. The balance under our currency system is very difficult to maintain. These difficulties were realized long ago in co-operative and early socialist circles, which accounts for the various attempts to displace currency by notes in terms of hours of labour.

Co-operators are faced with difficulties in relations with the trade union movement in so far as co-operation is essentially international. Restriction of imports from co-operative sources may be desirable in the interests of home producers' prices, but it is difficult to justify inflicting hardship on the overseas co-operators concerned. In recent years the National Government in this country has definitely embarked on a policy of restriction of imports of foodstuffs, frequently without too much regard to the effect on the normal export of manufactured goods which must be maintained for the welfare of the bulk of the population of Great Britain. In devising means for restricting imports the Government has had regard to tariffs, quotas, and some form of import board control. The latter is essentially a socialist idea, although it is doubtful if the Government would be pleased to acknowledge this. So far as tariffs are concerned, experience has shown that very frequently a tariff does not secure the rise in prices anticipated in the competitive imported commodity. The tariff idea frequently leads to a subsidy in the overseas country and possibly to a reduced standard of living among the producers concerned. In any case it seldom secures for any period a substantial increase over world price levels for the commodities received in this country. The quota principle can only really become operative if applied both to home produce and imported commodities. In such a case the quota idea very definitely stabilizes capitalism, and therefore strikes at the roots both of socialism and co-operation. In the first place, the import quota grants a monopoly to the licensed importers up to the quantities permitted in the licence. Such importers would be in a position, under a global quota, to purchase at world prices. They would obviously release their imports in this country at agreed stabilized prices with a guaranteed market and no particular necessity for an expensive selling organization, so that the importers would receive very considerable profits without competition. The home producers would also be stabilized on the basis of their licensed output, they would hold monopolies up to the limit of their licences, would have no competition, and guaranteed profits on the basis of the stabilized prices. Further, there would be no question of one producer or distributor extending his trade at the expense of another. Now, although the co-operative movement already handles approximately one-tenth of the essential food and household services of the country, it does not supply completely the requirements of its own members. Further, the movement, in the interests of the public welfare, definitely pursues a policy of extending its operations at the expense of private trade capitalism. Under a quota system the movement would not be permitted to extend even to the extent of supplying its own members. On the other hand, whilst it continuously would have to release part of its trade from overseas, it would only be permitted to extend its home trade in proportion to its quota. The result would be that the co-operative movement would actually be losing from year to year considerable quantities of import trade, and private trade organizations would be absorbing part of this trade which was formerly co-operative. From the co-operative point of view, the allocation of quotas really means the handing over of part of the existing co-operative trade to capitalism. Obviously the movement does not regard such a scheme as contributing to socialism or to the extension of the co-operative idea.

In the case of Import Boards there is a great deal of loose thinking. In theory the Import Board idea may be very sound, but the important question is the method of its practical application. If the State itself, by confiscation, took over the absolute control of imports for the benefit of the nation as a whole, co-operators would have less objection to the scheme. If, on the other hand, as is more likely, the State proposes to operate Import Board control on the basis of licences to existing importers, the State is, in fact, granting monopoly powers with guaranteed prices and uncontrollable profits to those importers. Just as in the case of the quota, licences would probably be granted in proportion to existing trade, so that the monopolists set up by statute would mainly be capitalists working for private profit. Such an arrangement would not be conducive to the expansion of co-operation nor to the welfare of the State. At the same time, the home producers, benefiting by an artificial raising of price levels, would either have to be controlled on a quota basis, with all the difficulties mentioned above, or would be at liberty to produce without limitation. In the latter case excess production would probably result in destroying the artificial level of prices completely, and it is difficult to see where the home producer would gain. Many co-operators, like socialists, believe that only on the basis of the national ownership of the land would any progress be possible for the welfare of the nation by a system of controlled production and import. On the other hand, it is difficult to see how such State control could be exercised except on a basis of confiscation or very heavy compensation. In the latter case, enormous credits would be placed in the hands of the existing capitalist owners, and it is rather difficult to forecast what the result of such large credits would be on the stabilization of prices in this country. The average co-operator is forced into a peculiar position. He realizes, as a practical man, that he lives under a competitive capitalist system. He believes that by the gradual permeation of the co-operative idea co-operative trading must advance and will advance on a basis of free and open competition. He feels convinced that no capitalist organization trading for private profit can ultimately withstand the attack of co-operative organization. For such reasons co-operators view with misgiving any immediate attempt to eliminate open competition or to restrict the importation of commodities at world prices. Under the co-operative plan the advantages must be shared by the members, and ultimately the full membership of the co-operative movement might conceivably be the full population of the whole country.

Meanwhile, within the capitalist competitive system, the co-operative movement is being forced into the position of a capitalist organization to some extent. In the first place, the principle of non-transferable capital prevents speculation of the Stock Exchange type and interest is normally above that paid on gilt-edged securities. The security of the assets of the movement is very substantial, and consequently there is a flow of capital to the movement very difficult to check. It is true that individual shareholding is restricted to £200 per individual, but there are no such restrictions on loan capital or shareholdings of societies in wholesale or productive undertakings. Up to a point the accumulating capital is a hindrance to co-operative but not to capitalist development. The general tendency of the movement is in the direction of cautious and safe investment, so that, instead of a bold but possibly speculative policy in the direction of large-scale production and manufacture, there is growing investment in gilt-edged securities or in large capitalist organizations holding key positions in industry. Probably little objection could be taken to holdings in Government stocks or corporation loans, but investments in capitalist organizations to secure a profit tends to commit the movement to the success of these organizations in the interests of the money invested. It is estimated that in 1934 the movement had about £85,000,000 invested in non-co-operative undertakings, shares, and bonds. All this may be regarded as money not being utilized in co-operative development. It is frankly admitted that for several years co-operative production and sales service of co-operative productions have lagged far behind the simpler business of factoring private trade goods supported by widespread private trade publicity. So far as the wholesale societies are concerned, inducements are given to societies to buy co-operative productions, but the societies are voluntary buyers and frequently take the easy course of buying goods of well-advertised types to effect easy sales. Possibly to some extent this course is encouraged by the fact that retail salesmen in the movement enjoy reasonable basic salaries and do not rely on commissions as do private trade competitors. Within the last few years excess capital of retail societies has been used more freely in the erection of up-to-date departmental stores, modern shop-fittings, etc., and the societies have consequently embarked more frequently into the sale of

luxury or fashionable articles. This in turn has made the
lag in co-operative production even more noticeable than
before and, for the time being, given added impetus to
factoring. In this development the movement has come into
sharper conflict with the private trade and has been compelled to develop a much livelier publicity sense. Wholesale
and retail societies, although newcomers to widespread
publicity, are developing in this department to an extent
never contemplated in the days when co-operative stores
were more or less grocers' shops. Further than this, there
is growing realization that service is largely the outcome of
intelligence behind the counter, and a very large-scale
system of education for salesmen and departmental managers
is being developed through the Co-operative Union. This
in turn will be bound to result in increased. co-operative
production, and probably in considerable reorganization of
this production. Already the Wholesales and Productive
Federation are endeavouring to construct a joint selling
agency, and a ten-year plan for retail expansion and increased centralization on co-operative production is in
operation. In line with private trade, there is considerable
expansion in credit trading (anathema to the old type
co-operator) on far better terms than those commonly
current. It is questionable as to whether the general level
of efficiency in the movement shows any considerable
saving over private trade ventures, but in the commodities
really developed on specialist lines, e.g. milk and bread,
there is no doubt that co-operative handling can be done
on a margin impossible for the general private trader. The
day will have to come for co-operative centralization and
specialization on many more commodities, and, in the
writer's opinion, this will have to be on the basis of commodity associations of the whole movement rather than
through the wholesale and retail societies acting as general
traders. The development in the milk trade, for example,
has largely been through the driving force and propaganda

of the Joint Co-operative Milk Trade Association. Other similar associations are now working for meat, bacon, coal, and drugs, and the list will probably be soon extended. In such associations representatives of wholesale and retail societies meet on level terms and act nationally in the formulation of policy.

WEAKNESSES OF THE CO-OPERATIVE MOVEMENT

Probably the chief weaknesses of the movement are unavoidable in any attempts to establish socialist communities on a localized basis within a competitive capitalist State. The co-operative unit, the retail society, with its own committee of management, looks first to an adequate return to its members. Therefore departments of the society are weighed up on a profit-making and turnover basis, so that departmental managers develop a competitive outlook, with a tendency to resent expenditure, even on service or sales organization, so long as there is no appreciable decline in turnover. The natural tendency is to copy distributive methods of private trade competitors in the district, and to rely more on the society's own astuteness in buying than on any scheme of national handling of commodities. It is seldom appreciated by local committees that a national organization, as a middleman, might be better fitted to cope with the requirements of all societies than a local society can, by apparently direct negotiations, secure its own requirements. The parochial outlook may have advantages in dealings with fashionable or luxury articles on some occasions, but the mainstay of co-operative production and distribution must be in essential commodities required on a national scale. This parochial outlook tends to enter into relations with neighbouring societies, with productive organizations, and with the co-operative wholesale houses. The parochial barrier has proved the most serious obstacle to

M

any attempt to co-ordinate the entire movement, either for its own development or for maximum advantage under any national schemes of control such as marketing schemes, coal organization, or transport regulation. The essentially voluntary nature of co-operation frequently prevents any representative body, even the Co-operative Union, from obtaining actual authority to negotiate on behalf of the entire movement, although, as in the case of milk, the Co-operative Union is usually able to obtain general co-operative application of any national arrangements negotiated for the movement. The democratic committee system tends to be slow moving on any national projects, but, on the other hand, the movement has not the danger of experimenting with incompletely tested and expensive experiments on a national scale. Here the progress of the movement differs from the spectacular developments of Public Utilities or Marketing Boards. Probably because of the steady development of co-operation, the effect of co-operative competition is not so readily perceived by the larger private trade organizations, but the competition is nevertheless growing. A more centralized co-operative movement would hasten matters considerably, but the private trade organizations were in less peril under *laissez-faire* conditions, as the movement had less incentive to organization on a national scale. Modern legislation forces the co-operative movement to act more as a national body and less as a voluntary association of local units in self-defence. It may well be that the outcome of national stabilization of capitalism by statute will lead to definite co-operative revolution and a tightening up of the whole co-operative structure. As a matter of fact, co-operative affairs are already moving in this direction. The attempts to restrict co-operative trading on a dividend basis by the Proprietary Articles Trade Association led to increased production by the movement itself in certain commodities and general boycott of others. Actions of the Pigs and Bacon Boards led to united co-operative action through the Co-operative Parliamentary Committee and extensions of co-operative bacon curing. Restrictions of manufacturing facilities are leading to centralizing of the movement's milk trade. These developments have led to a new policy in the movement.

FUTURE PROSPECTS OF CO-OPERATION

It is now recognized that the co-operative movement can best face the difficulties of modern methods of control of industry by some degree of reorganization. An association of wholesale, retail, and productive societies on a commodity basis paves the way for quick action in centralizing co-operative activities, resisting restrictions as a national body, and utilizing the wholesale societies as balancing agents between societies. It is probably true to say that the present views on planned and protected industries would have been far less important had the movement developed on present lines immediately after the war. The movement is now arranging to withdraw some of its imports gradually and replacing them by home production in co-operative factories. A centralized meat scheme is being developed in anticipation of regulation of the industry, and by means of federal dairies and wholesale creameries milk service is being extended to all parts of the country, so that manufacture of surplus will be centralized. Similarly, commodity association is being encouraged within the wholesale societies themselves. The question of a central selling agency for wholesale society and productive societies is under consideration, and the wholesale society is considering the reorganization of its agricultural commodities under a central sales department. Obviously the next step is closer association between organized home producers and a centralized co-operative distributive movement. Then, and only then, will the advantages of national control be shared by all parties with fair play for the consumers. Legislation in the form of capitalist monopoly must always be to the disadvantage of the public, even though there is a pretence of safeguards in the form of ineffective consumers' committees, with quasi-legal committees for investigation of complaints. The primary interest must always be the statutory monopoly board on which the success of the complete scheme must rest. Thus the tendency is to ensure reasonable returns to the marginal producer rather than to insist on efficiency of commodity production or service.

The movement is passing through a rather critical period. In common with the nation, the movement is considering the possibilities of centralization of commodity control. With such ideas, societies are developing federal organizations for laundries, bakeries, dairies, and abattoirs. Similarly, the wholesale societies are encouraging central selling agencies. Alongside this development there is a tendency for larger retail societies to absorb their smaller neighbours, although this is frequently stoutly resisted by the smaller independent societies. It is not yet clear, however, whether the enormous society is in fact the most economic or efficient society, and, further, the growth of a very large retail society may easily lead to wholesale decentralization in due course, unless actual co-operative production develops far more rapidly than at present. So far as goods of private trade manufacture are concerned, a very large society may obtain wholesale terms practically as good as those available to the wholesale societies. In such cases the retail society tends to resent the additional payment for middleman factoring by the wholesale society. On the other hand, the large retail society must ultimately force the wholesale society to develop in actual production and the necessary national publicity to create a *real* market for co-operative productions. In the opinion of the writer, greater distributive efficiency may be proved in time to be associated with the well-managed, medium-sized retail society, in which case centralized wholesale buying and certain federal activities for processing, etc., would become stabilized. Under such conditions, society amalgamations and co-operative production would not extend so rapidly, but the movement would retain more of its democratic character and suffer less from the weaknesses of mass production. The nation, as well as the co-operative movement, has to give attention to this problem, especially with regard to conditions of labour and unemployment. It is questionable whether large-scale industrial activities with prosperity for a few gigantic organizations and a limited labour market will lead to a general national prosperity so long as large numbers of unemployed have to be carried as a charge on industry. This is all the more unsatisfactory so long as a high percentage of the profits of industry passes into very few hands.

Co-operation has one outstanding advantage over all other forms of national development—prosperity for any section of the community can never be obtained at the expense of the community at large for co-operative membership is unlimited.

THE PUBLIC SERVICE BOARD: GENERAL CONCLUSIONS

by

WILLIAM A. ROBSON

THE rise of the public service board as a new type of concern for operating, organizing, or regulating industrial activities is the most important innovation in political organization and constitutional practice which has taken place in this country during the past twenty years. These boards grew up in a typically British fashion. They were not based on any clearly defined principle; they evolved in a haphazard and empirical manner; and until quite recently very few people were aware of their importance or even of their existence. Now suddenly they have become all the rage. Politicians of every creed, when confronted by an industry or a social service which is giving trouble or failing to operate efficiently, almost invariably propose the establishment of an independent public board. The idea appeals equally to the Right and to the Left. It may be recalled that the Bill setting up the London Passenger Transport Board was introduced into Parliament by a Labour Minister, continued by his Liberal successor in office, and piloted through its final stages by a Conservative Minister of Transport. In 1931 no less than 320 Members of Parliament (including 295 Conservatives) addressed a memorial to the Prime Minister suggesting a transfer of the functions of the Post Office to an organization of this kind. The Central Electricity Board was set up by a Conservative Government; and the Labour Party holds the view that a similar type of institution will be required for the operation of most socialized industries.

It can be seen, therefore, that the public service board

has made a deep impression among politicians of all parties. But despite this newly awakened interest, neither politicians nor the general public know very much more about the existing examples than they did five or ten years ago—which is not saying a great deal. There has been no attempt to study systematically actual institutions, to discover what lessons can be learnt from the experiments we have so far made. The studies presented in this book constitute a modest attempt to fill the gap in our knowledge. They claim to be no more than a preliminary survey, a first approximation subject to revision and expansion as information increases. In this chapter an effort will be made to survey the phenomena as a whole in order to ascertain what general conclusions can be drawn.

A RAPID RISE

One is impressed at the outset by the rapidity with which these new administrative organs have come into existence. Before the great war of 1914–18, there were already established such bodies as the National Health Insurance Commission, the Road Board, and the Port of London Authority. During the war a number of important public functions were entrusted to similar agencies. But they were regarded as irregularities of an exceptional kind, momentary deviations from the path of strict constitutional rectitude.

The Committee on the Machinery of Government, which numbered among its members such advanced and distinguished thinkers as Mrs. Sidney Webb and Lord Haldane, definitely set their faces against any departure from the ordinary principle of full parliamentary responsibility.

Attempts have been made [said the report] to distribute the burden of responsibility by other means. In some cases recourse has been had to the system of administrative boards. . . . We think that where, as in the case of the Insurance Commissioners, a Board is set up without explicit statutory provision for a

Minister responsible to Parliament for their work, the position is obviously unsatisfactory. We feel that all such proposals should be most carefully scrutinized, and that there should be no omission, in the case of any particular service, of those safeguards which ministerial responsibility alone provides.[1]

The Report appeared in 1918, but despite the clear warning which it contained and the great influence exerted by its signatories, these recommendations were ignored the very next year, when the Forestry Commission was established by the Forestry Act, 1919. From that time onwards the new trend towards independence has made increasing headway against the doctrine of pure ministerial responsibility. In 1926 the British Broadcasting Corporation and the Central Electricity Board were set up; in 1930 the Coal Mines Reorganization Commission and the Area Traffic Commissions came into being; in 1931 the first Agricultural Marketing Act was passed authorizing the establishment of the Agricultural Marketing Boards; in 1932 the Wheat Commission was organized; and in 1928 the Racecourse Betting Control Board came into existence to operate the totalisator. In 1934 the London Passenger Transport Board was established.

It has not been possible to include studies of all these organs in the present volume, but mention is made of them in order to show the full extent of the movement towards independent or semi-independent administrative agencies.

THE AREA TRAFFIC COMMISSIONS

It will be noticed that not all of these bodies are engaged in the operation of a public utility service or an industry. The functions of the Area Traffic Commissions, for example, are purely regulatory. They control the system of motor-bus and motor-coach services run for profit throughout the country by means of an elaborate system of licensing which gives them vast and loosely defined discretions at every

[1] *Report of Machinery of Government Committee*, 9230, 1918, p. 11.

point. The chairman of the Traffic Commission in each area is appointed by the Minister of Transport for a fixed term of years not exceeding seven.[1] One of the other two members is appointed from a panel nominated by the county borough and urban districts in the area, and the third member is appointed from a panel nominated by the county councils. All are removable for inability or misbehaviour, and the Statute requires them to act under "the general directions of the Minister." When the Bill was considered in committee in the Commons, Colonel Ashley, a former Minister of Transport, moved the omission of the word "general" in this clause. He urged that it was essential for the Minister to have complete control over the Commissioners. Otherwise trouble might arise between the Minister and a cantankerous Commissioner who refused to accept his orders. Mr. Herbert Morrison, the Minister of Transport who framed the Bill, resisted the amendment on the ground that it involved a misapprehension of what was intended. He explained that he had no intention as Minister of attempting to direct the Commissioners on every point of their duty. It appeared to have been assumed that he was to be answerable in Parliament for the specific actions of the Commissioners. That, however, was not the case. He could only answer for the general actions of the Commissioners, not for whether they had done right or wrong in any particular case.

The Coal Mines Reorganization Commission is, again, intended to be purely a planning body without responsibility for the actual operation of a mine, or the management of the coal industry as a whole. It is not possible, therefore, to draw a distinction between these modern bodies and the ordinary departments of state by saying that the former are performing service functions (i.e. those in which a direct service is rendered to the citizen) while the latter exercise control or regulatory powers.

[1] A Bill is now before Parliament to give the chairmen of the Traffic Commissioners a permanent tenure.

There have for long existed numerous organs in the body politic possessing varying degrees of independence from ministerial control of the orthodox kind. Such bodies as the Public Trustee, the Registrar of Friendly Societies, the Charity Commission, the British Museum, or the National Gallery, all form part of the system of public administration in Great Britain; yet they are in many respects autonomous or semi-autonomous institutions. But there is clearly a great difference between them and the public boards discussed in the preceding chapters. The fundamental distinction lies in the fact that the public board is primarily concerned with the control or operation of a great industry or a public utility.

This, indeed, is not merely the distinguishing characteristic of the boards, but also the essential explanation of their creation. The complex technological problems involved, the need for a spirit of boldness and enterprise, the desire to escape from the excessive caution and circumspection which day-to-day responsibility to Parliament necessitates, the recognition that the operation of public utilities and industrial undertakings requires a more flexible type of organization than that provided by the ordinary Whitehall department—these were the principal causes which led to the establishment of the independent public service board and helped it to gain public favour.

On the whole, the political instinct which led to the setting up of these boards has been amply justified by the results that have been achieved. Criticism has not been lacking in the preceding chapters, and it will not be spared in the following pages; but it is certain that electricity supply, broadcasting, metropolitan transport, and the docks and harbours of London have been substantially better managed and developed by their respective boards than would have been the case if the task had been given to an ordinary government department or left to the unregulated competition of private profit-making ownership.

It may be argued that the Post Office presents an exception to this statement, for the Post Office is admittedly a success in regard to the greater part of its activities, although it is the classic example of a department organized in strict accord with the traditional principles of full ministerial responsibility. This, however, is scarcely the position to-day. The Post Office reached its lowest point in public esteem and general efficiency when it adhered rigidly to the pattern of the ordinary Whitehall offices (other than the Defence Departments). It began to make a conspicuous advance, both in actual achievement and in public favour, after the Report of the Bridgeman Committee in 1932 had led to a series of reforms, which in two important respects had the effect of making it resemble a public board far more closely than hitherto.[1] In the first place, the Post Office is now organized internally as a board under the presidency of the Postmaster-General; and in the second place, it has acquired for the first time freedom to dispose as it considers best of any surplus revenue which remains after the payment of a fixed annual contribution to the Exchequer. Formerly, the whole surplus went to the Treasury, no matter how large it might be.

CONSTITUTIONAL TENDENCIES

Certain definite tendencies can be observed in all the boards dealt with in the preceding chapters. There is the tendency to divorce in greater or less degree the administration of industrial or economic services from the other activities of government. There is the complementary tendency to separate the finances of these boards from the national exchequer and to confer upon them a substantial measure of financial autonomy. There is the tendency to enlarge the area of operation to a national or regional basis in order to bring the administrative unit into conformity

[1] See "Post Office Progress," by W. A. Robson, *New Statesman and Nation*, June 16, 1934.

with technical needs. Another conspicuous feature in most instances is the tendency towards the establishment of a monopoly, in fact if not in law. Hence, the British Broadcasting Corporation, the Port of London Authority, the L.P.T.B., are without rivals in their respective areas of operation, although each is subject to certain kinds of competition from alternative services or from operators in outside areas. Thus, shippers can use the wharves or another port if dock facilities at London are unsatisfactory. Listeners can switch in to foreign stations;[1] and ultimately the L.P.T.B. could lose some of their passengers to motor cars, motor bicycles, or bicycles. The clear intention is, however, to dispense with competition in these socialized undertakings. The fixing of prices in agriculture and coal mining, combined with restrictions on output, are designed to attain the same object in the case of these privately owned industries. A similar aim is explicitly stated in the statute setting up the Area Traffic Commissioners.[2]

The constitutions of the boards present several interesting features. The members of the governing body are required in each case to be appointed for a fixed term of years, subject usually to removal for misconduct or inability—by which one understands the occurrence of one of those monstrous irregularities or formal disqualifications which occur so rarely in ordinary life as to be of slight practical importance. In most instances the tenure of office is not of the same length for all the members of the board, and the periods of service are staggered so as to preserve an element of continuity in the administration which would be lacking if all the members retired at the same moment. The principle of a fixed tenure is, of course, intended to secure

[1] Though the licence fee would still have to be paid to the Post Office.
[2] "The Commissioners may attach to a road service licence such conditions as they may think fit . . . for securing that . . .
(b) Where desirable in the public interest the fares shall be so fixed as to prevent wasteful competition with alternative forms of transport. . . ." Sec. 72 (4) Road Traffic Act, 1930.

independence for the board, since if the members could be dismissed at any moment they would be ultimately without an independent status.

At the same time, the principle of irremovability presents grave objections which might turn out to be highly detrimental to the public welfare. If a government came into conflict for some reason with one of the boards, it might result in the board deliberately deteriorating the service for which it was responsible or cultivating insolvency with the express intention of discrediting the government or its policy or a particular minister. Again, it is well within the bounds of possibility that a government of the Left which desired to pursue a vigorous policy of socialization and control of industry might find itself severely hampered by a board occupying a key position which was unwilling to go along in harmony with this policy or to expand at a sufficient rate. In certain circumstances a policy of merely doing nothing on the part of a board might be disastrous to the government of the day.[1]

Looking at the matter from a long-distance point of view, it would seem desirable to lay down a specific direction to the boards that they must carry out the general policies, if any, which may be prescribed by the government or by Parliament. To implement this it would be necessary to provide some further loophole against an obstructive board in addition to the right of removal for inability or misbehaviour. One possibility would be to make the members of the board removable by a resolution of the House of Commons. Another would be to give the government power to add extra members to the board, at their discretion, thereby enabling a recalcitrant or obstructive policy to be out-voted. This has been done in the new B.B.C. charter. Or, of course, one could give the appropriate minister a simple power of removal.

---

[1] The problem of co-ordinating the various boards under a national planning body is discussed later on page 399.

APPOINTMENT OF THE BOARD

In the case of the boards dealing with broadcasting, electricity supply, mining, and forestry, the government has the power of appointing the controlling executive; and this, without doubt, is the right method to adopt. It was the method proposed in the original Bill setting up the L.P.T.B.; but for political reasons the Bill was amended so as to introduce a body of appointing trustees consisting of such irrelevant persons as the president of the Law Society, the chairman of the Committee of London Clearing Bankers, the president of the Institute of Chartered Accountants, the chairman of the London County Council, and so forth. Anything more absurd than this device it would be hard to conceive. These *ex officio* trustees must in practice either rely on someone else's judgment, in which case there is no point in giving them the task, or they must form their own opinions, which in the case of most of them would not necessarily be based on any special knowledge either of transport in general, London transport in particular, or even of London. An excellent case can be made out for conferring on these public boards a measure of freedom from day-to-day parliamentary control; but just because they have a substantial degree of independence in the function of management, it is for that very reason of the utmost importance that the appointment to the highest positions should remain within the sphere of popular control, and this can only be done by leaving the decision in the hands of a responsible minister. The appointing trustees are utterly irresponsible from a political point of view. At no point do they have to answer to the general public for their decisions, and no way is open to the public to bring its grievances before them. An institution such as the B.B.C. may be regarded as democracy at one remove. The L.P.T.B., so far as popular control over the personnel of the board is concerned, is democracy at a hundred and fifty removes. In no circumstances should this method be followed in future instances.

In the case of the P.L.A., the principle has been followed of giving a controlling voice in the appointment of the board to the immediate consumers of the service, such as the wharfingers, payers of dues, and owners of river-craft. This has worked fairly well in the particular case, mainly because the port users form a small, coherent, easily defined group with similar interests. But the idea is of limited utility and cannot be regarded as suitable for widespread application. In most of the undertakings which are already under public ownership, or likely to be socialized during the next ten or twenty years, the consumers of the service form so large and heterogeneous a mass, with such diverse interests and so little knowledge of the special problems involved, that any attempt to form them into an *ad hoc* electorate for the purpose of appointing the control board would almost certainly end in confusion and general dissatisfaction. The most likely way of securing a measure of popular control combined with a reasonable probability of the special knowledge required for making the key appointments, is by entrusting the matter to a minister in charge of the appropriate department.

QUALIFICATIONS OF THE EXECUTIVE

Parliament has in some cases, such as the Electricity Board, the Forestry Commission, and the L.P.T.B., required that the members (or some of them) shall possess experience in particular fields, or be appointed after consultation with special interests, such as transport, local government, agriculture, electricity, forestry, industry, finance, and so forth. For the most part, however, the legislature has been content to give the appointing authority *carte blanche* as to who shall be selected, apart from a few self-denying ordinances disqualifying Members of Parliament[1] and persons with a financial interest in the industry affected.

The general practice has been to fill the principal posts in each concern with men of outstanding executive ability who have gained reputations in business or professional life, or the public service, and to select for the remaining places on the board a number of lesser lights of medium calibre and sound reputation. Sir Andrew Duncan, the first chairman of the Central Electricity Board, Sir John Snell, the chairman of the Electricity Commission, Sir John Reith of the B.B.C., Lord Ashfield and Mr. Frank Pick of the L.P.T.B., Sir Ernest Gowers of the Coal Mines Reorganization Commission, Colonel Banks, until recently Director-General of the Post Office, Lord Ritchie of the P.L.A., are all men of exceptional administrative capacity and unusually forceful character, who overshadow the other members of their respective boards. They were certainly not appointed on the grounds of their being either adherents of any political creed, representatives of the workers, or the spokesmen of vested interests, although in selecting their colleagues an attempt has been made to assemble various types of outlook and experience of a more sectional character. It was known at the time when Mr. Morrison introduced the London Passenger Transport Bill that strenuous efforts were made by the transport workers' unions to obtain representation for the employees on the board, and one part-time member is a former official of the Transport and General Workers' Union. This was regarded at the time as something of a concession. Shortly afterwards, however, the Labour Party's Annual Conference held in 1933 at Hastings passed a resolution declaring that wage earners of all grades and occupations have a right, which should be acknowledged by law, to an effective share in the control and direction of

---

[1] In the case of the Forestry Commission one Commissioner must be a Member of Parliament. It is not clear whether a governor of the B.B.C. can be a Member of Parliament. See Hansard, December 17, 1936.

socialized industries which their labour sustains. The resolution therefore called for direct representation of the workers, through their trade unions, on the boards of direction or control of such industries or services. I do not myself believe that this principle can be pursued to any large extent without endangering the efficiency of the enterprise and the interests of the consumer.

There is no doubt that the principle of selecting the chief executives on account of their administrative ability is fully justified by the overwhelming need for efficiency, vigour, and a go-ahead outlook in the conduct of these great undertakings. It is indisputable not only that the public boards dealt with in this volume are competently run, but also that much of the credit for their efficient management is due to the chief executive. The deliberate search for executive ability and the avoidance of political favouritism or sectional interest are tendencies to be definitely encouraged.

The remaining members of the controlling body vary in type and quality from board to board. The poorest example is to be found in the governing body of the B.B.C., mainly because technical qualifications are considered unimportant in selecting the governors, while political considerations have been permitted to carry considerable weight. The question is discussed at greater length in the chapter on broadcasting;[1] here it will suffice to say that the B.B.C. should in this respect serve as a warning rather than as an example to be followed. In general, it is undesirable that there should be too great a disparity of calibre between the chief executive (whether holding the title of chairman, vice-chairman, or director-general) and the other members of the board. Otherwise a relationship of domination on the one hand and subordination on the other may easily arise, and the whole virtue of the board system of organization disappears. Government by committee implies some

[1] See pages 85–88.

degree of equality of ability, or at least not an excessively gross inequality, among the committeemen.

Another aspect of the matter deserving of note is the practice, common to most of the boards, of appointing the chief executive on a full-time basis at a very high salary, while the remaining members of the board serve on a part-time basis at salaries of between £600 and £1,000 a year. This resembles the arrangement often found in large joint-stock companies; it contrasts with the organization of the Post Office Board, which consists only of full-time officials engaged exclusively on Post Office work.

The advantage of part-time members is that they bring an element of outside experience into the higher direction and ensure that the undertaking shall not determine its policy solely in terms of its own outlook and interests. In the case of the Post Office, an infiltration of fresh air from the outside world is introduced by the Postmaster-General, whose time is spent chiefly in political and parliamentary circles. The disadvantage of part-time members is that where the service is highly technical in character, or surrounded with a mass of detail not easily mastered by a cursory survey of occasional memoranda, the part-time members are unlikely to possess an adequate knowledge of the subject matter or sufficient grasp of the main problems to be able to play a part of real importance in influencing policy. The result is a formidable and sometimes excessive concentration of power in the hands of the individual occupying the chief full-time executive position.

In general, it is desirable that the chairman of the board should be the chief executive, as in the case of the C.E.B. The separation of the two offices in the B.B.C., for example, has been shown to have many disadvantages.

SALARIES DE LUXE

The question of salaries plays a significant rôle in this matter. Enormous salaries have been assigned to the prin-

cipal positions on these boards, judged by the standards
prevailing in the public service. The chairman and vice-
chairman of the L.P.T.B. receive £12,500 and £10,000 a
year respectively; the salary originally fixed for the chairman
of the Central Electricity Board was £8,000 a year. The
chairman of the Coal Mines Reorganization Commission
receives a salary of £7,000 a year, the director-general of
the B.B.C. £6,500 a year, and several of the principal
executives are remunerated on a similar scale. One is
prompted to ask why it should be considered necessary to
pay these individuals two, three, or four times as much as
the permanent secretary of one of the great departments of
state, whose responsibilities are at least as great, if not much
greater. The Post Office employs nearly a quarter of a
million servants and has a budget of seventy or eighty million
pounds a year, yet it operates quite efficiently under the
guidance of officials whose salaries in no instance exceed
£3,000 a year and are in most cases much lower.

The payment of extremely high salaries to the occupants
of official positions is likely to have far-reaching consequences. First, it will tend to magnify the power and
prestige of the recipient, not merely in the world generally,
but also vis-à-vis his colleagues on the board. They become,
in comparison, if not poor relations, at any rate humble
participants in the enterprise. Second, it leads almost
inevitably to the other members of the board being appointed
on a part-time basis, since it would be impossible to justify
more than one or two salaries on such a grandiose scale in
any public undertaking; and the only other practicable
alternative is to employ the remaining members of the
board on a part-time arrangement at a few hundreds a year.
Third, we run the risk of doing injury to the civil service
if we permit posts on these public boards to be rewarded
on a scale which bears no relation whatever to the salaries
paid to the men at the top of the civil service. How can
we expect the civil service to remain the loyal, devoted,

upright, and efficient body that it is to-day if we permit the members of it to find themselves surrounded with public boards controlled by men who are technically outside the civil service, but in fact very definitely within the public service, and who are remunerated on a scale far more lavish than anything offered to the civil servant. Discontent, jealousy, and envy are almost certain to arise, and when that occurs one of our most valuable national assets will have been damaged beyond repair.[1]

It may be argued that men of first-class business ability are indispensable for these public boards, and that salaries comparable to those paid in the commercial world must be offered in order to attract them. This argument is of doubtful validity. In at least one case a civil servant was taken out of his office to organize a board, and his salary was almost trebled for the purpose. The civil service has thrown up a sufficient number of men of outstanding business ability to show that high executive talent is not directly equated with princely incomes. The High Court judges are a standing demonstration of the possibility of persuading men accustomed to earn very large incomes to accept remuneration on a more modest scale on entering the public service.

From the political point of view, the establishment of these public boards would seem to be a move in the direction away from socialism if they involve the stabilization or intensification of the inequalities of income which have arisen under the conditions of private enterprise.

THE OFFICIAL STAFF

It is not only the appointments to the governing board which need consideration, but the entire staffing arrangements of these new institutions. They have grown up in a haphazard way and have in most cases been left free to

[1] See the essay on "The Public Service" in *The British Civil Servant* (edited by W. A. Robson).

make their own arrangements in regard to personnel. This
was no doubt due in part to the feeling that civil servants
were not likely to be the most suitable people to undertake
these new adventures in the spheres of electricity, broadcasting, and so forth. That there is a good ground for such
a belief can scarcely be doubted; and the criticism of the
civil servant which it implies is not unfounded.[1] But relatively small reforms in the civil service would suffice to
enable the staffs of the public boards to be brought within
the civil service and subjected, in the case of future appointments at any rate, to civil service standards as regards
methods of recruitment, professional qualifications, superannuation, remuneration, promotion, personal freedom, and
the right to form associations.[2] Admittedly a number of
changes in regard to pension policy, mobility, interchange
with private employment, methods of examination, and so
forth, are urgently called for; but more important still is
the need to integrate the personnel of these new public
boards with the regular civil service of the State, at any
rate so far as the leading principles of policy are
concerned.

A fundamental question which is raised by a consideration of the personnel problem is whether we are providing
in the university system of this country the kind of education
which is required for the higher appointments in these
socialized undertakings. In the civil service and the local
government service we make a rigid distinction between
technical men and administrative officials. The professional
class in the civil service consists of doctors, lawyers, chemists,
engineers, architects, accountants, and other experts, and
they are separated off into technical compartments subordinate to the authority of the higher command, which is
normally in the hands of members of the administrative

[1] See "The Public Service" by W. A. Robson in *The British Civil Servant*.
[2] See the House of Commons Debates on the B.B.C. (Hansard, July 6, 1936,
and December 17, 1936); also H. Finer, "The Semi-Public Services" in *The
British Civil Servant*.

class. A large proportion of the members of the administrative class, especially of those at the top of the service, have been educated in the humanities—in history, ethics, logic, philosophy, "Greats" at Oxford, or mathematics. An increasing number of the younger men have taken "Modern Greats" at Oxford, a course comprising economics, politics, and philosophy. For the most part they do not possess any knowledge of science, or even of its importance in the modern world; they have had no opportunity of obtaining an insight into technological methods or experimental research; and, apart from the "Modern Greats" men, they are not acquainted with the social sciences.

The professional men in the service, on the other hand, have received an inappropriate and narrow training in law or medicine, chemistry or engineering, or some other vocational discipline. The professional schools in the universities to-day take no account of the economic, political, or social aspects of modern life, even in so far as these have a bearing on the subject matter of the particular profession. The chief officials in the local government service are nearly all men who have received a professional training of this kind.

The public boards have in many cases avoided appointing men of the administrative class type to their leading positions, and have relied to a much greater extent on professionals and technicians. It is easy to understand the appeal of a good training and experience in engineering as a recommendation for an important job in a transport or electricity undertaking; but I venture to suggest that engineering, like patriotism, is not enough. The truth is that the traditional distinction between "administrative" and "professional" work is irrelevant and obsolete in the most important spheres of the public service to-day. The pure technician, who is ignorant of the economic, political, and social aspects of his work, is of small value in the highest positions; while the administrator who has to rely on other people to advise him about the elementary technical matters relating to the enterprise is unlikely to possess that mastery of the material which is required for the formulation of policy and far-sighted planning.

The problem which is here stated is one which must be solved primarily by educationists, and principally by those responsible for the conduct of our universities and other institutions of higher education. But if the character and dimensions of the problem are understood by the general public, and more especially by the public boards and departments charged with the running of the socialized services, great pressure can be brought to bear on the universities to cater for the essential needs of these bodies. The development of degrees and diplomas in public administration throughout the country during the past fifteen years is an indication that the universities are not unresponsive to a clear call from outside their walls, especially when vocational openings are likely to develop for graduates who have received an appropriate training. The Civil Service Commissioners could also play a large part in this matter, although it is doubtful whether they are alive to the issues involved.

RELATIONS WITH PARLIAMENT

We may turn now to a consideration of the constitutional position of these public boards and of their relations with other organs of government.

The elementary principle that everyone and every institution is in the last resort subject to the sovereignty of Parliament applies, of course, with undiminished force to the various organs discussed in these pages. Most of them were created by statute, but Parliament would not hesitate, if it desired, to control by legislation those which sprang into existence without legislative authority, such as the B.B.C. or the co-operative societies.

This ultimate power of control by Parliament is not,

however, of very substantial importance in the world of public affairs as it actually exists. What is of far greater moment is government control, with its correlative of ministerial responsibility to Parliament. It is here that the most striking change has occurred. Parliament has in effect abnegated the right to have a Minister of the Crown always available on the Treasury bench ready to answer questions concerning the day-to-day administration of the service. It has renounced the opportunity normally provided by the Estimates for obtaining information on, and a critical discussion of, every item of expenditure and revenue relating to the socialized service. It has denied itself the privilege, so little used in practice but so highly prized in theory, of compelling a minister to resign, or, indeed, of destroying the government, as a penalty for following a course of action disliked by a majority of the members of the House of Commons. It has forgone the various occasions offered by the procedure of Parliament for attacking, defending, expounding, and influencing policy in the various spheres of public administration comprised by the work of the boards.

There can be little doubt that on the whole the relinquishment by Parliament of its detailed day-to-day "control" over the undertakings run by public boards is an immense advantage. The so-called "control," even if nominally exercised, would certainly not be effective in any sphere of activity where the service is technical. The haphazard sniping which takes place during question time does not result in real control even in the case of the Post Office. What it does is to ensure the ventilation of comparatively minor abuses, injustices, stupidities, extravagances, and grievances, and thereby to reduce the likelihood of their occurrence.

Parliament is an excellent instrument for the formulation of new policy in legislative terms, but it is much less effective in supervising administration of a complex character.

Possibly its efficiency in this respect could be greatly enhanced if a series of advisory committees were set up in Parliament in association with particular departments or groups of functions. But here we are concerned with the parliamentary régime as it actually exists and not with a hypothetical state of affairs, so we must not take such possibilities into account. The most conspicuous fact about the present situation is the depressing effect on departmental initiative and administrative energy of continual liability to parliamentary inquisition on points of minor detail. An excessive caution becomes the indispensable passport to eminence in official life when even a slight deviation from established routine may land the minister in a quagmire of unforeseen difficulties. Routine, precedent, and the avoidance of risks tend to become the navigating lights by which the departmental ship is steered.

The result of this enervating discipline may be of no great consequence in a well-developed or fully mature field of activity in which most of the work is of a routine character. But in new or growing spheres of activity the whole tempo of administration is likely to be slowed down or even stopped entirely. It is difficult to believe that the broadcasting service, the production and wholesale supply of electricity, or the London dock and transport undertakings would have been handled with the thrust and energy which have been put into them in recent years if they had been subject to parliamentary control of the ordinary kind.

We may, therefore, conclude that the liberation of the public service boards from the obligations attaching to ordinary departments of government is thoroughly desirable. But this is by no means the end of the matter. The relinquishment of day-to-day supervision ought to be accompanied by a far more searching inquiry at periodic intervals than any which now occurs.

At present there is hardly any regular discussion in Parliament of the work of the public service boards. A chance debate may arise on the presentation of a Report by a departmental committee, or on the introduction of a new Bill, or on account of some incident which happens to arouse public attention. But there is no provision for regular inquiry and full discussion in Parliament of the policy and performance of these public service boards. It is obvious that a full-dress debate at least once a year is needed on each of these socialized services. In no other way can the political control over public undertakings which is essential to democracy find adequate expression.

THE ANNUAL REPORT

The basis of such debates should be the annual reports which the public boards are required to make either to Parliament or a minister. Here again there is evidence of the haphazard manner in which these bodies have been allowed to grow up, and the consequent lack of system in what should be an important part of their work. The annual reports of the various boards vary greatly in scope, fullness, frankness, and method of presentation. The annual report of the B.B.C., for example, is notoriously inadequate from almost every point of view, and has been rightly criticized for concealing more than it reveals. The annual report of the L.P.T.B., on the other hand, is a much more satisfactory document. It gives the impression that the Board is really endeavouring to enlighten the public as to its activities, and contains elaborate statistics, maps, and illustrations. The annual report of the Minister of Agriculture on the Marketing Boards is substantial in size but feeble in quality, and the vital questions are virtually ignored.

AN EFFICIENCY AUDIT

There is little doubt that if Parliament and the public desire to be adequately informed about the progress of these complex organizations, new machinery will have to be set up for the purpose of conducting audits or inspections on systematic lines. I do not think it is sufficient merely to call for an annual report, even if, as is sometimes the case, the minister is given power to specify the matters which must be dealt with therein or to prescribe the form in which the accounts must be rendered. It is asking too much to expect the responsible board of a great undertaking to draw attention to its weak points; they may even be unaware of them. If we are to develop effective methods of public criticism, permanent organs of scrutiny and investigation will have to be developed.

A possible method would be to establish an Audit Commission whose function it would be to hold efficiency audits at regular intervals. The audit would be incomparably wider in scope than the narrow accountancy check which now goes under that name. Its object would be to ascertain whether a board was conducting its work well or feebly, to call attention to merits and shortcomings, to make suggestions for improvement, and to act as the eyes and ears of the general public. Such a body would consider the character, quantity, and quality of service rendered; price policy and efficiency of administration; personnel questions, including pay, recruitment, and methods of promotion; relations between the board and the consumer; capital, expenditure and the methods of financing it; in short, all the most important problems involved in a socialized undertaking.

Such a task, it may be contended, would be beyond the capacity of an Audit Commission. But I do not believe this to be the case. The ideal body would consist, first, of a number of eminent specialists in such fields as applied economics, finance, industrial psychology, statistics, business organization, public relations, engineering, and so forth, giving their whole time to the work; second, of a number of persons engaged in outside occupations of varied kinds, accustomed to master the broad outlines of an administrative situation at short notice, who would form a panel to be drawn upon *ad hoc* as required. A staff of research assistants should be attached to the Audit Commission, partly in order to work through the relevant material relating to each board from the research standpoint, and partly in order to collect information about comparable undertakings at home or abroad. Only by some such method as this are we likely to build up a body of informed, critical, and disinterested opinion, available to Parliament and the public, concerning these socialized services.

ULTIMATE GOVERNMENT CONTROL

It has already been remarked that the relinquishment of ministerial responsibility to Parliament for the day-to-day administration of these boards is a constitutional innovation to be welcomed, having regard to the nature of their work. This, however, does not in any way dispense with the necessity for retaining the right of ultimate government control in time of emergency or in case of abuse of power or dereliction of duty. The best example of what is needed in this respect is the B.B.C. In time of emergency the government has the right to take over the transmitting stations and assume complete control of the undertaking. Even apart from this, the government could in fact gain control by omitting to collect the licence fees from listeners, or refusing to hand over that part of them which goes to the B.B.C. There is no similar power of control over the C.E.B., for instance, or the L.P.T.B., or the P.L.A., although in the event of war, civil conflict, a general strike, or a political crisis, it might be of the utmost importance for the Cabinet to have immediate control of such undertakings.

Apart from control in time of emergency, ministerial influence in the conduct of these public boards should remain restricted to major questions of policy. The power of appointing the members of the governing body should always vest in a minister; and, as I have already pointed out, the government should have at its disposal some means of overcoming an obstructive or hostile board. In appropriate cases a minister should have the power to issue regulations of a general or particular character appertaining to the service. Questions of a specially important nature likely to affect widespread public interests, such as the scale of charges, fines, byelaws, and service facilities, should be made subject to departmental approval or the sanction of an outside body such as the Railway Rates Tribunal or the Electricity Commission; but such reservations ought not to interfere with the substantial freedom of the undertaking in regard to day-to-day administration.

Since the political control which is exercisable over the public service boards is comparatively weak, it is desirable that judicial control over their activities should be strengthened, and be made, indeed, much stronger than it is in the case of an ordinary government department subject to full ministerial responsibility to Parliament. The ordinary courts of justice are, in my view (for reasons which I have explained at length elsewhere), incapable of exercising the degree and quality of judicial control which is called for in the case of these semi-independent boards. Neither the procedure nor the rules of law which they apply are suitable for the purpose. The judicial review of administrative decisions could be formulated effectively only by a tribunal which is adequately equipped to inquire into and evaluate the complicated administrative and technological issues involved; and which is above all capable of creating a body of new legal tissue to order on a satisfactory basis the relations between the citizen and the vast impersonal organizations which carry on the large-scale services in the modern state. The need for a system of administrative courts has grown apace with the emergence of each of the public boards described in these pages. It is not possible to deal with the question in detail here; the subject has been discussed at length elsewhere.[1]

TREASURY CONTROL

Most of the public boards are substantially free from the dominating authority which the Treasury normally exercises over an ordinary government department, though the degree of their emancipation varies considerably. The absence of Treasury control of the traditional kind is wholly desirable, having regard to the narrow outlook and antiquated doctrines commonly entertained by Treasury pundits on the subject of public finance, capital expenditure, economy in the social services, unemployment, and monetary policy. The Gladstonian tradition is still strong in Treasury Chambers, and that tradition is antithetic to the vigorous development of socialized enterprises. The Forestry Commission, Mr. Parker observes, "has suffered from being in a peculiarly weak position *vis-à-vis* the Treasury." By way of contrast, one has only to observe the leap forward which the Post Office was able to make in the expansion, cheapening, and general popularization of its services when the unimaginative and restraining influence of meticulous Treasury control was removed, as a result of the recommendations of the Bridgeman Committee, to realize how unadapted to public utility undertakings the habitual Treasury attitude is likely to be.

The Treasury has grown up as an instrument for imposing taxation on the one hand, and as a mechanism for avoiding extravagance, corruption, waste, and unauthorized disbursements by "spending" departments on the other. But these new public service boards are engaged neither in raising

---

[1] W. A. Robson, *Justice and Administrative Law*; Committee on Ministers' Powers: Report (Cmd. 4060/1932) and Minutes of Evidence. See especially evidence of W. A. Robson. Cf. article on the Report of the Committee in *Political Quarterly*, July 1932.

taxes nor in providing social services of the ordinary kind, such as public health. A good example of the inability of the Treasury to comprehend the essential distinction between a socialized utility and a profit-making industry on the one hand, or a "spending" department on the other, is to be found in the treatment of broadcasting. The B.B.C., a public service undertaking carried on without a divisible profit on a self-supporting basis, has been required over a long period of years to pay to the Treasury out of its licence revenue (a) a heavy percentage deduction amounting in 1934 to £1,134,315 out of £3,369,000; (b) a series of "emergency contributions" levied annually to meet the financial crisis of 1931, amounting in 1934 to £187,500; (c) a further sum by way of income tax amounting to £113,000 in the same year. All these payments are unjustifiable, and they have been drained out of the broadcasting revenue derived from the licence fee at the expense of the listener for no other reason than that the Treasury has an incurable habit of making predatory raids on every new and growing enterprise, regardless of the purposes for which it is run and without any coherent philosophy of public finance to guide its action. The Treasury is, therefore, not merely of little use as a controlling agent over the finance of public boards but likely to be positively detrimental to their future development.

To say this is, however, to arrive at the beginning of the problem of finance rather than at the end of it. Mention has already been made of the tendency to separate the finances of these boards from the national exchequer, to give them what may be called self-contained finance. This has the advantage of requiring each undertaking to accept responsibility for its own solvency, to determine price policy and general operating costs. It also permits a high degree of flexibility in financial policy and of adaptation to the peculiar needs of each service. There are, however, a number of points which require careful attention.

THE BASIS OF COMPENSATION

The first is the question of compensation. This only arises, of course, where private interests have been bought up or expropriated; but where it does exist it is of the utmost importance. As Mr. Davies remarks, "The success of the public corporation from the community's point of view turns on the extent of the capital burden it inherits from the companies it supplants." No one, I think, can read Mr. Davies' carefully documented account[1] of the relative position of the stockholders in the London Traffic Combine prior and subsequent to the setting up of the L.P.T.B. without feeling that the compensation terms were generous beyond the dreams of avarice. Yet the statute by which they were conferred was not the work of a tender-hearted sympathizer with the woes of shareholders, but the creation of a Labour Minister who is an outstanding opponent of capitalism. Nevertheless, the shareholders have come off much too well; their statutory rights bear little relation to the interest rates now prevailing; and the London transport undertaking will have to struggle along as best it can with a staggering burden of indebtedness round the neck. This encumbrance will severely hamper the service it can offer to the public for generations to come, and make many much-needed reductions of fares difficult if not impossible.

There is, unfortunately, nothing peculiar or exceptional about this arrangement. Compensation on an excessive scale is a common feature in the compulsory acquisition of public utility undertakings in this country. The proprietors and directors of the water companies which were taken over by the Metropolitan Water Board in 1904 received far too much for their rights and interests; and the same can be said of many smaller acquisitions by local authorities of water, gas, electricity, and tramway undertakings.

Compensation is both economically necessary and socially

[1] Infra, pages 193–4.

N

desirable, but the need remains for seeing that it is not excessive. Hitherto, two elementary mistakes have been made in determining the amount and basis of compensation. First, little or no allowance has been made for the financial value of a statutory monopoly. Thus, in the case of London transport, the shareholders of the companies which had been facing severe competition, that was almost certain to increase in the future, were given almost equivalent rights in a public concern enjoying an exclusive monopoly over a huge area, without due allowance being made for the enhanced security conferred on their holdings.

In the second place, no attempt has been made to ensure that the annual payments to bondholders should continue to occupy in the future the same position in the general scale of interest rates as they did prior to acquisition. Even if the rates of interest arranged to be paid on London Transport Stock were reasonable in 1930, when government securities yielded about 5 per cent, they certainly ceased to be reasonable after the great conversion operation performed by the government in 1932; but no provision was made in the Act for revising the rates in the event of such a contingency. Some device is clearly needed whereby compensation payments can be adjusted periodically to an index of interest fluctuations. There is an excellent opportunity for some ingenious economist to distinguish himself by devising a basic formula for this purpose.

In general, I find myself in substantial agreement with most of the ideas on the subject put forward by Mr. G. R. Mitchison in his pamphlet, *Industrial Compensation.*[1] He argues, first, that the proper form of compensation is a security bearing a limited dividend payable out of the profits of the socialized undertaking or industry. The rate of dividend should be determined according to the risk carried by the stock, which should not be guaranteed by

[1] Issued by the New Fabian Research Bureau, Now out of print. See also G. D. H. Cole, *The Essentials of Socialization*, issued by the Bureau, pp. 5-7.

the state. "But," he observes, "however risky the undertaking, the maximum dividend should still be fixed at such an amount as not to allow the dispossessed proprietors the benefit of the increased efficiency resulting from state co-ordination and state support. The object of socialization is to utilize the resources of the community for the benefit of the community and not for the benefit of the stockholders." A big step forward in this direction was made by transforming the shareholders of the London transport companies into bondholders without voting rights or any power of control in the management of the new L.P.T.B. Nevertheless, they have the right to apply for the appointment of a receiver in the event of the interest on the stock remaining unpaid for three years consecutively, and this is an unfortunate anomaly which should not be allowed to become a precedent.

The general principles which should be followed in fixing the terms of compensation are laid down by Mr. Mitchison as follows:

The normal form of compensation stock will be stock redeemable at a fixed date or earlier at the option of the issuer. The maximum dividend will be proportional to the risk involved, such dividend being only payable out of the year's profits. The rate of dividend will be subject to a reduction in the event of a reduction in the Bank Rate. The amount to be issued will depend on the average net profits of the socialized undertaking over a term of years (the length of the term varying according to the type of industry). In arriving at the net profits there will be an allowance for depreciation and, in some cases at any rate, for general reserve. In some cases compensation will take the form of terminable stock, which will not have in front of it any such depreciation allowance for reserve.[1]

THE RAISING OF LOANS

A financial aspect which deserves consideration is the question of raising capital. The public boards surveyed

[1] Op. cit.

herein enjoy varying degrees of freedom in this matter. There is usually a statutory limit placed on the total amount which can be raised—for example, £45,000,000 in the case of the P.L.A., £60,000,000 in the case of the C.E.B. Parliament increases these figures from time to time, and is usually willing to raise the permitted total to a sum well in excess of immediate needs. In most cases the capital debt is secured solely on the revenue of the undertaking and does not carry a government guarantee—which is quite as it should be. The stock of the C.E.B. could have received a Treasury guarantee if the Board had desired it and the Treasury were willing to agree. But in practice this has not been done. The stock is placed on the open market, the public is invited to subscribe, and thenceforth it can be dealt with in the ordinary way on the Stock Exchange. All this provides a sharp contrast to the traditional methods employed by the Post Office, which obtains its capital through loans raised by the Treasury from the National Debt Commissioners and repaid through annuities.

The weakness of the new methods has been the lack of a central organization competent to advise such bodies and, if necessary, to act on their behalf in raising money. It is believed that the Bank of England has advised the C.E.B. on its capital issues; and it is the opinion of many competent judges that its policy has not always been wise.[1] The advice tendered by the Bank to local authorities desiring to raise loans has on more than one occasion been notoriously bad—the case of Glasgow in 1935 is an outstanding example. I do not believe that the Bank of England is the right body on which to rely in such matters. There is a great need in the field of local government for a central organization of a disinterested and expert character to advise local authorities on their loan policy and assist them to float loans when required; and a loans bureau of this kind could easily and appropriately be combined with a similar organization for

[1] Infra, page 126.

the public boards. It might form the nucleus of a National Investment Board; at any rate it would work in close co-operation with such a body if one were set up.

PROFIT AND SURPLUS

The general lines on which the economic policy of these undertakings should be conducted are clear. They should, on the one hand, be financially self-supporting and not require any form of direct subsidy from public funds. On the other hand, they should not be expected to make a profit apart from the surplus required to pay interest and sinking fund charges.[1] Any surplus which does accrue should go to the improvement of the service, to raising the workers' wages, and to the redemption of outstanding indebtedness. In no circumstances should the boards be regarded as instruments of taxation for the purpose of contributing to the general revenue of national or local government. There is justification neither for levying a direct tax on their income or surplus nor an indirect tax on the sale of their commodities or services. Each board should be required to pay the full amount for all services rendered or commodities provided by other public authorities, including rent, rates, insurance, postal and telephone charges, and so forth.

CONCEALED TAXATION

It is possible that a Socialist society would find it desirable to provide some services or commodities at less than cost price and to make a profit out of others. Subsidization of this kind would be an open and avowed form of taxation based on a social policy discriminating between more urgent

[1] I have not attempted to deal with the question of financing capital expenditure out of the annual surplus made by a socialized industry. See G. D. H. Cole, *The Essentials of Socialization* (New Fabian Research Bureau), p. 14.

and less urgent needs. But this has nothing in common with the new and sinister forms of clandestine taxation which have recently been introduced into the British financial system.

One of the most pernicious features of the legislation designed to assist agriculture in recent years is the system of disguised taxation which it has introduced. An example of this is the Wheat Act, 1932. Under this Act a standard price is fixed in a quite arbitrary way for home-grown millable wheat (10s. per cwt. has been the actual figure so far), and registered growers in the United Kingdom are entitled to deficiency payments representing the difference between the standard price and the average price in the cereal year obtained by growers in the market for their product. The average price in 1933 was 5s. 4·46d. per cwt., so that (after deducting 0·68d. for administrative expenses) the deficiency payment was at the rate of 4s. 6·86d. per cwt., or more than 80 per cent of the market rate. A sum of about £5,000,000 is required for this purpose; and to provide the money millers and flour importers are called upon to make quota payments in accordance with an extremely complicated formula. The important po nt to note is that the whole scheme involves an elaborate system of concealed taxation designed to assist a particular set of producers at the expense of the rest of the community. The tax does not appear in the Budget, nor is it debated as part of the general system of taxation. The result is that the ordinary citizen has virtually no idea he is being mulcted in this way. Any tendency in the direction of concealed taxation is highly undesirable from every point of view and should in no circumstances be countenanced. Subventions to industry of any kind, if called for on social grounds, should be frankly treated as such and paid for out of undisguised taxation. No government would dare to ask the public to contribute permanently to wheat growers out of the income tax or the motor car licence fund; and the essential nature of the payment is not changed by financing it from a levy on a particular commodity.

THE POSITION OF THE CONSUMER

No observer of the experiments in public undertakings surveyed in this volume can fail to be struck by the relatively weak position of the consumer in the general scheme of control. The P.L.A. is an exception in this respect, since a large proportion of its members are elected by payers of dues and other persons immediately dependent on its services. In no other instance is the consumer as such directly represented on the governing body. The boards dealing with broadcasting, London transport, forestry, electricity, and mining are not elected at all; and there is, therefore, strictly speaking, no representation of any kind on them. There are, however, certain stipulations laid down by Parliament as to the qualifications of the members of the C.E.B. and the L.P.T.B. Thus, the Electricity Supply Act, 1926, requires that the members of the Board shall be appointed after consultation with bodies representing local government, electricity, commerce, industry, transport, agriculture, and labour; while the London Passenger Transport Act, 1933, contains somewhat similar provisions.

The inclusion of persons with a particular "point of view" or "experience" on the board, in the vague hope that they will safeguard certain special interests, is a poor substitute for systematic and carefully planned control by the consumer. In the case of the broadcasting service, I have shown in my essay[1] that while the B.B.C. has set up an elaborate network of committees, composed largely of vocational or producers' interests, there is practically no attempt to establish a living contact with the world of listeners. The C.E.B. has set up a number of consultative committees throughout the country which to some extent

[1] Infra, pages 100–103.

represent the bulk supply "consumers" of electricity sold by the Board; but these are not really consumers but distributing authorities.

The agriculture marketing schemes are based frankly on producers' organizations which entirely exclude any outside interest except in so far as this may be secured by co-option. Each agricultural marketing board is elected by the producers of the commodity with which it deals. A faint attempt has been made, in the case of the Milk Marketing Board and the Potato Marketing Board, to secure a slight foothold for the consumer by providing for the co-option of two persons after consultation with the Market Supply Committee appointed under Section 3 of the Agricultural Marketing Act, 1933. The duty of this committee is to review generally the circumstances affecting the supply of agricultural products, to make recommendations for regulating the supply, and to report on the working of the various Orders regulating the sale of the commodity.

The consumer is supposed to be protected by an entirely separate body called a Consumers' Committee, appointed by the Minister of Agriculture after consultation with the Board of Trade, and, as regards one member, with the Co-operative Union. This committee is to advise the Minister what is the effect of any agricultural marketing scheme on the consumers, and to report on any complaints made in this respect. The Minister may also appoint a Committee of Investigation to consider, at his request, any report made by a Consumers' Committee and any complaint made to the Minister which he considers could not be dealt with by a Consumers' Committee. If the Investigating Committee finds that any provision in a scheme, or any act or omission on the part of the board concerned, is contrary to the interests either of consumers or anyone affected by the scheme, and is not in the public interest, the Minister may amend the scheme, revoke it, or direct the board to rectify the matter in a specified manner; and the board has a duty to obey the Minister in such circumstances. There is an important provision to the effect that in carrying out these arrangements regard is to be had to the interests of the final consumer—that is, people who purchase the regulated product or any commodities made therefrom for their own consumption or use—and not to the interests of the intermediate consumer who purchases the article for the purpose of his trade or industry.

The fundamental defect in this elaborate and cumbersome machinery is that the consumer is organized in parallel with the producer, with the result that he is excluded from the vital processes of decision and policy making. At no stage is the consumer placed in a position to influence policy, at no point is he given an opportunity to get at the facts from the inside, to see the various alternatives which were available to the board, or to obtain an insight into the forces which determined the issue. Instead, he is left outside the ring fence which encircles the happy fraternity of producers, fluttering his wings in a vain attempt to discover grounds for complaint without any right of access to books, statistics, or other relevant information.

It is scarcely surprising that in these circumstances the mechanism described above appears to be working in a futile and utterly ineffective manner so far as the consumers' interests are concerned. A few instances, taken from the most recent Report[1] by the Minister on the Agricultural Marketing Schemes, may be given by way of illustration.

(a) An association of restaurant and hotel keepers known as the *Réunion des Gastronomes* claimed that their members should receive the manufacturing rebates in respect of milk used in their kitchens, notwithstanding the fact that they were unable to comply with the requirements of the Board as to the purchase of 500 gallons a day and the manufacture of 300 gallons. The Consumers' Committee reported that, so far as the interests of consumers (as defined above) were concerned, they saw no reason

[1] Cmd. 4913, 1935, H.M.S.O.

for recommending any alteration in the arrangements; and they added that the question whether there was a case for altering the arrangements in the interests of the hotel and restaurant trade did not fall within their province. The Minister then submitted that report to the Committee of Investigation, who found that the action of the Milk Marketing Board was reasonable, and gave no ground for the complaint. "On the broader issue, which was raised by the *Réunion* at the hearing, that their members are now having to pay higher prices for milk than in pre-scheme days, the Committee found (i) that it might be said that the provisions of the scheme in regard to prices and the action of the Board in putting these provisions into effect were contrary to the interests of members of the *Réunion*, but (ii) that the relevant provisions of the scheme and the action of the Board in putting them into force were in the interests of milk producers as a whole and might, *therefore*, in the absence of counter-balancing considerations, be said to be in the public interest."[1]

(b) The Consumers' Committee for Scotland heard complaints against the decision of the Scottish Milk Marketing Board to continue, during the summer months, the retail price for milk of 2s. a gallon. The Committee reported adversely on the Board's action and stated they could see no reason for departing from the long-established practice of differentiating between winter and summer prices. The report was then referred by the Secretary for Scotland to the Committee of Investigation, who found that the Board's action was neither unreasonable or against the public interest. The Board, they said, "had acted in a reasonable manner in a genuine endeavour to reconcile the conflicting interests of the producer, distributor, and consumer." The reasoning process by which this strange conclusion is arrived at is not divulged; the only information disclosed is the fluctuations in the average price paid to the producer through the year.[2]

(c) In 1933 the average price paid to merchants for hops under the Hops Marketing Scheme was £15 1s. 8d. a hundredweight for an output of 194,017 cwt. This compares with £8 17s. 2d. in 1932 for an output of 165,908 cwt. and £9 1s. 6d. in 1934 for an output of 245,496 cwt. A complaint made by the Brewers' Society as to the prices in 1933 was referred by the Minister to the Committee of Investigation, which merely

---

[1] Cmd. 4913, 1935, H.M.S.O., pp. 55–6. My italics.   [2] Ibid., p. 18

reported that the evidence and arguments placed before them disclosed no justification for the complaint.[1]

Many other instances could be given of the bland refusal of these committees to consider the consumers' pocket, and of their tendency to identify the public interest with the producers' ability to exploit a semi-monopolistic position to the utmost possible extent.

"BACK TO THE GILD"

A situation which is similar in its essential features exists in regard to the coal-mining industry. Here, again, a comprehensive cartel organization has been established on a statutory basis, armed with price-fixing and output-restricting powers, and authorized to impose disciplinary penalties of a severe kind on producers who fail to comply with its determinations. All this reminds one unpleasantly of medieval gild regulations. "Back to the Gild" seems indeed to be the watchword of many agricultural and industrial "reformers" in England to-day.

This type of producers' organization is fundamentally defective as an instrument of social control. It is the antithesis of socialization in the genuine sense. It is mainly a device for stabilizing the industry by giving the existing producers a permanent freehold in the *status quo* regardless of their efficiency. It is a means for removing the threat of competition from those who are unable to face it. It throws the mantle of statutory protection over the existing producer without securing any fundamental control in the public interest as a condition precedent. It is a smoke-screen for permitting profit-making *entrepreneurs* to join in the chorus against wasteful competition raised by the Socialist, on terms advantageous to themselves. It enables the individual producer to dig himself into a line of entrenched profits with the aid of statutory guarantees against the unpleasant

[1] Cmd. 4913, 1935, H.M.S.O., p. 9.

effects (to him) of lowered prices, falling markets, or improved methods on the part of rival producers.

It is abundantly clear that control by the consumer must take place at the very centre of operations if it is to be effective. An organization which merely enables consumers to lodge their complaints after the main principles of policy have been determined exclusively by profit-making producers is certain to be unsatisfactory and impotent. It follows that representatives of the consuming public, or special sections of it, must be appointed in effective numbers on the executive organization which is directing the actual productive or distributive operations.[1] How far this is likely to work harmoniously if the industry is left in private ownership I will not undertake to say. I merely emphasize the importance of recognizing the disadvantages and dangers of any other course, and of realizing how illusory or non-existent the benefits of any other policy are certain to be, so far as consuming public is concerned.

A penetrating exposure of the inherent defects and short-comings of the system represented by the Marketing Boards has been made recently in the case of the milk industry by the Reorganization Commission appointed for Great Britain by the Minister of Agriculture and the Secretary of State for Scotland jointly. "An examination of the decisions which the Boards have taken in the matter of price-fixing," states the Commission in its Report,[2] "shows that they are no different from what might have been expected from any body of business men engaged in selling a commodity and naturally intent upon obtaining for that commodity the best possible price. Each member must feel it incumbent upon him to have special regard to the views of those who

[1] For an alternative method of providing an element of consumer control see G. D. H. Cole, "The Essentials of Socialization," *The Political Quarterly*, July 1931 (also issued as a pamphlet by the New Fabian Research Bureau). Mr. Cole's scheme would apply equally to socialized services or utilities and to controlled industries. My suggestions concerning representation of the consumer refer only to the latter.

[2] Ministry of Agriculture and Fisheries. Economic Series, No. 44, H.M.S.O.

have elected him to represent them; and it is natural for the electors to consider that the chief aim of their representatives should be to secure the best possible price for producers. It would be unreasonable to expect the representatives of producers to give as much consideration to the interests of the 'Trade' or to the interests of the consumer, as to their own interests; further, as representatives, they must be tempted to strive after immediate benefits without due regard to the ultimate consequences."

"In this assessment of the position we cast no adverse reflection on the Boards; we merely decline to put them in a higher place than any other body of business men. The simple fact is, in our view, that it is impossible to expect them to fill the dual rôle of advocates and judges."[1]

Even the handful of "independent members" on the Boards cannot be relied upon, in the opinion of the Reorganization Commission, to take "a perfectly impartial view" on matters where the interests of parties other than producers are concerned. "They are members of a producers' board; they live in what may be called a 'producers' atmosphere'; and they are not specially charged with the duty of defending the interests of distributors, manufacturers, or consumers."[2]

The conclusion arrived at in this remarkable Report is that, where price-fixing in the milk industry is desirable, the prices prescribed should be approved by an impartial body appointed by the government. The body in question would be a permanent Milk Commission, and would consist of a chairman and four other members appointed by the ministers responsible for agriculture in England and Scotland respectively, after consultation with the ministers responsible for the other interests affected. The proposed Commission would become the central authority for the milk industry as a whole. It would be independent and impartial. It

[1] Report of the Milk Reorganization Commission, 1936, p. 189.
[2] Ibid.

would advise the government and operate in conformity with government policy. The Marketing Boards would continue to function, but would, of course, be relegated to a quite minor rôle.[1]

It is scarcely surprising that this excellent Report has aroused much opposition; but it is greatly to be hoped that its drastic and far-reaching proposals will be acted upon. It is certainly a step in the right direction.

GOVERNMENT BY COMMISSION

Looking at the diverse administrative organs surveyed in the foregoing pages, and bearing in mind the substantial number of other institutions, such as the Area Traffic Commissions and the Race Course Betting Control Board, which are similarly detached from the ordinary departments of state, it would seem as though we are definitely entering a phase which may be described as government by commission. By that I understand a system of boards which are not subject to the direction of a particular minister or of the Cabinet as a whole, nor liable to the normal incidents of the parliamentary régime. The members of such boards are appointed for a fixed term of years to carry on a service in the manner laid down in general and often vague terms by statute or charter.

There is nothing new in the conception on which these bodies are founded. The idea and the institution were both widely known in the Tudor era of centralized administration. "The Tudors relied heavily on such bodies, some of which functioned quite like modern administrative commissions."[2] A number of them appeared again in the nineteenth century to deal with poor law, public health, and other social services. The government of the United States operates on its regulatory side to a large extent

---

[1] Report of the Milk Reorganization Commission, 1936, p. 283.

[2] See the article on "Commissions" by John Dickinson in the *Encyclopaedia of the Social Services*, iv, p. 36.

through a series of commissions quite separate from the presidential cabinet. Among these are some of the most important Federal Agencies, such as the Federal Trade Commission, the Inter-state Commerce Commission, the Federal Power Commission, the Federal Radio Commission, and the Federal Reserve Board. The idea is also spreading to service organs such as the Tennessee Valley Authority. [1]

The novelty of the recent experiments in England lies in the nature of the functions dealt with rather than in the method adopted. There is something genuinely new and arresting in the attempt to adapt an old institutional form to the administration of complex modern industries or utilities such as electricity supply, broadcasting, the passenger transport system of the metropolis, the London docks, and so forth. The commercial or industrial character of the undertakings, their magnitude and technological complexity, the importance of their position in the social and economic life of the community, the vast scale of their financial operations, the monopolistic privileges which they enjoy, these and other factors make it necessary to place them in a category of their own distinct from all earlier precedents.

THE NEED FOR PLANNING MACHINERY

The most obvious weakness of the position as it now exists is the absence of any machinery for co-ordinating the work of the various boards or for harmonizing their activities in the light of a common plan. There is no central planning machinery for dealing with these or cognate undertakings, and, in consequence, there is no plan of any kind. The Electricity Commission was responsible for devising the regional and national schemes required to bring the grid into existence. The Coal Mines Reorganization Commission is supposed to be responsible for reorganizing the mining industry, though it has failed lamentably to achieve any-

[1] See the report of the President's Committee on Administrative Management (Washington, 1937).

thing whatever. The Post Office has entire control of telephones, telegraphs, and mails, including a complete underground railway of its own in London. The L.P.T.B. operates the tubes, trams, motor-buses and trolley-buses in the metropolitan region. The Forestry Commission has a general jurisdiction over afforestation throughout the country. The B.B.C. has an exclusive monopoly over radio transmission and the erection of wireless stations throughout Great Britain. Each of these bodies is supposed to operate in a watertight compartment, at best compelled to rely on whatever degree of haphazard and voluntary co-operation it can manage to secure from the others, at worst meeting with obstruction, secrecy, or even opposition.

It is obvious that there are numerous and important connections between these different services. The future demand for electrical power from the various coalfields is a matter of substantial interest to the C.E.B., and this depends on the future development and rationalization of the mining industry. The possibility of the telephone lines of the Post Office being used for relaying broadcasting programmes was discussed recently by the Ullswater Committee and also in Parliament.[1] In the London region there are vital relationships between the work of the P.L.A. and that of the L.P.T.B. The Post Office miniature tube railway will no doubt soon be in need of extension to keep pace with the immense expansion of the metropolis. Is this not a matter which concerns the L.P.T.B.? Forestry, again, is clearly linked with agriculture and, therefore, with the work of the agricultural marketing boards.

Quite apart from the interrelations between the work of these various organs, there is the problem of their relationship with other bodies, such as the highway authorities, the main line railways, the town and country planning authori-

---

[1] *Report of the Broadcasting Committee*, Cmd. 5091, 1936, pars. 130–6 and p. 52; Hansard: *Commons Debates*, vol. 311, No. 75 (April 29, 1936); vol. 314, No. 117 (July 6, 1936).

ties, the area traffic commissioners, the housing authorities, and so forth. There are innumerable points of contact between the work of all these bodies and the undertakings operated by the public service boards. To take one example, the future demand for electric power by the transport services is obviously a matter of substantial interest to the C.E.B.

There is a clear need for a central planning organization to deal with all these problems in a comprehensive way. Such an organization, I suggest, should be placed under the jurisdiction of a Cabinet minister free from other duties or a committee of the Cabinet.[1] Only in that way can it acquire sufficient authority to override sectional objections and secure conformity to the general lines of its policy. In the second place, the proposed method is the best means for securing a reasonable degree of public control in a situation which may easily get out of hand from a demo-cratic point of view, and lead us to a society not far removed from the authoritarian state. Democracy at one remove may be a desirable objective in the day-to-day operation of these highly technical services, but it should not be at more than one remove; and ministerial control over the large-scale plans and general lines of policy is essential just because the public boards are left free to work out the detailed application of these plans in their own manner.

It is, indeed, of crucial importance to reserve for the instruments of popular government the control over these commissions at their key points. That is why we should insist at all costs on the power of appointing members of the board residing with a Cabinet minister; on far more thoroughgoing and drastic methods of audit; on central planning; and on co-ordination under the direct control of the Cabinet. The relaxation of control over day-to-day

[1] The question of the best method of dealing with this problem is under consideration by a special committee of the New Fabian Research Bureau. See also G. D. H. Cole, *The Essentials of Socialization*, issued by the Bureau, p. 15.

administration should be accompanied at every point by a strengthening of the contingent controls over essential questions.

PUBLIC RELATIONS

The art of public relations, when it is more fully developed, may come ultimately to play a part of great importance in the operation of these socialized industries and utilities. At present it is scarcely more than an offshoot of commercial publicity, and it has not yet entirely shed the implications of its origin. But it is possible that one day it may facilitate the introduction of an entirely new kind of lay participation in the machinery of government.

The proper objectives of a public relations policy in the field of socialized industry are neither boosting nor ballyhoo. They are, on the one hand, to explain the policy and program of the undertaking to the body of consumers and citizens in terms which they can readily understand; and this includes, not a mere recital of present achievements and grandiose schemes for the future, but also an exposition of the problems and difficulties which confront the service, its aims and purposes, its hopes and aspirations, with a frank statement of its shortcomings and the efforts which are being made to overcome them. On the other hand, it should aim at providing lines of communication between the undertaking and the public along which grievances, complaints, criticism, and constructive suggestions or inventions may travel freely and quickly. There is room for much inventiveness and imagination in this new sphere. A not unpromising start has already been made by the L.P.T.B. and the Post Office, and the B.B.C. has followed suit, but it is so far a mere drop in the ocean compared with what is wanted.

CONCLUSION

In conclusion, we may say quite definitely that the future of socialization lies in the direction of the public board investigated in these pages, subject to the utmost care being taken to introduce the safeguards and ultimate controls discussed above. The public board is an institution capable of great flexibility, and can be adapted to the efficient discharge of a wide range of functions. It is possible, if we proceed with eyes open and mind alert, to reconcile the independent board with the fundamental assumptions and the essential requirements of our democracy; although, be it added, the board idea, wrongly used or misapplied, may equally well be employed to undermine the foundations of a democratic régime.

I believe that the proper function of the public service board consists in the operation of socialized undertakings, whether of an industrial or public utility character. The idea of setting up public boards to regulate or rationalize private industry or agriculture, while leaving the ownership and final responsibility for profit or loss in private hands, is likely to lead to confusion and conflict. Still more confused and dangerous is the practice of giving compulsory powers over output and price and the elimination of competition to gilds of producers, whether in the form of so-called marketing boards or of industrial cartels.

INDEX